Paraprofessionals
in the Classroom

Betty Y. Ashbaker, Ph.D.
Brigham Young University

Jill Morgan, Ph.D.

PEARSON

Boston   New York   San Francisco
Mexico City   Montreal   Toronto   London   Madrid   Munich   Paris
Hong Kong   Singapore   Tokyo   Cape Town   Sydney

Executive Editor: Virginia Lanigan
Series Editorial Assistant: Scott Blaszak
Marketing Manager: Kris Ellis-Levy
Production Editor: Greg Erb
Editorial Production Service: Nesbitt Graphics, Inc.
Composition Buyer: Linda Cox
Manufacturing Buyer: Andrew Turso
Electronic Composition: Nesbitt Graphics, Inc.
Interior Design: Nesbitt Graphics, Inc.
Cover Designer: Joel Gendron

For related titles and support materials, visit our online catalog at www.ablongman.com.

Between the time website information is gathered and then published, it is not unusual for some sites to have closed. Also, the transcription of URLs can result in typographical errors. The publisher would appreciate notification where these errors occur so that they may be corrected in subsequent editions.

Library of Congress Cataloging-in-Publication Data

Ashbaker, Betty Y., 1950-
  Paraprofessionals in the classroom / Betty Y. Ashbaker and Jill Morgan.
    p. cm.
  Includes index.
  ISBN 0-205-43688-9
   1. Teachers' assistants—United States. I. Morgan, Jill, 1956- II. Title.

LB2844.1.A8A74 2006
371.14'124—dc22   2005041247

Printed in the United States of America

10 9 8 7 6 5 4 3 2 1 VHP 10 09 08 07 06 05

Contents

Preface

Paraprofessionals in the Classroom is not merely a training course. Tested in the field, it directly addresses the many issues that paraprofessionals face every day: the need for clear role definitions; confidentiality and professionalism; how to carry out responsibilities effectively and efficiently, and so on. We stress that a paraprofessional's role should support rather than replace the teacher and that paraprofessionals should work under the direction of a professional supervisor. This legal requirement is explored and clarified early in the book, but is also translated into everyday practice throughout the text, as we provide many suggestions for how to actively seek supervision. Whole chapters are devoted to such critical areas as effective instruction and behavior management principles, time management, and evaluation of teaching and learning, making *Paraprofessionals in the Classroom* an eminently practical book.

The tone and level of writing is engaging and uncluttered with scholarly references and citations from research. Treatment of each topic is thorough but to the point, with interaction to keep it lively. Here are some of the outstanding features:

- **Clearly presented text** avoids research jargon and suggests approaches and techniques that paraprofessionals can apply in their classrooms immediately.
- **Reflective Activities** provide opportunities to consider the material presented and how the principles apply to each paraprofessional's particular situation.
- **Text boxes and tables** summarize information.
- Background information—including **legal terms**—demystifies the educational system and empowers paraprofessionals by increasing their knowledge.
- **Case studies** offer descriptions and follow-up questions about real-life situations, which ensure engagement and lively discussion.
- **Extending Your Learning** sections at the end of each chapter add opportunities for gaining more information and applying the principles learned.
- **Websites** that provide further information and resources for paraprofessionals are listed in the appendix. Additionally, the text's companion website can be found at www.ablongman.com/ashbaker1e.
- **A glossary and list of acronyms** explain terminology.

Paraprofessionals in the Classroom is excellent for formal college courses and school district staff development. For both initial and ongoing staff training, it will provide many hours of inservice credit for paraprofessionals. The textbook is intended as an introduction for paraprofessionals working in a wide variety of settings, and provides examples from both general and special education and across the K through 12 age range.

If this is your first formal class as a paraprofessional, it would be quite natural to be anxious. If you are not experiencing any feelings of anxiety—only excitement and eagerness to learn—be aware that many of your classmates may be a little nervous. Here are suggestions to help you survive—and enjoy—this experience:

■ *Feeling as if you're the only one who is new to studying and insecure about the class?* Most likely you are not alone in feeling this way. Lack of confidence is common for people who are in unfamiliar situations, and several other class members may feel the same way. Take courage. If you don't understand something—ask! Your confidence will grow as you get answers to your questions.

■ *Concerned about qualifications and college experience?* Even if you do not have formal training in education, you may have considerable classroom experience. This text enables you to think about your experiences in the context of educational theory; giving you a common vocabulary for discussion with other educators and helping you to see the principles underlying what you do for students. As new ideas are presented, relate them to what you already know and decide how they can be applied to your work with students.

■ *Talk to your classmates about their experiences.* Others may lack confidence about the class, and you can encourage them. They may work in situations different from yours, and you will be able to supplement each other's understanding through talking about your experiences.

■ *There may be those in the class who sound confident and who seem to be able to answer every question.* Be an active participant in the class—even if you don't feel confident—so that you too can benefit from the experience.

■ *Feelings of confidence often come from a sense of competence.* Think of an area in your life that makes you feel competent. Each of us draws motivation, satisfaction, and confidence from different aspects of success. Determine what it is that motivates you, and see how you can apply it to this class.

■ *Always ask if you're not sure about something.* Most of the questions that feel "silly" or trivial may be questions that other class members also want to ask, and they'll be very glad if you ask on their behalf. This is particularly true of unfamiliar words and terms that the instructor may use; so if the instructor uses a term or acronym you are unfamiliar with, ask for an explanation or definition.

■ *What if you are asked a question and you are unsure of the answer?* It is more helpful to try to answer, rather than just saying, "I don't know." Many questions that instructors ask will not have one "right" answer, and even if the answer you give is wrong, you will still learn from the experience.

■ *Know what is expected for assignments.* Make sure you ask: When is the assignment due? How should it be presented? How will it be graded? Then you will know what to focus on as you complete it. It takes courage and determination to be a successful student but there is a real sense of accomplishment to be found in mastering new material. We wish you enjoyment and success in meeting the challenge!

We would like to thank the following reviewers: Idell Adams, Baton Rouge Community College; Dick Heimann, Northland Pioneer College; Suzanne Koprowski, Waukesha County Technical College; Richard Malena, Mesa Community College; Eve Puhalla, Northampton Community College; Marjorie Schiller, Central Arizona College; Michael Shepherd, Mid-South Community College; Deborah Tschida, Community College of Denver; Merrill Watrous, Lane Community College; and Patricia Wojtowicz, Raritan Valley Community College.

Background and Context

In this introductory section, we set the stage for the remainder of the book. Chapter 1 discusses the definition of the term *paraprofessional* and looks at the national picture for paraprofessionals in the United States. We provide information on the many roles assumed by paraprofessionals and their typical working conditions and earnings, so you can gain a clearer understanding of the size of the workforce you belong to and the importance of the work you perform.

Chapter 2 provides an overview of the U.S. laws governing education and explains how they came into being. We focus particularly on the federal laws, which directly affect your employment as a paraprofessional.

Chapter 3 looks at role definition. We examine the federal, state, and local levels at which your role is defined and the restrictions placed on the roles you can be assigned at each of these levels. Perhaps most importantly, we look at how you can clarify your supervising teacher's expectations of your work, and how the fine detail of your responsibilities can be worked out with your supervisor.

Chapter 4 discusses the standards that have been set for paraprofessionals' work by various government or professional organizations.

Each of these chapters contributes to building a picture of the U.S. context for your work as a paraprofessional working in an educational setting.

1

What Is a Paraprofessional?

This chapter discusses the background leading to the employment of paraprofessionals and provides a context to help you better understand the regulations of the job. By the end of the chapter, you will be able to answer the following questions:

- What are the various titles used when referring to paraprofessionals?
- What are the various definitions of the term *paraprofessional*?
- What are some of the facts about paraprofessionals who are currently employed in the U.S. education system?
- What is the nationwide picture of work conditions, the job outlook, and earnings for paraprofessionals?

If you are currently employed as a paraprofessional, you already have information related to your job and the local conditions associated with your profession. Knowing about the variety of titles and assignments given to paraprofessionals across the country will give you a broader perspective of the work.

Paraprofessional Titles: A Rose by Any Other Name

Across the United States, at least fifteen different titles are used for paraprofessionals who work in education (see box). Some of them may be considered very

Titles by Which Paraprofessionals Are Known

Paraeducator	School assistant
Home visitor	Aide
Educational technician	Teaching assistant (TA)
Job coach	Learning support assistant (LSA)
Para	Paratherapist
Teacher aide	Occupational therapy aide
Instructional assistant (IA)	Transition trainer
Speech-language pathology aide	Physical therapy assistant

dated or politically incorrect in your school district or state, but most of them are still in use. *Aide* is probably one of the earliest titles, and *paraeducator* is one of the most recent. The term *paraprofessional* has been in use for some time.

Other paraprofessional assignments include Section 504 aide, gifted/talented enrichment paraprofessional, in-school suspension monitor, computer lab technician, and bus aide, among others. You may know of additional titles that are not listed here.

What Is a Paraprofessional?

This may seem a strange question to ask at the beginning of a book written for paraprofessionals whose readers are probably paraprofessionals. But it is a question that needs a clear answer, so you understand the rest of what is said in this book in its proper context. Typically, when we try to define someone who is a member of a group, we resort to describing what that person does. "What is a mother?" "A mother is someone who . . ." and then we list all the things a mother does. This is a useful way of defining a paraprofessional, and in this introductory chapter we look at some of the official definitions of paraprofessionals, as well as ask you to give your own definition. In fact, let's start with your definition. Imagine that someone has come from a different country or culture, where there are no paraprofessionals. In the Chinese education system, for example, there are only professional teachers, no paraprofessionals. So if someone from China asked what your job was, and you told him or her you were a paraprofessional, he or she would probably say, "I don't know that word. What is a paraprofessional?" What would you say to them?

A paraprofessional is someone who _____

_____

_____

_____

_____

Did you manage to define a paraprofessional without just describing what you do? How else could you define a paraprofessional?

_____

_____

_____

_____

_____

Try getting a second opinion on this question of defining a paraprofessional. Ask another paraprofessional—one in your class or who works in the same school as you—to define the term. Write the definition here.

_____

_____

_____

_____

_____

Are there differences between your definition and the definition your colleague gave? What points did your definitions have in common? What new insights did your colleague's definition offer?

_____

_____

_____

_____

_____

With so much variety in the work that paraprofessionals do, each paraprofessional would give a different definition if it were only a question of roles. So in order to get a more universal answer to the question "What is a paraprofessional?" let's first take a look at the word itself. It has two parts: para- and professional. We know a professional is someone who has a recognized set of qualifications for a particular job or profession. The word *professional* probably conjures up images of doctors, lawyers, dentists, and engineers. In the context of education, professional educators include teachers and administrators, as well as school psychologists and counselors and a variety of therapists who may work with individual students. The prefix *para-* means "alongside of." So a paraprofessional is literally someone who works alongside a professional.

If we only interpret the word *paraprofessional* in this way, our definition is still not very enlightening: a paraprofessional is someone who works alongside a professional. It gives no indication of what sort of work a paraprofessional might do and really only leads to another question: What sort of a professional? Paraprofessionals work in all sorts of settings—nursing, the health professions, and the law—not just in education. Many of those paraprofessionals have more descriptive titles that tell us exactly what sort of profession they are connected with, for example, paramedic and paralegal. We know a paramedic works with the medical profession and a paralegal works within a legal context. The term *para-educator* is sometimes used for paraprofessionals working in education settings, as a more descriptive term, and many of the terms we listed earlier in the chapter do help define the role that a paraprofessional may have been assigned (e.g., teaching assistant or job coach). However, the federal government has adopted the more general term *paraprofessional,* rather than *paraeducator.*

A Federal Definition

The federal government has also provided us with a definition for the term paraprofessional. The No Child Left Behind Act of 2001 defines a paraprofessional as "an individual who is employed in a preschool, elementary school or secondary school under the supervision of a certified or licensed teacher, including individuals employed in language instruction educational programs, special education, or migrant education."

Notice that this definition is a restatement of the translation of the word *paraprofessional* that we referred to earlier: a paraprofessional works alongside a professional. But this definition also clarifies the nature of the relationship between the paraprofessional and the professional. They are not merely working companionably side by side. There is a very definite difference in their roles. The paraprofessional is to be supervised, and the teacher (that is, the professional) is to be the supervisor. No Child Left Behind also stipulates training requirements for paraprofessionals (discussed in Chapter 3).

Facts about Paraprofessionals

A number of U.S. government agencies have published statistics about paraprofessionals. Before you read some of the facts we have gathered from these sources, take this short quiz to see how much you know about the people who work in your profession. These questions all relate to paraprofessionals who work in educational settings. You can check your answers as you read through the facts that follow the quiz. An answer key is also provided at the end of the chapter.

1. Approximately how many paraprofessionals were working in the U.S. education system in 2002?
   a. several hundred thousand (200,000 to 400,000)
   b. about 1.3 million
   c. 150,000

2. What percentage of paraprofessionals work in elementary schools?
   a. half, or 50 percent
   b. 75 percent
   c. 30 percent

3. What percentage of paraprofessionals work in special education?
   a. 35 percent
   b. 15 percent
   c. 50 percent

4. What was the average annual salary for a paraprofessional in the United States in 2002?
   a. $18,660
   b. $10,000
   c. $35,000

5. What proportion of paraprofessionals belong to unions?
    a. about 75 percent
    b. less than 10 percent
    c. about 33 percent, or one-third

6. What percentage of paraprofessionals work part time?
    a. over 90 percent
    b. about 40 percent
    c. about 33 percent, or one-third

Now check your answers as you read through the remainder of the chapter. According to the National Center for Education Statistics,

- In the 1993–1994 school year, most paraprofessionals (almost 90 percent) were employed in public schools.
- Seventy-five percent of those worked in elementary schools.
- Almost half of all paraprofessionals were involved in some aspects of special education, 15 percent in bilingual programs and 18 percent in Title I programs.

In a 1997 report prepared for the U.S. Department of Education—*Roles for Education Paraprofessionals in Effective Schools*—the following facts about paraprofessionals were highlighted:

- More than 500,000 classroom and library assistants were employed in the 1993–1994 school year.
- Almost 40 percent of paraprofessionals worked part time, which generally meant they did not receive benefits.
- In many districts, paraprofessionals were members of bargaining units represented by the American Federation of Teachers (AFT), the National Education Association (NEA), a state school employees association, or the Service Employees International Union (SEIU). In 1997 about 100,000 paraprofessionals belonged to AFT affiliates and almost 120,000 to NEA affiliates.
- Local affiliates negotiated paraprofessional salaries and benefits, promoted work-related professional development, initiated or supported legislation relating to credentialing standards, and helped establish career ladders.
- In major urban and rural areas, 60 to 75 percent of paraprofessionals were from racial and language minority groups. In the suburbs, paraprofessionals were predominantly white.

More recently, the Occupational Outlook Handbook, 2004-05 Edition, published by the Bureau of Labor Statistics in the U.S. Department of Labor, provided the following interesting statistics about paraprofessionals in the United States.

Nature of the Work

In keeping with their many and diverse titles, paraprofessionals take on a wide variety of roles, some of which are listed in the box.

Typical Roles of Paraprofessionals

Provide instructional and clerical support for classroom teachers.

Tutor and assist children, using the teacher's lesson plans.

Provide instructional reinforcement under the direction and guidance of teachers.

Specialize in a subject, such as math or science, at the secondary level.

Operate audiovisual equipment and keep classroom equipment in order.

Listen while students read.

Take charge of special projects or exhibits, such as a science demonstration.

Supervise students in the schoolyard, cafeteria, hallways, or on field trips.

Set up equipment and help prepare materials for instruction.

Review class lessons or help students find information for reports.

Grade tests and papers; check homework.

Keep health and attendance records.

Work in computer labs.

Complete typing and filing assignments, duplicate materials, and stock supplies.

The *Occupational Outlook Handbook* also makes the following statement:

Many paraprofessionals work extensively with special education students. As schools become more inclusive, integrating special education students into general education classrooms, paraprofessionals in general education and special education classrooms increasingly assist students with disabilities. Paraprofessionals attend to a disabled student's physical needs, including feeding, teaching good grooming habits, or assisting students riding the school bus. They also provide personal attention to students with other special needs, such as those from disadvantaged families, those who speak English as a second language, or those who need remedial education. Paraprofessionals help assess a student's progress by observing performance and recording relevant data. Paraprofessionals also work with infants and toddlers who have developmental delays or other disabilities. Under the guidance of a teacher or therapist, paraprofessionals perform exercises or play games to help the child develop physically and behaviorally. Some paraprofessionals work with young adults to help them obtain a job or to apply for community services for the disabled. (p. 2)

Working Conditions

- Even among full-time workers, nearly 40 percent work less than eight hours per day.
- Most paraprofessionals who provide educational instruction work the traditional nine- to ten-month school year.
- Paraprofessionals work in a variety of settings, including private homes, preschools, and local government offices, but most work in classrooms in elementary, middle, and secondary schools.

- Paraprofessionals also work outdoors supervising recess, and they spend much of their time standing, walking, or kneeling.
- Paraprofessionals who work with students in special education settings often perform more strenuous tasks, including lifting, as they help students with their daily routines.
- Paraprofessionals held almost 1.3 million jobs in 2002, with nearly three-fourths working in education institutions at the state and local level; private schools, day-care centers, and religious organizations hired most of the remainder.

Training, Other Qualifications, and Advancement

- Paraprofessionals with instructional responsibilities usually require more training than do those who do not perform teaching tasks. The No Child Left Behind Act of 2001 now requires paraprofessionals in Title 1 schools and programs to meet a more rigorous standard of qualification.
- Many schools also require previous experience in working with children, a valid driver's license, and/or a background check.
- Most paraprofessionals receive their training on the job.
- Those who tutor and review lessons with students must have a thorough understanding of class materials and instructional methods, and they should be familiar with the organization and operation of a school.
- Paraprofessionals must know how to keep records, operate audiovisual equipment, prepare instructional materials, and have adequate computer skills.
- Advancement usually takes the form of higher earnings or increased responsibility and comes primarily with experience or additional education. Some school districts provide time away from the job or tuition reimbursement so paraprofessionals can earn a bachelor's degree or pursue teaching qualifications. Paraprofessionals are often required to teach a certain length of time for the school district in return for tuition reimbursement.

Attributes Required of Paraprofessionals

- Enjoy working with children from a wide range of abilities and cultural backgrounds.
- Be able to handle classroom situations with fairness and patience.
- Demonstrate initiative and a willingness to follow a teacher's directions.
- Possess good writing and communication skills.

Job Outlook

- Employment of paraprofessionals is expected to grow faster than the average for all occupations through 2012.
- Although school enrollments are projected to increase only slowly over the next decade, the student population for which paraprofessionals are most needed (students in special education and those for whom English is not the first language) is expected to increase more rapidly. Legislation requires

these students to receive an education equal to that of other students, and this will generate jobs for paraprofessionals to accommodate these special needs.

■ The greater focus on educational quality and accountability required by the No Child Left Behind Act is likely to lead to an increased demand for paraprofessionals: to help prepare students for standardized testing and to provide extra assistance to students who perform poorly on tests.

■ An increasing number of after-school programs and summer programs will create new opportunities for paraprofessionals.

■ Numerous job openings will arise as paraprofessionals transfer to other occupations or leave the labor force to assume family responsibilities, to return to school, or for other reasons characteristic of occupations that require limited formal education and offer relatively low pay.

■ Opportunities for paraprofessionals are expected to be best for persons with at least two years of formal education after high school. Those who can speak a foreign language should be in particular demand.

■ Demand for paraprofessionals is expected to vary by region of the United States. Areas such as the South and West, where population and school enrollments are expanding rapidly, should have rapid growth in the demand for paraprofessionals.

Earnings

■ Average annual earnings of paraprofessionals in 2002 were $18,660. About 50 percent of paraprofessionals earned between $14,900 and $23,600. Ten percent earned less than $12,900, and 10 percent earned more than $29,000.

■ Paraprofessionals who work part time ordinarily do not receive benefits. Full-time workers usually receive health coverage and other benefits.

■ In 2002 about 30 percent of paraprofessionals belonged to unions, mainly the American Federation of Teachers or the National Education Association.

Related Occupations

■ Paraprofessionals who instruct children have duties similar to those of *preschool, kindergarten, elementary, middle,* and *secondary school teachers, special education teachers,* and *school librarians,* although paraprofessionals do not have the same level of responsibility or training.

■ The roles of paraprofessionals and their educational backgrounds are similar to those of child-care workers, library technicians, and library assistants.

■ Paraprofessionals who work with children with disabilities perform many of the same functions as occupational therapy assistants and aides.

Lastly, the statistic available in every document that describes paraprofessionals and their work is that overwhelmingly paraprofessionals are women. Typically, more than 95 percent of the paraprofessional workforce is female.

C-H-A-P-T-E-R S-U-M-M-A-R-Y

This chapter gives an overview of the nature of the work paraprofessionals perform under the various titles used throughout the United States. Now that you have read the chapter, and compared the national information with your own job, you should be able to answer the questions at the beginning of the chapter. You have learned about:

- The many terms that are used across the United States for paraprofessionals.
- The definitions of what a paraprofessional is and what she or he does, according to government and other sources.
- Facts about the work of paraprofessionals who are currently employed in U.S. schools.
- The nationwide picture of work conditions, the job outlook, and earnings for paraprofessionals.

Some of the facts may already be familiar to you, matching your own experience and work situation. However, few paraprofessionals have a real sense of belonging to such a large part of the workforce, with such widespread influence in education across the United States. Many paraprofessionals work in relative isolation with few opportunities to network with peers in their own school districts, let alone those from other districts in the state or other states in the nation. Remember, as a paraprofessional, you are literally "one in a million"—and certainly not alone in the work you do or the challenges you face.

E-X-T-E-N-D-I-N-G Y-O-U-R L-E-A-R-N-I-N-G

Paraprofessionals in Other Countries

You may be interested to know that paraprofessionals work in the education systems of many other countries around the world, most notably in Great Britain and Canada, where the situations are remarkably similar to the United States. Using a search engine such as Google or Yahoo, conduct an Internet search for information on paraprofessionals in other countries. You can use some of the titles listed in the first part of this chapter as you conduct your search. In Great Britain, paraprofessionals are now known as *teaching assistants (TAs)* but were formerly called *LSAs,* or *learning support assistants.* In Canada, the most common terms are *classroom assistant* or *teaching assistant.*

A-N-S-W-E-R-S

1. B.
2. B.
3. C.
4. A.
5. C.
6. B.

2 The U.S. Educational System

This chapter discusses the public educational system of the United States at the federal, state, and local levels and identifies where paraprofessionals fit into that system. The federal government has recently passed legislation that impacts paraprofessionals in the schools and is changing the way state offices and local school districts provide for their paraprofessionals. In this chapter, we look at how these changes have come about.

Government regulations are discussed at the federal, state, and school-district levels. In later chapters, we look at school-level programs and how they impact your work in the classroom. By the end of this chapter, you will have an understanding of the historical and legal influences that have shaped the roles and responsibilities of paraprofessionals. You will also be able to answer these questions:

- Where did state governments get the authority to become involved in education?
- How did the federal government get involved in education?
- What laws have shaped the programs under which paraprofessionals are hired?
- What are the important concepts of the law that affect your job at the classroom level and define the basic educational terminology corresponding to those laws (e.g., due process, least restrictive environment, and confidentiality)?

Many forces outside the school impact your job. Although we do not expect you to use the vocabulary of a lawyer in discussing the important laws affecting your work, this chapter explains the laws and terminology that may seriously affect your success as a paraprofessional. First, we look at education at the national level and identify where state governments obtained the authority to become involved in education. Figure 2.1 outlines the levels in the U.S. educational system.

Education at the National Level

You may find it interesting to know that education in the United States is not required by the Constitution and the United States has no national system of education. Perhaps you remember from high school history classes that the Constitution provides for the establishment of legislative, executive, and judicial powers. In addition to the Articles of the Constitution are twenty-six amendments; the first ten are called the Bill of Rights. Although education is not mentioned in the Constitu-

---

Levels in the U.S. Educational System

Federal Government: Tenth and Fourteenth Amendments
■ Americans with Disabilities Education Act
■ Education of All Handicapped Children's Act (PL 94-142)
   Reauthorized as the Individuals with Disabilities Education Improvement Act
      (IDEIA '04)
■ Section 504 of the Rehabilitation Act
■ Title I of the Elementary and Secondary Education Act
   Reauthorized as the No Child Left Behind Act (NCLB)

State Office of Education administration of state compliance plans for:
   special education programs, ELL and Bilingual Programs, Head Start Programs,
   and 504 plans
Local school districts' administration of program funds for school programs: special
   education, ELL and Bilingual, Head Start, 504
Schools' delivery of services to students eligible for services in special education, ELL
   and Bilingual, Head Start, 504

Figure 2.1

---

tion or its amendments, two amendments have been interpreted to give authority to states to provide for public education: the Tenth Amendment and the Fourteenth Amendment (see Figure 2.2).

The Tenth Amendment to the U.S. Constitution states, "powers not delegated to the U.S. by the Constitution, nor prohibited by it to the States, are reserved to the States." It is by virtue of this authority that all states have chosen to provide public education. Essentially the law *allows* each state to assume the power to

---

The Tenth and Fourteenth Amendments

Amendment Ten
The powers not delegated to the United States by the Constitution, nor prohibited by it to the states, are reserved to the states respectively, or to the people.

Amendment Fourteen
All persons born or naturalized in the United States, and subject to the jurisdiction thereof, are citizens of the United States and of the state wherein they reside. No state shall make or enforce any law, which shall abridge the privileges or immunities of citizens of the United States; *nor shall any state deprive any person of life, liberty, or property, without due process of law; nor deny to any person within its jurisdiction the equal protection of the laws.* (emphasis added).

Figure 2.2

provide educational services to its children, and all states have made the decision to do that.

The Fourteenth Amendment requires all states to provide *due process and equal protection*. In connection with education, this clause has been interpreted to mean that if states choose to provide education services, they are required to provide them to all students on an equal basis and to provide due process before denying equivalent educational programming to any student or group of students. Because of this amendment, the state constitutions of all fifty states provide for public education for all students.

How Did the Federal Government Become Involved in Education?

Although the decision to provide educational services to all American children was first taken at the state level, now we do have substantial federal legislation relating to education. We briefly describe the development of the Education of All Handicapped Children Act of 1975 as a good example of how the federal government became involved in the educational system.

The Education of All Handicapped Children Act, also called Public Law (PL) 94-142, was the first law to be passed on behalf of children with disabilities. It was strongly influenced by the 1954 court case of *Brown v. Board of Education of Topeka*, which was not directly related to disability but challenged the practice of segregating schools according to race. This case was taken to the U.S. Supreme Court, and in its ruling, the Court declared that education must be made available to *all* children on equal terms:

> Today, education is perhaps the most important function of state and local governments. Compulsory school attendance laws and the great expenditure for education both demonstrate our recognition of the importance of education to our democratic society. It is required in the performance of our most basic responsibilities. . . . In these days, it is doubtful that any child may reasonably be expected to succeed in life if he is denied the opportunity of an education.

The *Brown* decision, with its effect of extending public school education to African American children on equal terms with white children, began a period of intense questioning among parents of children with disabilities. Tax-paying parents noted the similarities between the education provided to their children with disabilities and that provided to African American children. They asked why their children with disabilities were being denied an education or, when they were being educated, why they were in segregated programs. They noted that these segregated classrooms were often substandard. They questioned why the same principles of equal access to education for all children—whatever their race—did not seem to apply to all children, whatever their abilities.

Legal cases brought by the parents showed their growing dissatisfaction. Eventually some of these cases reached the U.S. Supreme Court. Generally, the arguments were based on the principles of the Fourteenth Amendment to the Constitution: no state should deny anyone equal protection of the law, or deprive any person of life, liberty, or property without due process. The Supreme Court agreed, stating,

> Education services such as special education follow the requirement of the 14th Amendment, which states that no state shall "deprive any person of life, liberty, or property, without due process of law . . . nor deny . . . equal protection of the laws." Education is part of the clause designated to "protect the general welfare."

Thus the Education of All Handicapped Children Act eventually came into force in 1975, as PL 94-142. In 1990 it was reauthorized and renamed the Individuals with Disabilities Education Act (IDEA). It was again reauthorized in 1997, thus it is commonly referred to as IDEA '97, but the most recent reauthorization (2004) renamed it the Individuals with Disabilities Education Improvement Act (IDEIA). The concepts of *equal protection* and *due process* remain fundamental today in special education under IDEA. The process of case law is generally the means whereby the federal government becomes directly involved in educational issues as landmark cases are heard and ruled on, particularly those that reach the Supreme Court.

IDEA was not the first piece of legislation that impacted paraprofessionals, but it was the first to be explicit about the paraprofessional's role. As you read the next section about how IDEA and other federal laws affect paraprofessionals, try to identify important concepts in these laws that affect your job at the classroom level. Also, see if you can define the basic educational terminology corresponding to those laws, for example, confidentiality, due process, and least restrictive environment.

Recent Federal Law Affecting Paraprofessionals

Paraprofessionals have been working in classrooms for many decades, and they continue to be employed in increasing numbers. During the 1960s there was a strong national focus on civil rights and the legal rights of children with disabilities to receive an education. Paraprofessionals were hired in increasing numbers to assist in education, mental health, and health and human services. In the early 1970s, national attention focused on the need to support women and senior citizens in their quest for financial and political equity, and some federal financial support was added to schools to employ paraprofessionals. Head Start and Title I programs initiated at this time mostly hired mothers of children enrolled in the programs as paraprofessionals. The rationale for hiring family members was to both increase educational and support services for economically and educationally disadvantaged children and youth and also to provide employment for their families. At about the same time, special education services were being established, which increased the number of paraprofessionals hired to meet the legal push for inclusionary settings and additional support for students with disabilities.

So why after so many years as a classroom assistant is there an urgency expressed for classes, training programs, and activities to help your effectiveness in the classroom? Whereas the earlier laws led to the creation of classroom positions for paraprofessionals, only recently have laws specified training and qualification requirements for them. The two most notable are IDEA '97, which we have already described, and Title I of the Elementary and Secondary Education Act (ESEA).

IDEA '97 and IDEIA '04 The Individuals with Disabilities Education Act (IDEA) makes the following specific reference to paraprofessionals:

> A state may allow paraprofessionals who *are appropriately trained and supervised* under state standards to assist in the provision of special education and related services (Individuals with Disabilities Education Act Amendments, 1997, PL 105-17).

Although the original act had required school districts to provide special education services for over twenty-two years, IDEA '97 was the first piece of education legislation that specifically mentioned paraprofessionals and their role in providing those services. Training sessions on IDEA '97 from the federal Office of Special Education Programs (OSEP) informed states that the use of paraprofessionals and assistants was contingent on state law and regulation. Thus states were given the option of determining the extent to which paraprofessionals could assist in the provision of special education and related services, and they had flexibility in determining the scope of paraprofessionals' responsibilities (U.S. Department of Education, 1999). The language used in IDEA to refer to paraprofessionals being "appropriately trained and supervised" was very general. It may seem strange that the law would be so vague and lacking in detail. However, this is quite common when a new aspect of a law is introduced. The fine details of any law are gradually worked out and better defined through cases brought against organizations or individuals on the basis of the law. This has certainly been true of special education.

Building on case law, IDEA '97 included six principles, or elements. Although they describe the rights of students with disabilities and their parents, they have a direct bearing on your work as a paraprofessional, whether you work in special education or not. You will find a brief definition of each of these here because they are not all self-explanatory. If you are currently working as a paraprofessional, you will probably recognize these terms, particularly if you work in a special education setting. You may wish to list those terms you have heard or used at the end of this section, and note where the definitions we provide increase your understanding of the concepts as they have been applied to your work with students and parents.

These are the six principles of IDEA (see box for summary):

1. Free and appropriate public education (FAPE). As the name suggests, this principle requires states to provide education services that meet the individual needs of each student at no cost.
2. Nondiscriminatory evaluation. This principle requires that all students be evaluated or tested in ways that allow them to show their true abilities, and it requires schools to provide supports such as a scribe, assistive technology, or additional time, if the student needs them. The law also requires a comprehensive school evaluation involving all areas of the suspected disability. Testing must be in the native language of the child, a team of professionals rather than a single individual must give the tests, and the testing must be administered one to one, not in a group.

3. Individualized education program (IEP). When a student is identified as needing special education services, the school is required to write an IEP for that student, including specific goals and objectives; curriculum modifications; behavioral goals, if needed; and additional supports that may be needed to help the student achieve those goals. Parents, teachers, and the student (when able) should all participate in writing and reviewing the IEP. The IEP team must also determine which setting will best help the student reach educational goals.

4. Least Restrictive Environment (LRE). LRE provides for mainstreaming into general education programs and classrooms so students with disabilities can have access to the general curriculum. It means that students with disabilities must be educated with their nondisabled peers to the maximum extent appropriate. The LRE may be different for each student. For some, it will be the general classroom with additional support provided; for others, it may be a pullout program for part of the day; still others may benefit most from a separate classroom within the school. The principle of LRE discourages educating students with disabilities in segregated settings away from their nondisabled peers, unless it is absolutely necessary for the education and safety of all students.

5. Procedural safeguards. The law guarantees to parents that their rights will be safeguarded; that is, all procedures will be properly followed. One example of a required procedure is that all options must be considered when looking at the least restrictive environment for a student. Another example is the school must inform parents of every step in the IEP process, including upcoming evaluations and meetings.

6. Due process. This principle requires school districts to set up a system of trained mediators and due process hearing officers, so parents who are dissatisfied with the services (or a lack of services) for their child can challenge the provision and request changes. They are first referred to a mediator, but if they cannot reach agreement, they may engage in the due process procedure and have their case heard by a due process hearing officer. Because of the hearing, the school district may be required to change the provisions made for the student, but each case is judged individually against the requirements of IDEA.

The Six Principles/Elements of IDEA and IDEIA '04

1. Free and appropriate public education (FAPE)
2. Nondiscriminatory evaluation
3. Individualized education program (IEP)
4. Least restrictive environment (LRE)
5. Procedural safeguards
6. Due process

FAPE: The Right to a Free and Appropriate Public Education

In the case of *Mills v. Board of Education* (1972), a twelve-year-old African American student named Peter Mills was excluded from the fourth grade because he was allegedly a "behavior problem." The principal approved his exclusion from school. During the ensuing court case, the school district contended that it did not have enough money to provide special education programs for such students. The Court held that lack of funds is no excuse for failing to educate children and ordered the school to readmit the boy and serve him—and other such students—appropriately.

Even if funds are limited (often the case today), children with disabilities must not be denied access to the public schools. Among other provisions, the *Mills* case ruled that children with disabilities have a right to a *free public education* and a right to *due process*. In 27 states, another 36 court decisions were made affirming the *right* to education. It became clear that a federal standard was needed. As a result, a bill was introduced in the U.S. Senate in 1972, reintroduced during the next two legislative sessions, and finally emerged as PL 94-142, the Education for All Handicapped Children Act (1975).

We have not covered these elements in any great detail, but you will find examples of cases that helped define the law for the principles of FAPE and due process in the text boxes.

Title I of the Elementary and Secondary Education Act (ESEA) Title I refers to a section or title within a law—in this case, the Elementary and Secondary Education Act (ESEA). This federal law first began as the Eisenhower Education Act (PL 107-110) and has had several content changes and new names over the years. It has had a significant impact on America's schools and children since it was first enacted in 1965, when provisions in the act called for intensive efforts to increase parent involvement in education. Title I of the act was designed to provide additional instructional support for disadvantaged students. Federal funding for Title I programs is now used to provide tuition in basic skills (literacy and numeracy), with the majority of funding targeting the early elementary grades.

Title I programs have traditionally relied on paraprofessionals as key players in delivery of educational services. In fact, by the year 2000, paraprofessionals, rather than professional educators, comprised about one-half of all Title I instructional staff in the United States. As ESEA approached its 2001 reauthorization, a great deal of concern was expressed nationally about accepting such a low level of qualifications for Title I instructional staff, many of whom were performing the same instructional functions as fully certified teachers but had few if any formal qualifications. The chairman of the U.S. Department of Education advisory board, Christopher Cross, told a 1999 Senate hearing committee that teacher aide positions were originally intended to serve as interim positions for people on their way

Due Process

As little as forty years ago, children with disabilities were treated very differently from their nondisabled peers. Considered "uneducable," they either remained at home or were given a "special" education in segregated settings. Parents questioned why their disabled children were being excluded from training and education that could better their lives. As legal action was taken against this practice, courts were required to determine whether or not such treatment was rational. One of the landmark cases to examine these questions related to disabilities was *Pennsylvania Association for Retarded Children (PARC) v. Commonwealth of Pennsylvania* (1972).

PARC challenged a state law that denied public school education to children who were considered unable to profit from attendance in schools. Lawyers and parents supporting *PARC* argued that, although the children had intellectual disabilities, it was not rational to assume they were uneducable or untrainable and the state was unable to demonstrate a rational basis for excluding them. The Court not only ruled that the children were entitled to receive free public education but also that the parents had a right to be notified before any change was made in their child's educational program. It stated that certain procedures known as *due process of law* must be followed to ensure that parents are fully and fairly informed. *All* states now have the responsibility to ensure that each public agency establishes, maintains, and implements procedural safeguards that meet the due process requirements of IDEA.

to teacher licensure, but it had rarely happened because of the lack of professional incentives that would make teacher training affordable to paraprofessionals.

The reauthorization of ESEA, signed into law by President George W. Bush, was called the No Child Left Behind Act (NCLB) of 2001. The NCLB Act affected every program authorized under ESEA, ranging from Title I and efforts to improve teacher quality, to initiatives for limited English proficient (LEP) students and safe and drug-free schools. It also required considerable accountability from schools, requiring testing of student achievement and annual measurable objectives for each district and school. The act's impact on paraprofessionals came in the clause that called for "highly qualified" teachers and paraprofessionals in America's schools. For teachers this meant new requirements to ensure that those who taught core academic subjects had the appropriate academic qualifications. For paraprofessionals it was very specific about the need to meet more rigorous training and skill requirements.

The NCLB provisions for paraprofessionals were similar to the IDEA requirements in stating that paraprofessionals should receive appropriate training and supervision, but they took training requirements much further.

▪ Higher qualifications for paraprofessionals. Paraprofessionals in Title I programs must have at least two years of postsecondary education or, for an existing paraprofessional with only a high school diploma, demonstrate necessary skills through a formal state or local academic assessment. All new hires in Title I programs after January 8, 2002, had to meet these requirements; existing paraprofessionals were given four years from January 8, 2002, to comply. These requirements did not apply to paraprofessionals used only for translation services or parent involvement. However, all paraprofessionals in programs funded by Title I money have to meet the requirements, even if their positions are funded by special education or 504 monies.

■ Appropriate roles for paraprofessionals. The law specified that paraprofessionals should not provide instructional support except under the direct supervision of a teacher (U.S. Department of Education, 2002).

IDEA and No Child Left Behind have been the most influential pieces of education legislation affecting paraprofessionals. Other legislative influences have included Head Start, Even Start, the Americans with Disabilities Act (ADA), and Section 504 of the Vocational Rehabilitation Act. Because these are laws that have a significant general effect on schools, and not just on paraprofessionals, we have provided some detail on each of them.

Head Start and Even Start

Early childhood education is critically important because children who have good vocabularies and who are taught early reading skills before they start school are more likely to become good readers and achieve academic success throughout their school careers. Head Start and Even Start are federal programs that have had a long-standing reputation of involving parents in their programs, often hiring mothers of the children enrolled in the program to work as paraprofessionals.

Head Start Staff Requirements Although many Head Start staff may have the title of "teacher," many of them have the qualifications of paraprofessionals, rather than teachers. In 1998 a mandate in the Head Start Act required that by September 2003, at least half of all Head Start teachers in center-based programs should have an associate's, bachelor's, or advanced degree in early childhood education or a degree in a related field with preschool teaching experience. When a classroom in a center-based program does not have a teacher with a degree in early childhood education or in a related field, with experience in teaching preschool children, the act requires the teacher to have a child development associate (CDA) credential or a state-awarded certificate for preschool teachers.

The Even Start Family Literacy Program Even Start provides services to low-income families with young children (birth through age seven). The program's purpose is to break the cycle of illiteracy and poverty. Goals of the Even Start program are adult education (for the parents), early childhood education (for the children), parenting education, and interactive literacy activities for parents and children together. Even Start serves about thirty thousand families every year and was reauthorized and consolidated into the No Child Left Behind Act. Here are some of the changes in Even Start that may be important to you and your school program:

■ Local programs must use instructional programs based on scientific research relating to reading and the prevention of reading difficulties.

■ Instructional services must be offered during the summer months.

■ By December 2004 a majority of the instructional staff must have obtained an associate's, bachelor's, or graduate degree in a field related to early childhood education, elementary or secondary education, or adult education; they must also meet state qualifications for providing these services. All instructional staff hired since December 2000 must meet these qualifications when hired.

■ By December 2004 the local administrator must receive training in operating a family literacy program, *and all paraprofessionals who provide support for academic instruction must have a high school diploma or the equivalent*. (emphasis added)

Section 504 and the ADA

Many paraprofessionals are hired under what is commonly known as Section 504, properly called Section 504 of the Vocational Rehabilitation Act of 1973, a broad civil rights law that protects individuals with disabilities from discrimination in programs and activities that receive federal financial assistance. Section 504 of this law requires state and local governments to assure that accommodations and/or services are provided for people with disabilities, if they are needed. The Department of Education's Office for Civil Rights (OCR) enforces the law at the nation's educational institutions. Under this law a person is identified as having a disability if she or he has (1) an impairment that substantially limits a major life activity, (2) a history of a disability, or (3) been regarded by others as having a disability.

The law applies to any business or agency (such as school districts) with more than fifteen employees. Because most school districts have more than fifteen employees, most also have a Section 504 coordinator who assures the requirements of the section are met. Because this law applies to both employees and students, the Section 504 coordinator may work with individual students, their parents, and teachers to develop a 504 plan that will adapt the learning environment to accommodate the environmental or learning needs of the student. The influence of Section 504 goes beyond individuals with disabilities, however. Requirements to make building and transportation accessible have made a big difference for all Americans. Ramps and sidewalk curb cuts designed for wheelchair users, for example, also allow easy access to buildings and street crossings for adults pushing baby strollers.

Section 504 of the Vocational Rehabilitation Act served as a springboard for the Americans with Disabilities Act of 1990 (ADA). Like Section 504, the ADA is a civil rights law. It uses the same definition of disability but is much broader because it applies to state and local government entities, private-sector employment— whether it is federally funded or not—public services, public transportation, and telecommunications. It requires that employers do not discriminate on the basis of a person having a disability. If the person with a disability, given the proper support, can perform the activities required for the job as well as a nondisabled person, the employer may not eliminate the person who has a disability as a candidate for employment. Moreover, the employer must be prepared to make reasonable accommodations to enable the person with a disability to do the job. These protections apply in a school setting to students and employees. It has been suggested that school districts assign the Section 504 coordinator to oversee the provisions of the ADA.

Section 504, ADA, and Paraprofessionals Section 504 of the Vocational Reha-bilitation Act of 1973 and the Americans with Disabilities Act (1990) also led to the hiring of paraprofessionals, and millions of students with disabilities have seen doors of opportunity open because of these acts. They are particularly important pieces of legislation for students because some students with disabilities can only receive limited support under IDEA. For example, some students use a wheelchair because of cerebral palsy, but the condition may only affect their physical function-ing and not their cognitive abilities. In this case they may not need or be eligible for assistance from special education personnel (i.e., under IDEA), but Section 504 re-quires they be provided with a physically accessible classroom and may also provide them with a paraprofessional to help with their physical needs, rather than their ed-ucational needs. Thus Section 504 complements IDEA. It also extends from cradle to grave, whereas IDEA is only designed for pre- and school-aged population.

Three decades ago, more than a million school-aged children received no edu-cational services because they had disabilities; and only one out of five of the stu-dents who received services was educated in a regular public school building. To-day, more than six million children with disabilities receive special education and regular education with services, virtually all of them in regular school buildings. In addition, studies of postsecondary education indicate that in the last two decades of the twentieth century, college enrollment rates of students with disabilities tripled, and those students completed their programs at a rate nearly as high as that of other students. These changes have come about because of the types of federal legislation we have described here and the many programs initiated be-cause of the legislation, many of which rely heavily on paraprofessionals.

Two other areas of the law deserve a mention before we consider education at state- and school-district levels: (1) Equal Opportunities and other civil rights leg-islation, and (2) the Family Educational Rights and Privacy Act (FERPA), which addresses the issue of confidentiality.

Civil Rights, Equal Educational Opportunities, and Title III of NCLB

The national effort to guarantee equal educational opportunities for all students in the United States, and in particular the rights of language minority students, draws heavily on the Fourteenth Amendment to the Constitution and the Civil Rights Act of 1964. Title VI of the Civil Rights Act of 1964 declares, "No person in the United States shall, on the grounds of race, color or national origin . . . be denied the ben-efits of, or be subjected to discrimination under any program or activity receiving federal financial assistance." In addition, the Equal Educational Opportunities Act of 1974 makes educational institutions responsible for taking the necessary steps to overcome linguistic and/or cultural barriers that keep students from equal par-ticipation in instructional programs. It states,

> [N]o State shall deny an equal educational opportunity to an individual on account of his or her race, color, sex or national origin, by . . . the failure of an educational agency to take appropriate action to overcome language barriers that impede equal participation by its students in its instructional programs.

Title III of the Elementary and Secondary Education Act (No Child Left Behind) addresses the issues of students whose first or home language is not English. The major goals of Title III are to help students who are considered limited English proficient (LEP) to attain English proficiency, develop high levels of academic competence in English, and meet the same academic content and achievement standards that all students are expected to meet. Title III requires states to establish English language proficiency standards, to develop and implement English language proficiency assessments, and to define annual achievement objectives for measuring and increasing levels of English proficiency. The English language proficiency standards are based on the four areas of speaking, reading, writing, and listening. However, the local school district or LEA (Local Education Agency) must assess LEP students in five areas: speaking, reading, writing, listening, and comprehension. Many paraprofessionals have been hired under the requirements of Title III to provide support for students with limited English proficiency. The value of the service provided is enhanced when the paraprofessional comes from the same background as the student and can provide social and linguistic support, as well as instruction in English proficiency.

The Family Educational Rights and Privacy Act (FERPA)

The Family Educational Rights and Privacy Act (FERPA) is a federal law that protects the privacy of student education records. The law applies to any school that receives funds under a program of the U.S. Department of Education. FERPA gives parents certain rights with respect to their children's education records; these rights transfer to the student when he or she reaches the age of eighteen or attends a school beyond the high school level. Students to whom the rights have transferred are termed *eligible students*. Parents have the right to (1) inspect and review the student's education records maintained by the school, although schools may charge a fee for copies, and (2) request that a school correct records they believe to be inaccurate or misleading.

Generally, the law states that schools must have written permission from the parent in order to release any information from a student's education record. However, FERPA does allow schools to disclose those records, without consent and under certain conditions, to school officials with a legitimate educational interest. For example, records may be given to the following people:

- Officials at another school to which the student is transferring.
- Specified officials for audit or evaluation purposes.
- Appropriate parties in connection with financial aid to a student.
- Individuals acting in compliance with a judicial order or lawfully issued subpoena.
- Appropriate officials in cases of health and safety emergencies.
- State and local authorities within a juvenile justice system.

Schools may disclose, without consent, directory information such as a student's name, address, telephone number, date and place of birth, honors or awards, and dates of attendance. However, schools must tell parents the directory information exists, and they must allow a reasonable amount of time for parents to request that the school not disclose directory information about their child. Schools must also notify parents each year of their rights under FERPA. This notification can be sent home in a letter, PTA bulletin, student handbook, newsletter article, and so on.

The critical aspect of FERPA for paraprofessionals is the responsibility it assigns for keeping confidentiality. We discuss confidentiality at length later in the book, but you must realize that confidentiality is not just a question of professionalism. It is a legal requirement, established at the level of the federal government.

Education at the State Level

Based on laws such as NCLB and IDEA, each state must develop a plan that describes how it will respond to the federal legislation, and the federal education office must approve this plan before it is implemented. State plans are usually compiled from individual plans received from school districts within the state. The plan must also include proposals for how the state will show compliance and measure progress toward the goals it has set. This is true of all programs funded by the federal government (e.g., special education, Title I, Head Start). For example, under No Child Left Behind, the law requires state education agencies to "ensure that schools provide instruction by highly qualified instructional staff." A state must outline its plan for ensuring highly qualified staff, including training programs it may put in place or incentives for attracting highly qualified candidates from outside the state. It must also provide statistics for the current situation and set targets for increasing or retaining highly qualified staff members. Continued funding from the federal government usually depends on a state showing it has realistic plans in place for complying with federal requirements.

Education at the School-District Level

Officials in school districts are required by their state Office of Education to develop a plan describing how they will meet the state and federal mandates. They must outline how they will implement the plan and what measures they will use at the end of the year to determine whether or not they have done what they said they would. This plan is particularly important if the school district is to receive federal and state monies to help support continuing implementation of the plan.

Out of the funds received from the federal government, or those collected at the state level through taxation, a state typically allocates funds to school districts according to the number of students served, that is, on a per capita basis. However, a portion of the federal or state money is often retained, either to provide a service at the state level or to offer additional discretionary funds for districts to provide that service at the local level. Training for paraprofessionals or teachers is a good example of this. It is expensive to conduct training classes for educators.

Even Start: How Funding Flows Through to Individual Programs

Even Start is primarily a state-administered discretionary grant program in which states hold competitions to fund integrated family literacy services. The U.S. Department of Education allocates Even Start funding to states based on a mathematical formula, which is largely based on numbers of students and economic need. States then award subgrants to partnerships of local school districts and other organizations.

In many locations throughout the country, school district personnel take responsibility for advertising positions and interviewing, and hiring staff. This is similar to most special education and Title I programs in which a supervisor located at the school district offices oversees these programs. In other locations, individual schools or programs take the responsibility for interviewing and hiring.

Costs can include a trainer's time, training materials, pay for substitutes, and mileage reimbursement for travel to the training location. Large school districts may have the personnel and resources to organize and provide such training, but it is usually beyond the scope of small school districts. A state may choose to provide these services at the state level for all school district personnel within the state, or it may offer funds to the school districts directly to provide the service locally.

CHAPTER SUMMARY

The U.S. educational system, particularly as it relates to paraprofessionals, is a complex system with many different programs and agencies involved. It is helpful for you to have a context for what you do and understand where your work fits into the national educational picture. It is also important to know as a taxpayer and parent that what you do can have an impact on the system, and to know the system is there to ensure appropriate education services to students.

Here are the basic points from this chapter:

- Although there is no constitutional requirement to provide educational services, the federal government has made a significant impact on educational provision through legislation and allocation of funds to states.
- All states have taken on the responsibility for providing educational services, prompted initially by the freedoms of the Tenth Amendment.
- States are required to provide equally for all students under the requirements of the Fourteenth Amendment, which has led to civil rights legislation affecting education (such as the Americans with Disabilities Act) and to legislation that directly addresses educational issues (such as the Individuals with Disabilities Education Act).

- With each successive reauthorization, greater detail has been added to laws such as IDEIA and NCLB as cases have been brought challenging the provisions of the law and causing the law to become better defined.
- States and school districts receive federal funding to implement programs and policies required by education legislation, and they must present plans for compliance with regulations in order to receive that funding.
- Changes in requirements for paraprofessionals have only been introduced into law in recent years. They have included better definition of appropriate roles and the level of qualifications and skill required of paraprofessionals working in instructional roles.

Perhaps most importantly, the changes in education law at the federal level are a reflection of the valuable instructional services you offer students as a paraprofessional and the extent to which educational programs depend on your efforts. Although the requirements of the law may seem demanding and appear difficult to accommodate, they are in keeping with the high levels of responsibility you have been assigned. In addition, the law now clearly states some principles that have always made sense even though they have not been mandated: you should have appropriate levels of qualification and training for your work, and you must be supervised by a professional. Thus the law protects students both in requiring that they receive an education and in requiring they receive it from "highly qualified" personnel.

This chapter on federal education law provides a framework and an understanding of where the authority lies in establishing requirements for services, along with training standards for paraprofessionals and other school staff. Having considered the larger, national context for education, we look at classroom-level influences in the following chapters.

E-X-T-E-N-D-I-N-G—Y-O-U-R—L-E-A-R-N-I-N-G

Self-Evaluation Exercise

To assess your current knowledge of the government, answer the following questions:

1. From which two amendments of the U.S. Constitution does the government derive its authority to pass laws regulating education?

   _____

2. The special education law called the Handicapped Children's Education Act, or Public Law 94-142, was reauthorized and renamed IDEIA. What do the letters I-D-E-I-A stand for?

   _____

3. Title I of the Elementary and Secondary Education Act was reauthorized and signed into law by President George W. Bush as the

_____

4. Circle the correct answer:

State Offices of Education have which of the following responsibilities?

a. Administration of state funds to school districts

b. Development of plans to show how they will comply with federal laws

c. Programs such as Special Education, Title I, Head Start and Even Start, and 504

d. Monitoring of federal programs to assure compliance

e. All of the above

f. None of the above

5. Local school districts must administer the program funds for federal programs offered to children in the schools. True? _____ False? _____

6. The delivery of services to students who are eligible for services in federal programs, such as Special Education, Head Start, Even Start, and 504, happens at the school level. True? _____ False? _____

Answers are listed at the end of the chapter. If you answered one of the questions incorrectly, refer back to the chapter and reread the relevant section.

You may also wish to ask yourself these questions: How does this knowledge of federal law affect my work with students? What might I do differently because of this knowledge? Take a moment to reflect on these questions and then write your thoughts in the space provided.

_____

_____

_____

_____

_____

_____

_____

_____

_____

CEC Standards

In Chapter 4 we discuss the Council for Exceptional Children (CEC)'s knowledge and skill standards for special education paraprofessionals. Because two of the CEC standards relate directly to the laws we have been discussing in this chapter, it would be appropriate for you to begin to consider those standards here.

CEC Standard 3: Know the rights and responsibilities of families and children as they relate to individuals.

Given the requirements of IDEIA you have read about in this chapter, what could you do to meet this standard?

_____

_____

_____

_____

_____

_____

CEC Standard 9: Demonstrate sensitivity to the diversity of individuals and families.

Some of the requirements of the laws discussed in this chapter include equal educational opportunities, free and appropriate public education, and nondiscriminatory practices toward individuals with disabilities or those from minority cultures. These are high moral principles, but they must be implemented at the classroom level and every day by educators like you. What are some of the ways in which you can demonstrate "sensitivity to the diversity of individuals and families" by implementing the principles required by law?

_____

_____

_____

_____

_____

_____

A-N-S-W-E-R-S————————————————————————————

1. Amendment Ten and Amendment Fourteen

2. Individuals with Disabilities Education Improvement Act

3. No Child Left Behind Act

4. E

5. True

6. True

3 How Are Paraprofessional Duties Assigned and Defined?

We consider clearly defined roles and responsibilities to be such an important topic that we have dedicated a whole chapter to it. After discussing some of the essential aspects of role definition, this chapter suggests practical ways for you to obtain the information you need to be clear about the extent and limits of your roles, and thus provide more efficiently for student needs as a member of the instructional team.

When you have read and responded to the activities in this chapter, you will be able to answer the following questions:

- In what ways does the federal government define and restrict the work of paraprofessionals?
- What are the state requirements for paraprofessional roles?
- What school-district and school guidelines exist for my job as a paraprofessional?
- What exactly are my duties at the classroom level?

Understanding the importance of having a clearly defined job will help you better support student learning. Knowing how to learn what you are expected to do and what you are restricted from doing is vital to your continuing employment and a good relationship with your supervisors.

Role Definitions and Restrictions at Federal Levels

In 1997 the U.S. Department of Education sponsored a report by the Policy Studies Associates, *Roles for Education Paraprofessionals in Effective Schools*. As the title suggests, the report offered a set of recommendations regarding appropriate roles assigned to paraprofessionals by schools and school districts. The recommendations also included the statement that in order to be most effective in their roles, paraprofessionals need support from schools and districts in the form of appropriate training, instructional team support, and supervision. Here are some of the roles that paraprofessionals assume and the report highlighted:

- Nurturing the social and cognitive competence of preschoolers.
- Engaging parents in discussions about raising healthy and successful children.

- Providing academic support through Title I programs.
- Serving as mentors in programs for at-risk youth.
- Serving as advocates in the community and as coaches for migrant or immigrant students and their families.
- Contributing to adult education programs associated with the school.

This is a nice reminder of the wide variety of roles that paraprofessionals assume, and it adds to the list in Chapter 1. However, it does seem to play down a major role: providing academic and instructional support.

The report goes on to suggest that the effectiveness of paraprofessional staff largely depends on the adequacy of the curriculum, the instructional methods used, and the general organization of the school, not just on the qualifications of the paraprofessionals themselves. We discuss how curriculum is selected in a later chapter because the principles involved are important. We also devote considerable space to discussing effective instructional methods in Chapter 8. But otherwise, these areas are well beyond your control as a paraprofessional. You have little or no say in the curriculum that is followed or the way the school as a whole is run, and you are generally required to use teaching methods that your supervisor requests. But it is interesting to note that such a report would make a point of highlighting the critical place you hold as part of the larger structure of a successful school or other educational establishment.

Supporting the School and Students

Seasoned veteran paraprofessionals agree that the most important—and rewarding—part of their job is providing direct support to students. This is perhaps the most important way in which they support the mission of a school. Members of a 1997 U.S. Department of Education task force looked at what they considered effective practices for paraprofessionals in education. The task force represented the National Education Association, the American Federation of Teachers, and the National Resource Center for Paraprofessionals, as well as paraprofessionals themselves. At the conclusion of their work they made five recommendations. They identified the following areas as necessary to ensure that a paraprofessional's work contributes appropriately to achieving a school's mission:

- Clear definitions of roles and responsibilities.
- Appropriate job qualifications and methods for demonstrating competencies.
- Ongoing professional development that is directly related to skills and knowledge needed by paraprofessionals.
- Organizational support for the paraprofessional's work as these roles are performed under the supportive direction of a certified teacher.
- Development of a career ladder for those aspiring to be certified teachers.

We are only concerned with the first of these areas in this chapter—clear definition of roles and responsibilities—although later chapters deal with some of the other areas.

Clear Definitions of Roles and Responsibilities

The 1997 government report recognized the difficulty of balancing each staff member's responsibilities against tight schedules and the need for supervision, but it emphasized the importance of establishing clear expectations as a foundation for effective teamwork between paraprofessionals and their professional supervisors. This is a point that many other authors have made: *paraprofessionals need to know exactly what is expected of them.* It almost seems too simple to be so important. But the truth is, because it seems so obvious, this sort of clarification of roles and expectations often does not happen. Time and energy are wasted as paraprofessionals guess and interpret a teacher's requirements, and of course they do not always get it right because paraprofessionals are no better at mind reading than anyone else.

Later in the chapter we discuss how your roles are defined at the state, local, and school level, but first we look at the federal level. Federal legislation is beginning to provide more insight into appropriate roles for paraprofessionals working in a variety of settings. We discuss two of the foremost laws: No Child Left Behind (NCLB) and the Individuals with Disabilities Education Act (IDEA). We already discussed these laws and the foundation they provide for the U.S. educational system in Chapter 2. Here we look at the ways in which they influence the roles assigned to paraprofessionals.

No Child Left Behind (NCLB)

Title I of the No Child Left Behind Act of 2001 defines a paraprofessional as an "individual with instructional duties," and it specifically states that a paraprofessional may not provide instructional support services without the direct supervision of a professional. No Child Left Behind is the major piece of federal general education legislation covering the elementary and secondary years. It is understandable therefore that the major role referred to is "instructional support." In fact, NCLB goes so far as to state that individuals who work solely in noninstructional roles (food service, cafeteria or playground supervision, personal care services, and noninstructional computer assistance) are not considered paraprofessionals at all for the purposes of Title I. Within this general category of "instructional support," no further clarification of roles is provided by No Child Left Behind. Additionally, paraprofessional roles are only referred to in the sections of the law that deal with Title I, which provides support in the areas of reading, writing, and math.

Individuals with Disabilities Education Act (IDEA) 1997 and 2004

The 1997 reauthorization of the Individuals with Disabilities Education Act (IDEA) makes the following specific reference to paraprofessionals and their roles: "A state may allow paraprofessionals who are appropriately trained and supervised under state standards to assist in the provision of special education and related services."

The IDEA is the major piece of federal special education legislation. The role definition here is to *assist in the provision of special education and related services.* In the 2004 reauthorization the regulations remained essentially unchanged, and still somewhat vague. Not only does it allow for paraprofessionals to assume instructional roles, but also a wide variety of other roles that provide support to students in special education settings. These may include the following:

- Academic support in the general education classroom for a student with mild learning difficulties.
- One-on-one tutoring in a resource room for a student with more severe learning difficulties or with attention deficit disorder.
- Interpreting for a student who has sensory impairments (hearing loss or deafness).
- Toileting, feeding, and/or suctioning for a student with severe physical disabilities.
- Providing physical therapy sessions under the direction of a professional physical therapist.
- Acting as a job coach for an older student with disabilities: training the student in the skills required for work in a school environment and at a work placement.
- Facilitating friendships and other socially appropriate behaviors for students who have limited social skills.

All of these roles constitute *assisting in the provision of special education and related services* as allowed by IDEA, and the list could be much longer. If you work as a paraprofessional in special education, you may find your particular role is not included in the list, and there may be many other paraprofessionals in the class whose roles could also be added to the list. IDEA 2004 is discussed in Chapter 4.

Restrictions for Paraprofessional Roles. IDEA places only two restrictions on the paraprofessional's role. First, when this law was reauthorized in 1997, many state departments of education asked for clarification because this was the first time the law specifically referred to paraprofessionals. The U.S. Department of Education issued a statement to the effect that the employment of paraprofessionals should be governed by state laws. Thus each state could decide the extent to which paraprofessionals would be allowed to perform different duties. This reading gave the states considerable flexibility in assigning roles to paraprofessionals. We discuss the states' interpretation of these requirements in Chapter 4, but interestingly, when the U.S. Department of Education gave that clarification, fewer than half of the states had any standards or guidelines in place for the employment, duties, training, or supervision of paraprofessionals.

The role of paratherapist, an example of a role not permitted in all the states, is discussed in the nearby box.

The second restriction in IDEA relating to the roles of paraprofessionals consists of the phrase *who are appropriately trained and supervised.* This is not really a restriction on the *type* of role that can be assigned to a paraprofessional

---

Paratherapist: A Paraprofessional Role Not Permitted in All States

Paratherapists carry out physical therapy duties, but because of the expert nature of the work they must undergo special training and have continual supervision as they provide physical therapy. This is largely in response to a professional organization that represents physical therapists and expressed strong objections to paraprofessionals being allowed to carry out duties for which professionals are required to have several years of training. A compromise was reached by requiring training and close supervision for the paraprofessionals. Even in states where the role is considered acceptable, paratherapists are not permitted to carry out the full range of a professional therapist's duties or to prescribe treatment for a student. In some states, however, the role of paratherapist is not considered appropriate for paraprofessionals at all.

---

but a condition for *any* assigned role. However, it is a very important point, which mirrors the recommendation in the report referred to at the beginning of this chapter: no paraprofessional should be expected to take on any role without receiving the appropriate training and supervision for that role. IDEA is legislation that covers special education only, so these restrictions are not binding on the work of all paraprofessionals, only those hired under special education programs and funding. We discuss supervision later in the book; however, all paraprofessionals should have a designated supervisor, and there are many ways in which you can be proactive in seeking supervision and working more effectively with your supervisor.

Individual State Requirements

As mentioned in relation to IDEA, individual states can decide what sort of restrictions to place on the roles that can be assigned to special education paraprofessionals. To find out what your state allows and does not allow, check your state's Department of Education website, and look for the special education pages, where information on paraprofessionals can most often be found. Or check with the local branch of your union or professional organization. The American Federation of Teachers (AFT) website, for example, has a section specifically for paraprofessionals, under the heading Paraprofessional and School-Related Personnel (PSRP), which also contains information on the various laws affecting the employment of paraprofessionals. The National Education Association (NEA) has similar information on its website under the section for Education Support Personnel (ESP). In states where union involvement is strong, paraprofessional roles are most often defined in conjunction with union membership and negotiated pay and employment conditions.

When you have checked local requirements and restrictions, check other states to see what differences there may be. (Several websites are listed at the end of the chapter to help you get started.) Even if you do not work in special education, you can learn about the differences that can exist within the dictates of the law. If you are employed in a special education setting, it will be particularly interesting for you to see the differences between what you are allowed to do and what special education paraprofessionals in surrounding states are and are not allowed to do. Make a note here of your state's requirements as well as those of surrounding states.

My State's Requirements or Restrictions:

_____

_____

_____

_____

_____

Requirements or Restrictions of Neighboring States:

_____

_____

_____

_____

_____

School-District and School Guidelines

Written guidelines at the school and school-district level, likely quite generalized, state what types of responsibilities should and should not be assigned to paraprofessionals. In addition, you should have an individual written job description that details what is expected of you personally. Some groups of paraprofessionals have a common job description (e.g., those working for Title I programs, with duties that include supporting basic literacy and numeracy in the school). But all paraprofessionals should have a copy of their own job descriptions. If you do not, ask for one from your supervising teacher or if necessary from the school building administrator or the school-district office. Check one of the two boxes here to indicate you have a written job description.

☐ Yes, I already have a written job description.

☐ No, I did not have a written job description, but I have since obtained one from my school or school district.

You will need a copy of your job description for an activity in the next section of the chapter, so make every effort to obtain a copy as soon as possible.

Classroom Level

We have talked about the national, state, and local contexts for paraprofessional roles and responsibilities, so this is a good point to begin looking more closely at your assigned roles. In the space provided, list the duties you have been assigned, as you understand them. If you have a written job description, refer to it, but take a very careful look and add any duties you feel you carry out, even if they are not actually mentioned in the written job description. Most people have a clause in their contract that states "and other duties as assigned," which allows individual teachers and administrators to ask you to take on additional responsibilities as needed. However, most of your regular assigned duties should be listed on your job description.

These are my duties as a paraprofessional:

1. _____

2. _____

3. _____

4. _____

5. _____

6. _____

Before you move on to the next part of this section, look back at what you have written to check whether you have included any behavior management responsibilities that have been assigned to you. Even if nothing specific is listed on your job description about managing student behavior, everyone who works with students has some responsibility for student behavior. After all, if you are not actively managing their behavior, they are probably managing yours! So make sure you add something about your behavior management responsibilities as you see them.

Clarifying Classroom Roles: A Case Study

Companion Website

View the following scenario by going to the companion website Scene A, or read the case study below before answering the questions that follow. The case study consists of a conversation between a kindergarten teacher and her new paraprofessional as they discuss the paraprofessional's responsibilities in the classroom. As you read, take note of the roles that the teacher assigns to the paraprofessional and the paraprofessional's expectations of the teacher. Read the case study more than once if necessary in order to understand exactly what is going on as these two adults discuss the paraprofessional's responsibilities.

Case Study: The New Paraprofessional and Her Duties
Scene A: By the Pop Machine
Teacher: Oh, there you are. I didn't know if we would meet here or in the faculty
    room. Did you get a drink?
Para: Oh no, there wasn't time.
Teacher: Well go ahead and get one. I can wait.
Para: Oh, I'm fine, thanks. I did tell you I needed to leave by four, didn't I?

> Teacher: Yes, but I think we can get through by then. Um . . . I brought that list of questions that you wrote down. Let's see . . . maybe you better just tell me. What were they?
>
> Para: Well, what I really need to know are the guidelines you need me to do.
>
> Teacher: Well that's easy. Just come in and make yourself useful. And if you see something that needs to be done, go ahead and do it. With 30 kindergarteners, I'm just so glad you're going to be in there with your new ideas.
>
> Para: Is there a copy of the timetable I could get?
>
> Teacher: Yes, I have that hanging up in the room. But we don't always go by it; because, uh, you know, we get on a subject . . . and I hate to, uh, stop the children when they're excited about something.
>
> Para: Well, maybe I could get a copy of the timetable. Does the district have guidelines of what I should and shouldn't do?
>
> Teacher: Yes, I did bring that for you. It's, uh, in here . . . Oh, maybe it's still in my room . . . I'll get it for you.
>
> Para: Okay.

Write here what you would understand your responsibilities to be if you were the paraprofessional in the case study:

_____

_____

_____

_____

Now write a brief description of what you think the paraprofessional in the case study expects of the teacher:

_____

_____

_____

_____

At the end of the discussion, the paraprofessional is obviously not satisfied. Take a moment to reflect on the possible source of the paraprofessional's dissatisfaction. Ask yourself these questions:

- Did the paraprofessional come away from the meeting with a clear idea of her role?
- Did the teacher present her expectations clearly?
- Does the paraprofessional have a clear idea of what she can expect of the teacher?
- How might the meeting affect their working relationship and the effectiveness and efficiency of the classroom environment?

Some of the confusion for the paraprofessional seems to stem from the differing personalities and styles of the teacher and paraprofessional. The teacher appears very relaxed and spontaneous in her work; the paraprofessional seems to need a much more structured approach. It is all too common to have such different approaches and preferences, and neither one is essentially right or wrong. Such differences can be considered a real strength in a classroom team, rather than an obstacle. But very few strong teams are made in heaven. Most need to be carefully nurtured and cultivated. In a later chapter we discuss how you can turn the differences among team members into strengths. Establishing clear expectations and roles is one of the first ways to begin that process.

Is It OK to Ask? You may feel it is inappropriate for a paraprofessional to insist on some sort of framework or formal description of her responsibilities as the paraprofessional in the case study was trying to do. However, it is perfectly reasonable for you, as a paraprofessional, to ask your supervisor for clarification. Your teacher should provide a clear definition of your roles and what is expected of you, but if this does not happen, you must ask—for your own peace of mind and to avoid future conflict and even legal vulnerability. Very few teachers have received training on supervising paraprofessionals, and they may therefore not appreciate the importance of first establishing your duties. There is nothing inappropriate about your prompting this first step.

The Devil in the Detail

You may feel your duties are clear, and writing a list of your responsibilities in general terms may not have been difficult. However, it is a good idea to take this exercise a step further, so you can list your duties in finer detail, rather than just in general terms. This is particularly important, because if you overstep the bounds of your responsibilities there can be negative consequences for your relationships with your supervisor or other adults you work with. They may see you as taking too much initiative or encroaching on their roles, and the worst case scenario would be that you could be legally vulnerable if you carried out duties that strictly belong to a professional rather than a paraprofessional. Likewise, if you do less than what is expected of you, you can jeopardize your working relationships and be perceived as lacking in commitment and accuracy in your work.

The next step in defining your responsibilities is to break down, or dissect, each general role or responsibility into its component parts. We have provided three examples of roles common to paraprofessionals and the possible components of each. The questions we ask about each of the roles might be answered differently by individual paraprofessionals because each situation is different. Only you and your supervising teacher can answer for your own situation. But if any of these roles are part of your assignment, ask yourself the questions. They will help you complete the next part of the role clarification exercise.

Example 1. Role: Assist in maintaining an orderly classroom
Does this mean . . .

- Keeping the teacher's desk clear? Or would your supervising teacher consider the desk to be outside of your responsibility?
- Reorganizing the classroom closets and drawers? Or would your supervisor be somewhat surprised and even irritated at not finding things where they used to be?

- Taking down bulletin boards you think are badly designed or have been there long enough, and replacing them with your own displays?
- Gathering a small group of children together to play a game or read a story if they have finished an assignment and seem to be at loose ends?
- Moving chairs and tables to what you think is a more efficient classroom layout?
- Sending a student to time-out for disrupting other students' work?
- Phoning a parent about a student's lack of homework?
- Redesigning a worksheet the teacher has written because you think your group of students would find it difficult to use?
- Taking a child aside to read through a passage he obviously cannot understand?

All of these are appropriate tasks for you to perform as a paraprofessional, but only if your supervising teacher has assigned you to do them. Some teachers would be horrified if you were to interpret the role *assist in maintaining an orderly classroom* in some of these ways. Other teachers would be delighted. Some teachers would not object, provided you cleared it with them first; others would be happy to see you taking the initiative and assisting in so many helpful and innovative ways. One paraprofessional felt she was being helpful by cleaning off the teacher's desk that was covered with bits of paper of all different sizes. It turns out the teacher was saving odd scraps of paper because of the limited budget the school had allocated for paper that semester.

Example 2. Role: Assisting with student reading
Does this mean . . .

- You decide when the student is to move on to the next reading book? Or is that the teacher's responsibility?
- You administer mastery tests at the end of each basal reader?
- You record the results of the tests in the teacher's grade book? Or should you just pass the results on for the teacher to record?
- If parents ask you how their child is progressing in reading, you let them know the results of the tests? Or do you refer any such questions to the teacher?

Again, any of these components of the role *assisting with student reading* would be appropriate for a paraprofessional, provided the supervising teacher had specifically assigned them.

Example 3. Role: Assist in classroom behavior management
Does this mean . . .

- Giving students tokens or rewards for good work and/or appropriate behavior?
- Imposing sanctions or consequences for inappropriate student behavior or poor standards of work?
- Reporting serious behavior problems to a school administrator?
- Reporting or discussing serious behavior problems with the student's parent(s)?
- Monitoring student behavior plans?

You can apply this type of analysis to any of your roles and responsibilities. As you can see, there are two parts to this issue: first, what exactly is your role? and second, to what extent should you take initiative and interpret your teacher's instructions? The first part is essential. You must be proactive and seek clarification of your responsibilities. The second part of the question may only be answered with time. As you see things that need to be done, check with your supervisor whether it is OK for you to go ahead and do them, and judge by the response whether you interpreted expectations and instructions accurately. As time goes on, you are likely to have to make many small adjustments to your work as you become better acquainted with your supervisor and the way your supervisor manages the classroom. However, an initial proactive approach of seeking a clear understanding of your role and your teacher's expectations will help establish a good relationship between the two of you, which will make any future changes easier to handle for both of you.

Dissecting Your Own Roles and Responsibilities

Using the form provided, take time to explore the extent and limits of your own roles and responsibilities. List in the left-hand column each of the roles you have already identified, and then list in one of the two right-hand columns the possible components of each of those roles, according to whether you believe that component is or is not included within your area of responsibility. We have included an example to start you off. If this particular role is applicable to you, make adjustments as necessary to the components that are or are not part of your responsibility.

When you have completed this exercise and feel confident you have carefully examined and analyzed the various roles and responsibilities you have been assigned, ask your supervising teacher to review what you have written. Explain the purpose of the exercise, and then ask your supervisor to check whether your interpretation of your roles is accurate. You need to know:

1. If your supervisor feels any roles or responsibilities are missing from the list (i.e., in the left-hand column),
2. Whether your supervisor feels the components you have identified for each role are accurately placed in the middle or right-hand column, according to whether they are part of your role or not, and
3. Whether your supervisor feels there are other components of any of the roles you have not identified but should be included.

A Special Case: Substitute Teaching

We would like to add a cautionary note here about substitute teaching. Many paraprofessionals tell us they substitute regularly for their teacher. Paraprofessionals know the students and the current curriculum. The students know them and know what is expected. They say it provides continuity, and it saves the time of bringing a substitute teacher up to speed. There are apparently many good arguments for paraprofessionals working as substitutes. However, we have also talked to

Defining and Clarifying Your Roles and Responsibilities

Roles I have been assigned	This *does* include . . .	This *does not* include . . .
Example: Supporting student in ninth-grade math class.	Helping him to keep track of where the teacher is in the text. Reading text-based problems to him during practice sessions in class.	Giving him the answers to questions. Writing the answers on the worksheet.

administrators in the schools and school districts where these paraprofessionals work, and they often tell us their paraprofessionals do *not* substitute for teachers because it is against school or district policy. This mismatch between the theory, or policy, and the classroom practice is of serious concern. It could mean paraprofessionals are performing duties (in this case substitute teaching) that are not allowed by school-district policy, which is obviously inappropriate, but if the policy is based on state law, it is also illegal for a paraprofessional to assume that duty.

We strongly recommend you clarify your position regarding substitute teaching in your school district because it is a very common practice for paraprofessionals to be asked to substitute, often at short notice. If you discover school-district policy or state law does not allow paraprofessionals to substitute teach, approach your administrator and give notice that you will no longer be able to undertake this responsibility and when you did so previously, you were unaware it was disallowed. It may cause inconvenience and some ill feeling if it is a common practice in your school, but you have the force of the law behind you, and ethically you must refuse if you know local policy does not allow you to perform that particular duty. If you have teaching qualifications but are working as a paraprofessional, this caution may not apply to you.

C-H-A-P-T-E-R—S-U-M-M-A-R-Y

This chapter discussed these topics:

- The importance of having clearly defined roles and responsibilities.
- Some of the aspects of role definition to consider.
- Practical ways to obtain the information needed to understand the extent and limits of paraprofessional roles.

This information should help you to be more effective in providing for student needs. It will enhance your working relationship with your supervising teacher and give you confidence that you are carrying out the duties assigned to you.

E-X-T-E-N-D-I-N-G—Y-O-U-R—L-E-A-R-N-I-N-G

A Case Study

The following case study will give you the opportunity to reflect on what you have learned about the role of paraprofessionals. It is a real-life story that occurred in a middle school. Like most of life's experiences, you do not have access to all of the information at the beginning, so to simulate life, we give you the first scenario to respond to. Then you will receive more information and review your response (modifying if needed), then more information. Sometimes in hindsight we wish we had all of the information at the beginning, but this is rarely the case.

> **Part One**
> Hello, I'm James, a special education teacher of sixth- and seventh-grade students. Last year I had two full-time paraprofessionals (Karen and Tiffany) working with me. We functioned very well as a team, letting each other take turns teaching the whole class, and we set up a system that helped the students work well. Last year's students had quite a lot of self-discipline, but this year I received a sixth-grade student named Roy. The IEP team decided Roy should have a full-time paraprofessional (Alice) to work with him exclusively. Alice was to collaborate with Roy's mother and me to work on discipline and to modify his curriculum.
>
> In the first part of October, Karen and Tiffany started to complain to me about Alice. They said she was trying to take over their jobs. Admittedly, I had a few reservations about Alice. She had shared some good ideas, so I let her teach the art class a couple of times. But then she showed up one Monday and announced she had planned the art for the rest of the month. Alice's ideas were very good and I didn't want to discourage her helpfulness. Yet I needed her to focus on Roy and let the other two paraprofessionals do what they were assigned to do.

From what you have learned in the chapter, what do you think needs to be done about this situation? And who should take responsibility for it, the two paraprofessionals who are experiencing difficulty with Alice or the teacher?

_____

_____

_____

_____

_____

_____

Part Two

I decided that as the teacher, I should take on the responsibility of changing some of the ways I managed the class. I divided the class into three groups, excluding Roy, and assigned each group to a different paraprofessional (or to me) for twenty-minute rotations during the morning hour before recess. I explained to the class that they were to stay, work with, and talk only to that "teacher" for the allotted time. I told the paraprofessionals to work only with the students assigned to them during each time period. I also told Alice that Karen, Tiffany, and I would be the only ones teaching in this way during that hour, and meanwhile she would work one on one with Roy on a variety of curriculum areas in which he needed individual help.

What do you think of the changes the teacher made? Has he addressed the problem, or is there more that could be done? If you were one of the original paraprofessionals—Tiffany or Karen—would his solution seem reasonable to you?

_____

_____

_____

_____

_____

_____

Part Three

We tried this new routine for a few days, noticing that things were much better during the time we did rotations. Alice stayed with Roy and worked on the curriculum areas she and I had selected. However, a few days later, Tiffany was working with her group and asked the students a question. The students gave various answers and Tiffany was about to elaborate on those answers when Alice blurted out her own responses to the students' comments—across the room from where she was working with Roy. This really disturbed the class and upset Tiffany, who later said she felt she was being "walked all over." She said she just couldn't work in the same room with Alice anymore. I told her that Alice was in the classroom to stay, at least for the rest of the school year. The work she does with Roy is actually very good, and we were lucky to get her. She was the only person who applied for the job who had any classroom experience.

If you were the paraprofessional Karen, what could you do (if anything) to help resolve the difficulties that have arisen between Alice and Tiffany?

_____

_____

_____

_____

_____

_____

_____

_____

Part Four

I could see Tiffany was still very upset, and because Alice is likely to stay with us for the school year, I thought I'd better talk to Alice again, to remind her to let the person who is in charge of a group teach them without interruption. But I also stressed that Roy is her main responsibility. I told her how much I valued her work with Roy, and we listed all the things she does for him that I don't have time to do as the teacher, so I'm relying heavily on her. Then she and I talked about the things Karen and Tiffany do for the other students, and she said she'd really like to be allowed to do some of them, that perhaps they could help with Roy sometimes and they could switch roles. I don't know what Tiffany and Karen will think about that, but in theory I have no objections, so I said I'd ask them and let her know.

If the teacher came to you to ask what you thought about swapping roles with Alice some of the time, what would you say? Would you have any reservations about taking on Alice's work with Roy? Why or why not?

_____

_____

_____

_____

_____

_____

_____

_____

Authors' Comments

Understanding Expectations. An important aspect of establishing clear expectations is to understand your duties and responsibilities. It is vital to communicate with your supervisor so you have a clear understanding of the knowledge and skills expected of you. Obviously if you are working with students in developing reading and math skills, you should have those skills yourself; if you are supporting students in a work environment you may need networking and collaborative skills, in addition to basic levels of numeracy and literacy, as you facilitate work placements and mentor students; if you support bilingual students the main emphasis of your work may be on their home language or on English, but you are likely to need knowledge and skills in both. It is the primary responsibility of your supervising teacher to ensure you have the skills and knowledge you need to carry out your assigned duties because you cannot be effective without those skills and knowledge. An effective supervisor will make an initial assessment of your skills and only assign duties you can carry out effectively, and then provide any training necessary to enhance your skills so you can be assigned more complex or technically difficult tasks as your skills increase.

If the teacher in the case study asked you to swap roles with Alice, you might not feel competent enough to take on Alice's responsibilities, particularly if you have not worked with a student like Roy before. In that case, you should approach the teacher and tell him about your concerns. He may just offer reassurance, but you may also need training, or at least close supervision, until you feel confident in carrying out your new duties. In later chapters we discuss ways in which you can evaluate your own performance and make continuous self-assessments, reflecting on the quality of your work and setting goals for improvement. At this point we would just say that if you feel you lack the necessary skills and need more support to carry out your responsibilities, you should talk to your supervisor and ask for direction and assistance.

Websites

Earlier we suggested you conduct an Internet search to identify any restrictions that may be placed on the roles that paraprofessionals can assume. These websites will help you get started, but you can also conduct a general search using a search engine such as Google or Yahoo.

The National Education Association (NEA) includes paraprofessionals under Education Support Professionals (ESP). The website can be found at **www.nea.org**.

The American Federation of Teachers (AFT) refers to paraprofessionals as Paraprofessionals and School-Related Personnel (PSRP). The website can be found at **www.aft.org**.

Your state's Department of Education will have a website of its own. It may be known as a state Office/Department of Education/Instruction. If you do not know the URL, you should be able to find it quite easily using a search engine. The same is true for Departments of Education in neighboring states.

4 Standards for the Paraprofessional Roles

This chapter discusses standards for paraprofessionals including entry-level requirements—that is, the certificates and other qualifications that paraprofessionals must have to enter the profession—as well as standards of knowledge and skill needed to perform effectively on the job. You will learn the importance of identifying additional training available to help you refine your skills, to maintain and enhance your employment, and to perform more effectively in helping students learn. You should also be able to identify where you can get information about new standards or standards as they change over time. As we did earlier, we review legislation that influences the employment of paraprofessionals—in this case regarding standards for employment—before asking you to examine your own situation and then suggesting ways in which you can move forward in your profession.

By the end of this chapter you should be able to answer these questions:

- What standards have IDEA and NCLB set for paraprofessionals?
- What are some of the ways to satisfy the requirements of NCLB's option C?
- What skills are necessary for paraprofessionals to be effective on the job?
- What standards has the Council for Exceptional Children (CEC) established for paraprofessionals working in special education?

Entry-Level Job Requirements

In the same way that a variety of titles are used for paraprofessionals, hiring guidelines and employment standards also vary among programs and funding bodies. We look first at the standards prescribed by IDEA and No Child Left Behind.

Individuals with Disabilities Education Act of 1997 and IDEIA of 2004

As we noted in Chapter 2, the 1997 reauthorization of IDEA outlined that "a state may allow paraprofessionals who are *appropriately trained and supervised under state standards* to assist in the provision of special education and related services" (emphasis added). This requirement for training and supervision was made without reference to a time frame. There is no indication of what constitutes appropriate training or supervision for newly hired paraprofessionals as opposed to paraprofessionals who were already working in schools when the legislation was enacted.

As we stated earlier, this is a very general statement and open to interpretation. The exact meaning and intent of the law will only become clear through case law.

The 108th session of the House of Representatives passed the Improving Education Results for Children with Disabilities Act of 2003, referred to as HR 1350. Regarding the employment of paraprofessionals, this move toward the next reauthorization of IDEA was very similar to the 1997 version. It has only a few changes that define compliance. It reads that the state standards shall "allow paraprofessionals and assistants who are *appropriately trained and supervised, in accordance with state law, regulations, or written policy* . . . to be used to assist in the provision of special education and related services to children with disabilities" (emphasis added). The Individuals with Disabilities Education Improvement Act of 2004 was signed into law December 3, 2004 (see Figure 4.1).

The intention of this change during the reauthorization process was to create congruency among NCLB, IDEA, and the states' interpretation and implementation of the law. However, it remains a very general statement, allowing individual states to set standards for training and supervision of paraprofessionals, both at entry level as they are hired and as they continue their employment in the school district.

No Child Left Behind Act of 2001

The Elementary and Secondary Education Act (reauthorized as the No Child Left Behind [NCLB] Act of 2001) made very specific demands regarding the credentials of paraprofessionals working in Title I schools and programs. The general requirements of NCLB are designed to ensure that paraprofessionals are competent for the following types of responsibilities: one-on-one tutoring, assisting with class-

---

IDEA 97 and IDEIA 2004: Requirements for Paraprofessionals

Individuals with Disabilities Act of 1997	Individuals with Disabilities Improvement Act of 2004
"A state may allow paraprofessionals who are appropriately trained and supervised under state standards to assist in the provision of special education and related services." (IDEA, section 186(f)).	State standards shall "allow para-professionals and assistants who are appropriately trained and supervised, in accordance with State Law, regulations, or written policy, in meeting the requirements of this part to be used to assist in the provision of special education and related services to children with disabilities under this part." (Part B, Section 612)

Figure 4.1

room management, assisting in computer labs, supporting parental involvement activities, acting as a translator or interpreter, providing support in a library or media center, and providing instructional services to students under the direct supervision of a highly qualified teacher. These general requirements form the basis of the federal standards for paraprofessionals' work.

More specifically, the NCLB Act of 2001 requires that paraprofessional staff hired in Title I programs must be "highly qualified" for their responsibilities. This is to be accomplished by 2006 through one of three means:

> "(A) at least two years of study completed at an institution of higher education; (B) an associate's (or higher) degree; or (C) meeting a rigorous standard of quality and demonstrating (through a formal state/local academic assessment) knowledge of, and the ability to assist in instructing reading, writing, and mathematics, or reading readiness, writing readiness, and mathematics readiness."

These three options are all considered acceptable as proof that a paraprofessional is "highly qualified," but here are some interesting points about each one of them:

- Option A: two years of higher education. This requirement is fairly straightforward at first glance, but within a year of its publication, individual states were applying different definitions to "two years of study," with some states stipulating forty-eight credit hours and others as much as sixty credit hours to meet it.
- Option B: an associate's or higher degree. Again, the number of credit hours required for a two-year degree can vary quite substantially across individual institutions of higher education, making the requirement more or less demanding according to the institution where the degree is sought and granted.
- Neither option A nor option B specify a subject of study for the two years of study or degree, although government guidelines subsequently suggested there should be some connection with education.
- Although option C appeared to be a godsend to paraprofessionals who did not have the time or funds to meet options A or B, it has caused the greatest practical difficulties for states and school districts because no "formal state or local academic assessment" existed for paraprofessionals at the time the law came into force. We take a closer look at option C once we have considered the implications of these NCLB requirements as well as those of IDEA.

Who Must Meet These Requirements?
The requirements of No Child Left Behind apply to the following people:

- Individuals providing instructional support, but *not* those individuals with only noninstructional duties (e.g., supervision in the lunchroom or at recess).
- Paraprofessionals in targeted assisted programs paid with Title I funds.
- All paraprofessionals hired before January 8, 2002, although they were given four years to meet the requirements.
- All paraprofessionals hired after January 8, 2002, as a condition of being hired.

No Child Left Behind: Qualifications for Paraprofessionals

A. Complete at least 2 years of study at an institution of higher education

OR

B. Obtain an associate or higher degree

OR

C. Meet a rigorous standard of quality and demonstrate your knowledge and ability to assist in instruction of reading, writing, and math; or (as appropriate) readiness skills for these subjects. This may be demonstrated through formal state or academic tests.

Figure 4.2

NCLB made an exception for paraprofessionals working solely on parent involvement activities or those working only as translators/interpreters, rather than in direct instructional roles. They are only required to have a high school diploma or the equivalent. Note that although these requirements of NCLB appear in the portion of the law that applies to Title I (the education of disadvantaged students), the qualifications are required for all paraprofessionals working in Title I funded programs, especially schoolwide programs, and this includes those hired for special education, bilingual education, or under 504 funding. Also, regardless of hiring dates, NCLB stipulates that all paraprofessionals working in Title I programs must have a high school diploma or its equivalent.

So let's review what the law says. There are two entry-level requirements that a person must meet *before* applying for a job as an instructional paraprofessional. What are they?

1. _____

2. _____

What is the entry-level requirement for a person applying to work with parents in school-related activities?

_____

_____

Now let's look at where you are in this process. Were you hired before January 8, 2002? Yes / No

If you were hired before 2002, how long do you have to meet the full requirements of NCLB?

_____

_____

What are the requirements you must meet?

_____

_____

What are the requirements to work in a schoolwide Title I program if you are an instructional paraprofessional in special education and you were hired after January 8, 2002?

_____

_____

What is the requirement for a paraprofessional who is proficient in English and a language other than English and who provides services to enhance the participation of students primarily by acting as a translator?

_____

_____

Who Is Responsible for Making This Happen? Although the federal government has set these requirements, the individual states must develop and implement a plan of accountability that certifies compliance with federal requirements: paraprofessionals hired within the state can be considered "highly qualified" as interpreted through state law. States are required to submit an accountability plan to the U.S. Department of Education to inform them—and the public—of both the state education agency (SEA) and the local education agency (LEA) progress toward compliance. The accountability plan is a system that is "tied directly to a state's standards and assessments." All schools and districts should be included in the system and have the opportunity to be identified as "high performing" or "low performing." Once the system is created and showing a functional flow of accountability between states and local authorities (such as school districts), the U.S. Department of Education reviews and sanctions the plan. As of early 2004, out of the fifty states and the District of Columbia, forty-six had responded by creating credentialing standards for paraprofessionals.

Accountability Flow Chart

   I. U.S. Department of Education
      A. State accountability plans are reviewed and sanctioned
  II. State Education Agency (SEA)
      A. Creates accountability plan
         1. Statement of standards and assessments
         2. Functional flow between SEA and LEA
         3. Report compliance
 III. Local Education Agency (LEA)
      A. Implements standards and assessments
      B. Reports compliance
         1. Paraprofessionals
            a. Written notice from principals of schools operating a program under NCLB sec. 1114 and 1115.
            b. Attestations are preserved at the school, with a copy on file at the main office of the LEA (NCLB, 2001).

Option C: A Paraprofessional Assessment

According to the NCLB Act, paraprofessionals should have at least an associate's degree in order to be considered "highly qualified." However, lawmakers understood that it was unlikely every paraprofessional would be able to meet the higher education standard; therefore the use of an alternative assessment was also approved. We highlight two such alternative assessments here that were developed in direct response to option C and have been widely adopted by states: the ETS *ParaPro* and ACT's *WorkKeys Proficiency Certificate for Teacher Assistants.* ETS (Educational Testing Services) is a national for-profit organization; ACT (formerly the American College Testing Program) is an independent not-for-profit organization. Both have developed numerous academic tests for students in both K–12 and higher education.

ETS ParaPro

The ParaPro Assessment is a paper-and-pencil test that measures knowledge in six content categories. Each category represents either the paraprofessional's basic knowledge of the skills of reading, writing, or math (remember, this test was developed in response to Title I requirements) or the paraprofessional's ability to implement the skills in an instructional setting. The basic knowledge questions represent approximately 60 percent of the test, and the implementation of skills

Areas Covered by the ParaPro Test

Content Areas	Approximate Number of Questions	Approximate % of Test
I. Reading skills and knowledge	18	20%
II. Application of reading skills and knowledge of classroom instruction	12	13%
III. Mathematics skills and knowledge	18	20%
IV. Application of mathematics skills and knowledge of classroom instruction	12	13%
V. Writing skills and knowledge	18	20%
VI. Application of writing skills and knowledge of classroom instruction	12	13%

questions cover the remaining 40 percent. The table shows each of the six areas covered, the number of questions involved, and the proportion of the final score for each area. The test consists of ninety multiple-choice questions and has a 2.5-hour time limit.

Although the ParaPro is not a required test, thirty-seven states had chosen to adopt it by early 2004 as their option C (see Extending Your Learning section at the end of the chapter for information on each state's required scores for paraprofessionals taking the ETS ParaPro).

WorkKeys Proficiency Certificate for Teacher Assistants

The WorkKeys Proficiency Certificate for Teacher Assistants was built around ACT's *WorkKeys* job skills assessment, which schools, businesses, and other organizations had already been using for more than a decade. The WorkKeys job assessment evaluates initial skills of new hires or college students and a person's suitability for a particular occupation. Tests are available in such areas as applied mathematics, applied technology, locating information, reading for information, and business writing. The three main areas featured in the WorkKeys Proficiency Certificate for Teacher Assistants are reading for information, writing or business writing, and applied mathematics, in line with the Title I emphasis on literacy and numeracy. In addition, a knowledgeable observer completes the Instructional Support Inventory, which assesses a paraprofessional's classroom teaching skills. The ACT tests are available in both computer and paper-and-pencil formats; each test takes between thirty and fifty-five minutes to complete. As of early 2004, more than a dozen states had approved this test for assessing their paraprofessionals.

The U.S. Department of Education requires each state and local district/LEA to have an assessment in place for paraprofessionals. States may choose to require a standardized test for all paraprofessionals or they may allow the local authorities/school districts to adopt their own assessment. Note: The law does not require a paper-and-pencil test, only that the assessment be valid and reliable, meaning it tests what it claims to test, and the answers to questions must be clear and indisputable.

Other Evidence of Highly Qualified Status

In their accountability plans submitted to the federal government, two states cited assessments unique to their own state as a measure of paraprofessional credentialing. Kentucky chose its own previously developed *Kentucky Paraprofessional Assessment* (KPA), and Michigan referenced the *Michigan Test for Teacher Certification—Basic Skills* (MTTC). Three states—Maine, Massachusetts, and New Mexico—opted to use a portfolio as a measure of the proficiency of their paraprofessionals. Details of the Kentucky and Michigan assessments can be found on the individual websites for those states. Check to see what your state is doing by visiting **www.ecs.org/clearinghouse/42/65/4265.htm**. This site lists state accountability plans and consolidated plans for meeting regulations of the No Child Left Behind law.

Other Assessments Selected as Evidence of Highly Qualified Status

Portfolio

Maine, Massachusetts, New Mexico

(Others are using this for current paraprofessionals.)

KPA: Kentucky Paraprofessional Assessment

Kentucky

MTTC: Michigan Test for Teacher Certification—Basic Skills

Michigan

Portfolios. NCLB allows states to use a portfolio as a way to measure a paraprofessional's knowledge and skill level, provided a standardized rubric or set of guidelines is in place to ensure fairness. A portfolio allows paraprofessionals to display their knowledge and ability to assist in instruction through certificates of attendance at training, evidence of work completed with students, personal philosophy of education statements, or other documentation. The portfolio route is appealing for paraprofessionals who are not able to complete college courses and who may have many years of experience to support their claim of being "highly qualified," but the difficulty lies in assessing the relative value of the content, when there is likely to be a great variety of evidence in each paraprofessional's portfolio.

In the early 1990s, portfolios began to appear in education to help teachers set goals, reflect on their learning/teaching, and assess their continuing professional development needs. With the more recent focus on training and assessment of paraprofessionals, portfolios are being adopted in many states as a way for you to reflect on your work and to develop evidence that you perform your work effectively.

A portfolio generally consists of a selection of artifacts, that is, examples of the type of work you do or something that represents you as a person who provides support to students' learning. Through the portfolio, you can also demonstrate your achievement of any standards that have been set for paraprofessionals. As a state or school district elects to follow the portfolio route for showing evidence of competence, the portfolio program must clearly define its purpose. For example, the portfolio may be used to meet the requirements of No Child Left Behind, or it may be used to show how a paraprofessional is meeting the standards set for progressing through a career ladder program. Thus it is incumbent on the paraprofessionals involved in the portfolio program to make sure they respond to that purpose when compiling their evidence.

The Extending Your Learning section at the end of the chapter contains guidelines for building a portfolio. Even if there is no portfolio program in your school district or state, it is a useful way for you to build a case for your competence and skills as a paraprofessional. Should you make a change in your employment you will be well equipped to demonstrate your marketable skills.

Skills Necessary to Be Effective on the Job

Some have expressed concern that even though paraprofessionals may pass testing requirements or earn the associate's degree, teaching is a practical skill and cannot be measured through academic activities. As an example, the 40 percent of items on the ParaPro test that deal with the application of knowledge to an instructional setting are answered on paper. No practicum or classroom observation is required. So like any paper-and-pencil test, ParaPro is not a test of how paraprofessionals work with students; it can only test how they *say* they would work with students. In addition, other skills and knowledge are needed to perform effectively and efficiently in the classroom with students.

In addition to demonstrating your knowledge as a paraprofessional, you should be able to do the following:

- Serve as an effective member of a program implementation team.
- Assist teachers in maintaining learner-centered, supportive environments.
- Assist teachers with planning and organizing learning experiences and environments.
- Assist teachers in engaging students in learning experiences.
- Assist teachers with assessing learner needs, progress, and achievements.
- Meet standards of professional and ethical conduct.

Council for Exceptional Children Standards

In an attempt to address standards for paraprofessionals at the practical, classroom level, the Council for Exceptional Children (CEC), the national organization for special education, also established standards for paraprofessionals (although CEC uses the term *paraeducators*). The standards indicate the desired knowledge base and application of skills for paraprofessionals working with exceptional children or students with disabilities. Each standard has a *knowledge content* and *skill application*. Some of the skills cited refer to the "Common Core," each individual state's common core curriculum.

CEC Performance-Based Standards for Paraeducators

Knowledge	Skills
Standard 1: Foundations	
*Purposes of programs for individuals with exceptional learning needs.	*None in addition to the Common Core.
*Basic educational terminology regarding students, programs, roles, and instructional activities.	*(continued)*

Knowledge	Skills
Standard 2: Development and Characteristics of Learners	
*Effects an exceptional condition(s) can have on an individual's life.	*None in addition to the Common Core.
Standard 3: Individual Learning Differences	
*Rights and responsibilities of families and children as they relate to individual learning needs. *Indicators of abuse and neglect.	*Demonstrate sensitivity to the diversity of individuals and families.
Standard 4: Instructional Strategies	
*Basic instructional and remedial strategies and materials. *Basic technologies appropriate to individuals with exceptional learning needs.	As directed . . . *Use strategies, equipment, materials, and technologies to accomplish instructional objectives. *Assist in adapting instructional strategies and materials. *Use strategies to facilitate effective integration into various settings. *Use strategies that promote the learner's independence. *Use strategies to increase individuals' independence and confidence.
Standard 5: Learning Environments/Social Interactions	
*Demands of various learning environments. *Rules and procedural safeguards regarding the management of behaviors of individuals with exceptional learning needs.	*Establish and maintain rapport with learners. *Use universal precautions and assist in maintaining a safe, healthy learning environment. *Use strategies for managing behavior as directed. *Use strategies as directed, in a variety of settings, to assist in the development of social skills.
Standard 6: Language	
*Characteristics of appropriate communication with stakeholders.	*None in addition to Common Core.

(continued)

Knowledge	Skills
Standard 7: Instructional Planning	
*None in addition to Common Core.	*Follow written plans, seeking clarification as needed. *Prepare and organize materials to support teaching and learning as directed.
Standard 8: Assessment	
*Rationale for assessment	*Demonstrate basic collection techniques as directed. *Make and document objective observations as directed.
Standard 9: Professional and Ethical Practice	
*Ethical practices for confidential communication about individuals with exceptional learning needs. *Personal cultural biases and differences that affect one's ability to work with others.	*Perform responsibilities as directed in a manner consistent with laws and policies. *Follow instructions of the professional. *Demonstrate problem solving, flexible thinking, and conflict management techniques, and analysis of personal strengths and preferences. *Act as a role model for individuals with exceptional learning needs. *Demonstrate commitment to assisting learners in achieving their highest potential. *Demonstrate the ability to separate personal issues from one's responsibilities as a paraeducator. *Maintain a high level of competence and integrity. *Exercise objective and prudent judgment. *Demonstrate proficiency in academic skills, including oral and written communication. *Engage in activities to increase personal knowledge and skills. *Engage in self-assessment. *Accept and use constructive feedback. *Demonstrate ethical practices as guided by the CEC Code of Ethics and other standards and policies.

As you can see from the chart, these CEC standards are very comprehensive. They are voluntary, however. Neither state nor school districts are legally obligated to ensure that paraprofessionals meet these standards. Many states and districts have used the CEC standards as a basis for setting their own state standards for paraprofessionals, although this has been mainly in special education.

Whether you work in special or general education, there is a level at which standards (in terms of required skills and knowledge) have greater significance for you as an individual. As you carry out your responsibilities—or contemplate new responsibilities that have been assigned to you—you may feel very inadequate and ill qualified for the job. This may only be a question of self-confidence. However, it is very appropriate for you to consider seriously the extent to which you have the knowledge and skills required for the roles assigned to you. We referred to this earlier and suggested you approach your supervising teacher if you feel inadequate to the tasks you have been assigned and ask for support and training to enhance your skills.

CHAPTER SUMMARY

In this chapter we discussed the NCLB and IDEA regulations and standards. Now you should be able to answer the questions posed at the beginning of the chapter. You have learned:

- The entry-level requirements for paraprofessionals working in Title I programs, as dictated by the NCLB Act of 2001 and IDEIA of 2004.
- Some of the possible alternatives available to meet the requirements of NCLB's option C.
- The standards for special education paraprofessionals developed by the Council for Exceptional Children (CEC).
- Some of the additional skills needed for job success.

EXTENDING YOUR LEARNING

ParaPro and WorkKeys

You may be curious to see what the ETS ParaPro and the ACT WorkKeys Proficiency Certificate look like. You can find sample questions for each of them on their websites: **www.ets.org/parapro/** and **www.act.org/workkeys/**.

If you plan to take the ParaPro assessment, verify what your state considers a qualifying score on the test because different states have set different standards for a passing grade. The American Federation of Teachers website has links to many of the State Department of Education web pages, where you should be able to find the details.

Paraprofessional Portfolios

Under the NCLB, parents have a "right to know" as part of the law, which includes the right to know about the qualifications of teachers and paraprofessionals providing services. Whether your employment is governed by the NCLB Act or not, you may wish to begin a portfolio as evidence of your qualifications and practical skills. Here is a list of suggestions for items to include.

A High School Diploma

If you are a paraprofessional and providing student support services, you need a high school diploma or its equivalent. Put a copy of your diploma or general equivalency diploma (GED) in the portfolio.

Evidence of Postsecondary Education

If you have instructional duties, you need to supply evidence (by 2006, according to NCLB) of one of the following: a transcript showing you have completed two academic years of postsecondary education or an associate's degree (in the form of a certificate or license). Include any evidence of college-level classes, whether they meet the full requirements of NCLB or not.

Evidence of Demonstrated Mastery

A portfolio permits you to show mastery of your subject area based on your experience. You might add letters of recommendation you have received, evaluations from your supervisor(s), and other objective measures. If you have been evaluated—formally or informally—in any way, ask for a copy of the evaluation for your own files.

Staff Development Certificates

Save copies of certificates, letters, or other evidence that shows you have attended in-service or staff development classes and met the requirements for achieving the course objectives. Include these in your portfolio. If you have attended many classes, you might summarize them in a table. Here's an example:

Classes Attended

Title of Class Attended	Dates/Times	Objectives Completed
Paraprofessionals Supporting Reading in Third Grade.	April 2, 9, 16, 23, (include the year) 3 hours each session	■ Learned to use Instructor's Manual ■ Identified how to provide support to the teacher and her students ■ Demonstrated effective tutoring techniques
CPR training	September (include the year) 3 hours	■ Learned basic techniques

II

The Learning Environment

In this section we look at the context for the work you perform as a paraprofessional, the learning environment you have been assigned. The traditional learning environment is a classroom with a teacher and perhaps other paraprofessionals present, but you may work in very different surroundings, depending on your duties and the students you serve. The nature of your responsibilities and your students will determine your approach to the learning environment.

Chapter 5 looks at both how the learning environment can be organized and managed effectively and the influences that shape the environment, including curriculum requirements, achievement standards, and testing procedures. Although not all of these areas come under your jurisdiction, you need to be aware of them and how your supervising teacher takes them into consideration as he or she organizes the classroom environment.

Chapter 6 examines the different characteristics of learners and the ways those characteristics influence the learning environment. We look at diversity in terms of the varying abilities of students, as well as the social influences that students bring with them into the classroom: ethnic, cultural, and linguistic backgrounds; socioeconomic status; and the influence of abuse and neglect.

Chapter 7 explores the need for instructional supervision as you work under the direction of your supervising teacher or other professional. The chapter provides you with multiple opportunities to consider the supervision you currently receive, as well as ways in which you can seek additional supervision if you feel you need it, and how you can enhance your relationship with your supervisor.

5 Organization and Management of the Learning Environment

This chapter looks at the structure of the learning environment and the factors that influence its organization. The first factor we explore is the teacher's role as classroom manager and your perceptions of teachers' and paraprofessionals' roles. We then move on to curriculum—its selection and how curriculum requirements and associated achievement standards affect the organization of the learning environment. Last, we look at testing and the way it affects the learning environment. By the end of the chapter, you will be able to answer these questions:

- Why is it now appropriate to consider the teacher a classroom manager, and what changes have created this change in role?
- What is my supporting role as a paraprofessional in the classroom?
- How do curriculum requirements influence classroom organization?
- How do achievement standards and testing impact classroom organization?
- How does testing of student achievement influence the management of the learning environment?

The Teacher's Role as Classroom Manager

It is the teacher's responsibility, as a professional, to take charge of the learning environment, which may take many different forms according to the students being served. The learning environment may be a traditional classroom in general or special education or it may be a resource room where students attend for differing amounts of time and purposes during the course of the week. Or it may not be the same place every day, if you are taking students out for job coaching or other applied experiences. So the learning environment is wherever you and your students find yourselves working together. But whether the teacher is present in that setting or not, he or she has ultimate responsibility for it. You carry out your assigned responsibilities—and this is a point we make more than once because it is so crucial—under the teacher's direction. A teacher or other professional is always assigned to manage the learning environment in which you work.

Different Teachers, Different Styles

If you have already worked with more than one teacher, you know that teachers, like students, vary enormously in their preferences, their approach to their work, and what we might call their philosophy: how they view education and their role in the educational system. This can be true even for two teachers who have received exactly the same training. They may have quite different perspectives on what is most important about their work. Later we look at ways you can work most effectively with your supervising teacher, which includes a discussion of the impact of differing approaches to work and differing priorities. However, this is a good point to begin asking these questions:

1. How do I view my role in the educational system?
2. What are my priorities for the students I work with?

To help you think this through, consider an idea described by David Berliner, a teacher educator from Arizona State University. In the mid-1980s Dr. Berliner described how he had used metaphors to explain his view of the teacher's role, given the changes he had observed in U.S. classrooms over the years. Metaphors, a type of comparison in which one thing is used to describe another, are a useful tool for stimulating thought and exploring the possible connections between the two things. They generate discussion, which is one of the ways we learn. But the really useful thing about metaphors is that the object we choose for the comparison is often quite different from the thing we are comparing it to—at least on the surface—and may surprise people who hear it. So the first reaction to a metaphor may be: *No! It's not like that! Why would you say that?* But because of that reaction to a comparison that they are not expecting, discussion is stimulated.

Dr. Berliner used the metaphor *teacher as executive,* and many teachers reacted with surprise: *We're not executives! We're teachers.* Over the years, teachers have been seen as Mother Earth figures, gathering and caring for children, and nurturing their education and growth. This is particularly true in elementary education where the majority of teachers are women. Teachers have also been viewed as *information givers,* passing on knowledge and wisdom, a perception quite typical of teachers at the secondary level, where students need to acquire large amounts of new knowledge and information. Dr. Berliner saw these two metaphors—teacher as Mother Earth and teacher as information giver—as much too simplistic, with the changes in a teacher's role and the additional responsibilities of today's teachers. Think about some of the changes in classrooms over the past decades and how they have affected the teacher's role.

You: The Major Change

You represent one of the major changes in the classroom: a teacher's responsibility for supervising other adults. Paraprofessionals began to appear in U.S. classrooms after the Second World War because of the national shortage of teachers. Then, as we discussed earlier, with the introduction of special education law in the 1970s, the numbers of paraprofessionals grew substantially and have continued to increase steadily as different educational programs have been introduced (504, Title I, etc.) to provide additional support for students. So those who were hired many years ago have seen enormous changes in the way classrooms work and the different members of staff who have been added to the typical classroom.

Your Role: The Second Major Change

The second part of your influence as a paraprofessional has been the change in your role. Paraprofessionals were initially employed to carry out housekeeping and clerical duties such as making copies, creating bulletin boards, toileting and feeding students with severe impairments, and generally helping keep the classroom looking orderly. Although many paraprofessionals still carry out these important duties, over the years the role of many paraprofessionals has developed to include much more technical and sophisticated responsibilities. The majority of paraprofessionals are now closely involved in providing instruction and other direct services to students, as well as seeing to their physical needs and providing clerical support for teachers. Now teachers are not only supervising other adults in the classroom; they supervise other adults who are also teaching or providing expert help to students. And that means they should be sharing students' educational goals, coordinating lesson plans, getting feedback on students' progress, and making sure paraprofessionals use good teaching and behavior management methods. This is much more complex than just requesting that a paraprofessional make copies or help with paperwork.

Curriculum Requirements: Another Major Change

The other major influence on a teacher's role is the introduction of stricter curriculum and testing requirements over the years. Teachers now have a much greater responsibility for organizing and planning work, making sure curriculum requirements are met, and preparing students for formal tests. In addition, with the greater sensitivity we now have to the emotional and social needs of students, teachers are required to have classrooms that are not just functional, but pleasant environments, where children feel safe and motivated.

All in all, a teacher wears many hats and is much more of a classroom manager, or executive, than a person who passes on information or nurtures student learning. Although the metaphor *teacher as executive* may strike teachers as unusual, when they discuss their various responsibilities, most can see the similarities that Berliner pointed out between their role and that of a business executive. They recognize that they serve as a manager of people and events in the work environment.

Understanding the nature of the teacher's role affects what we expect of teachers, gives us an indication of the training required, and helps school and school district administrators understand what resources and support they need to carry out their responsibilities. As teachers themselves gain a clearer understanding of what is expected, it helps them set priorities, plan their work, and organize their work environment. The same is true of your role as a paraprofessional. As you gain a clearer understanding of your role in the educational system and in the learning environment you have been assigned, you will be better equipped to set priorities and organize your work—and communicate this to your supervising teacher.

To return to the questions we asked previously,

- How do you see your role in the classroom?
- What do you think are the most important aspects of education for your students?

Take a moment to write your thoughts: first, on what you think is the most important for students to learn, and then what role you play in making that happen.

I think the most important things that students come to school for are:

_____

_____

_____

_____

_____

Now consider where you fit into this picture. What part do you play as a paraprofessional in ensuring that students benefit from their education, in the ways you think are important? If possible, describe your role in terms of a metaphor, such as Berliner used. Do you see yourself as a go-fer, picking up after the teacher and generally making yourself useful? Or do you see yourself as a copilot, working alongside the teacher on similar tasks? When you have written your thoughts, suggest a metaphor for today's paraprofessionals and explain why you think that metaphor is appropriate.

I see my role as _____

_____

_____

The metaphor I would propose is *paraprofessional as* _____

_____

_____

_____

_____

I think this metaphor is appropriate because _____

_____

_____

_____

_____

We revisit metaphors later in this section, but we hope these questions will have helped focus your thinking on what you consider a priority for your students and how you can contribute to their achievements.

How Curriculum Requirements Impact Classroom Organization

Now that we have established the teacher is the professional assigned responsibility for the learning environment, and the learning environment is influenced by the

Interaction of Curriculum, Instructional Strategies, and Management Techniques
Curriculum Instructional Strategies Management Techniques

personal philosophies and priorities of the adults who work in it, we need to consider some of the other major influences on your workplace. Curriculum (that is, what we teach) and instructional strategies (how we teach) both help determine our classroom management techniques. In this context, we refer to classroom management as the literal physical management of the learning environment, not the management of student behavior. These three elements are discussed here according to how they interrelate. Instructional strategies and techniques for managing student behavior are covered in detail in Section III.

Curriculum

First you need to know about curriculum requirements. *Curriculum* is a word that essentially means "'what we are supposed to teach students." But who decides what students should learn? And how do they decide?

The term *curriculum* is a Latin word that means the courses of study at a particular school or a particular course of study. Most students could not tell you the meaning of the word, but almost all can tell you the names of the school subjects they are taking: reading, math, social studies, history, and so on. Curriculum is most commonly defined as the *scope and sequence* of courses or classes offered in a school's program. The *scope* of a course is the range of activities, the extent of the subject matter to be covered. It is *what* and *how much* a teacher needs to teach. *Sequence* is the process of following in space, time, or thought. Curriculum sequence dictates *when* a teacher should teach specific subject matter. For example, early or basic math skills include learning to recognize number symbols; a later, more complex, skill is to combine numbers in mathematical problem solving. These skills are often assigned to different grades, so the early basic math skills are learned in a preschool or kindergarten class or early in the first grade, and combining numbers to solve a problem such as multiplication may be learned in the third grade. In other words, when a teacher is given a curriculum to follow, that curriculum has been designed to match a typical child's developmental phase (sequence), as well as an adult perception of what children of that age should know and be able to do (scope).

In the United States, we do not have a prescribed curriculum for all schools and all teachers, unlike many other countries. We discussed earlier how the federal government has had considerable influence over public schools, but the primary authority for education rests with the states, which have traditionally honored the concept of local control. School boards, elected by the people, represent local control. Typically, the federal government only intervenes and dictates local practice on rare and critical issues, for example, during the 1950s and 1960s when schools were segregated by race or color and not offering quality education on an equal basis to all students. Otherwise, the school board takes overall responsibility for issues relating to the running of the local school district. The Board oversees such activities as negotiating employee salaries and establishing policies (e.g., the number of days of sick leave available and whether or not staff receives holiday pay), although in many states and districts where employees are represented by employee associations or unions, these items are negotiated jointly by representatives of the employees' union and representatives of the school board.

School boards delegate the responsibility for overseeing the selection of appropriate curriculum to the superintendent of schools. Typically, this responsibility is then assigned to a director of curriculum who invites parents and teachers from a variety of backgrounds to serve on a curriculum selection committee. The committee identifies the goals of the content area—that is, what they feel the students should learn—with input from various stakeholder groups. The committee then reviews various textbooks from publishers, along with other programs or materials (such as those developed by teachers), to determine which materials will help students meet those goals. Depending on the subject taught (math, reading, science, etc.) and the availability of textbooks that meet the learning/teaching goals, a list is composed of adopted or approved textbooks and made available for schools to use. This is an arduous task, and cost is a consideration when school districts select curriculum materials, so changes in textbook and material adoptions typically do not happen frequently. Parents and other community members who are interested in details of curriculum content and standards can request information from their local school district. Many state Offices of Education now also provide curriculum information on their websites.

The Teacher's Role in Selecting Curriculum

Traditionally the determination of what was taught and when it was taught was entirely at the teacher's discretion. However, in recent decades there has been a national movement toward curriculum alignment and a call for national standards. Selection of the exact textbook(s) used in individual classrooms or schools is still generally considered the responsibility of the teacher—from the textbook adoption list and under the guidelines of the local education authority. Teachers receive extensive training regarding use of textbooks and modifications to the curriculum in their teacher licensure or certification programs. This is an important part of the professional teacher training programs that are offered through universities and colleges. Teachers also receive in-service training (training offered by the school district or state) when they are implementing new programs. Paraprofessionals generally are not involved in this process of curriculum and textbook selection because when you are hired to work in a classroom or with a student, the curriculum is already in place.

Interaction of Curriculum, Instruction, and Management

The curriculum provides teachers with guidelines for *what* they need to teach and *when* it should be taught but not *how* the students receive the information, that is, which instructional strategies should be used. The teacher must take all of this into consideration, and so must you as a paraprofessional. For example, for some students who learn more slowly, the pace of the curriculum should be slowed, the scope narrowed, and the sequence may also need to be adjusted. Other students may be able to handle a much greater scope of curriculum and can be given materials typically used with older students. Still other students may require specialized instructional techniques to meet their unique learning needs. Specific instructional strategies are discussed in detail in the next section, but the important point to remember here is that curriculum, instructional strategies, and management techniques all interact with each other and must be considered together. Here are some examples of how curriculum, management of the physical environment, and instruction interact to influence classrooms.

Scenario 1. Management problems can prevent students from learning and engender inappropriate behavior, no matter how appropriate the curriculum may be or how good the instructional strategies used.

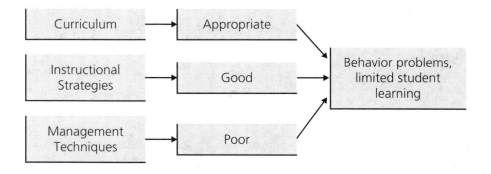

Scenario 2. Instruction that uses only a limited range of techniques and is poorly organized may also elicit behavior and/or classroom management problems, even if the curriculum is at the appropriate level.

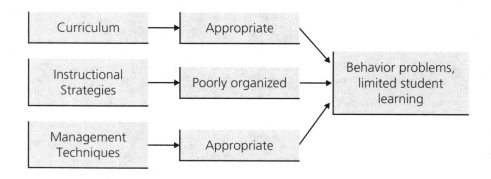

Scenario 3. Curriculum that does not match the students' abilities can prevent students from learning, no matter how appropriate the instruction and the management techniques used. When the curriculum is too difficult, or too easy, eventually students will act out to avoid the work.

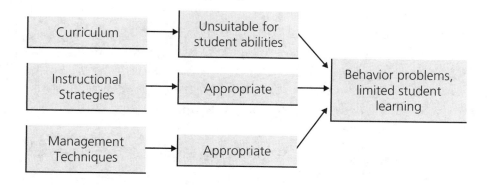

Curriculum and Management

Whether large or small numbers of students are in a classroom or group, effective techniques are required to manage their movement within the learning environment and their learning activities and to enable them to meet behavioral expectations. Transitioning students from one activity to the next is important, as is the safety of students as they transition from the classroom to the lunchroom or other parts of the school. But management within the classroom, or other parts of the learning environment, during learning activities is just as critical for enhancing student learning. This type of management is directly affected by the curriculum that students are following and whether the instructional techniques are appropriate to the age and abilities of the students. We look at two examples.

The math curriculum for almost any age requires students to "add, subtract, multiply, and divide numbers." However, for second-grade students it may specify they should be able to do the following:

- Solve whole number problems using addition and subtraction in vertical and horizontal notation.
- Use fractions to identify parts of the whole.
- Model and illustrate meanings of the operations of addition and subtraction and describe how they relate.

Here is what would be considered a developmentally appropriate *scope* of the curriculum for children who are approximately seven to eight years old.

In terms of instructional techniques, at this age and grade level:

- Students may still be using manipulatives (physical equipment to help them visualize the mathematical concepts they are using) for some of their work.
- They may still need to count on their fingers and talk to themselves as they work to help them think.
- They often are taught in small groups rather than as a whole class.

- They also often complete their work in their own workbook or on worksheets because this reduces the errors they might make in copying from a textbook or from the chalkboard and allows them to get on with the math work itself rather than spending unnecessary time on laborious copying.

All of these factors affect the management of the physical arrangements of the classroom, which have to accommodate the instructional tasks and developmental needs of the students:

- Desks/tables are grouped rather than set in rows.
- Storage space is available for workbooks and manipulatives.
- The classroom often buzzes with the voices of students working in small groups with a teacher or paraprofessional and the other students talking themselves through their work.

Compare this with a ninth-grade math class. The curriculum may state that students should be able to do the following:

- Draw conclusions using concepts of probability after collecting, organizing, and analyzing a data set.
- Understand and apply measurement tools, formulas, and techniques.
- Recognize, describe, and identify geometric shapes, and solve problems using spatial and logical reasoning, applications of geometric principles, and modeling.

These students will usually be taught as a whole class, they will be using calculators for basic operations and textbooks for information, and they will usually be expected to copy practice problems from the textbook or chalkboard into their exercise books. Unlike students in the elementary grades, ninth-grade students also move from one classroom to another for each class period, and they are expected to bring their own books and equipment with them. As a result, in ninth-grade (and in many other secondary-level) math classrooms,

- Desks tend to be in orderly rows facing the teacher and chalkboard at the front of the room, rather than in groups.
- Students work without manipulatives to help visualize concepts (because they should now understand those concepts without the physical prompt).
- Classes generally have larger numbers of students and desks.
- Relatively little storage is needed for books and equipment.
- The classroom tends to be quieter, with only one voice heard at a time as the teacher lectures or circulates to provide assistance and students respond.

Thus, although the curriculum is strictly only concerned with the content and sequence of what you teach, it also influences the physical arrangements that teachers make in their classrooms and other learning environments. The learning environment must be designed to meet the developmental needs of the students as they work through the assigned curriculum. If we consider the math curriculum for a ninth-grade student who is receiving special education services, we would find yet another arrangement. The learning environment could be a supported employment setting where (with the support of a paraprofessional) the student is making change. In this case, there would be no desks or other students; no pencils, paper, or textbooks; and the manipulatives would be actual money. This shows the extent to which curriculum influences the management of the physical arrangement in the learning environment.

The Influence of Curriculum on Your Work

Think through the curriculum content and the developmentally appropriate activities you use with the students you work with (choose only one class if you work with several) and plot how that affects the way the classroom or work space is organized. List some of the physical arrangements made to accommodate the curriculum activities you and your students engage in regularly.

Class or group of students you work with: _____

Organizational features that are necessary because of the curriculum and teaching

methods used: _____

_____

_____

_____

_____

_____

Curriculum and Special Education

As you learned earlier, students who receive education and services under special education should have access to the same curriculum as their nondisabled peers, to the greatest extent possible. However, that curriculum may have to be modified so they can access it, and the type and extent of the modifications will depend on their abilities and identified disability. Modification may take several forms.

The first type of adaptation is to *modify instructional materials and activities*. The learning task remains the same, but the way in which the necessary skills and information are presented is changed. Some recommendations for working with students for whom the curriculum has been modified are contained in the box. Note that these would be appropriate for students with learning or behavioral difficulties and can often be helpful for students who have no difficulties at all.

Recommendations for Working with Students Who Have a Modified Curriculum

- Make sure directions are clear. Consider giving instructions both in written and oral form. When giving directions orally, simplify and only give one direction at a time. Written directions should be on the student's reading level and can be written on the board so students can keep referring back to them if necessary.
- Break larger tasks into their smaller components and assign one component at a time. If you ask students to write a story or report, rather than asking them to complete the whole task at once, have them write just the introduction or a first

paragraph (or a first sentence) before you check their work, and provide encouragement and feedback. Then have them write the next section or sentence. In math, this may take the form of asking the student to complete the first three problems on the page (or first computation) before checking their work. If the student is working from a worksheet, draw a line across the page to denote how many problems the students need to complete before showing you their work or before the end of the class period.

▪ Enlarge the font on worksheets. This makes reading easier for some students. If a student is embarrassed by what appears to be childishly large writing on the worksheet, the sheet can be copied onto a colored paper, which also tends to be easier to read.

Another type of modification is to *reduce the level of difficulty* in relation to the student's age. This means that although the student will learn the same concepts (e.g., adding and subtracting in math), the level of difficulty will be lower and more like the curriculum for much younger students.

A third type of modification is to *reduce the breadth of the curriculum;* that is, expectations for performance—quantity, speed, and accuracy—are reduced. For example, the requirement for a one-page assignment for other students in the class may be reduced to a half page for the student needing modifications. However, the same time limit may be imposed. Or the student may be allowed a little longer than age- and grade-level peers to complete the same assignment. Accuracy may also be adjusted, and the measure of successful performance may be set at 75 percent correct instead of the 95 to 100 percent set for the majority of the class.

The final type of modification we mention—and it is perhaps the most common for students with moderate or severe disabilities—is *an increased emphasis on practical and vocational skills,* rather than academic knowledge. When students plan to go from school to supported employment rather than to college, the curriculum may have more of an applied orientation in which students have many hands-on experiences to support their ability to learn the curriculum.

Many paraprofessionals who work with students in special education settings are directly involved with these types of curriculum modifications. In fact, many of the paraprofessional positions available in special education exist because students need modifications that require one-on-one help or additional support that cannot be supplied by a teacher working in the classroom alone. However, the supervising professional should decide the nature of the modifications. Although you may present a modified curriculum to your students, you should not have to design those modifications, only deliver them.

How Achievement Standards and Testing Impact Classroom Organization

Another major influence on the management of the learning environment is the need to test student achievement. First we take a look at the rationale behind testing—formal and informal—and then we briefly examine some of the pitfalls with tests, before identifying how testing impacts the learning environment in which you work.

Testing: Knowing Whether We Are Getting It Right

Recent years have seen a substantial increase in the emphasis placed on accountability in schools; that is, schools and teachers should be able to show they are doing the job they are paid to do. This is only reasonable because the U.S. educational system consumes millions of dollars every year, and those who provide the money (federal and local governments and taxpayers, some of whom are represented by the school board) want to see evidence the money is not being wasted and children really are learning. Of course, teachers continually look for evidence that their students are learning, so they give frequent tests such as spelling tests at

Criterion-Referenced and Norm-Referenced Tests

Criterion-referenced tests are designed to match the curriculum that students are currently following. A teacher has certain expectations of what students know or certain criteria that must be met to show a student has learned the assigned curriculum material, and the students are tested against these expectations or criteria. The score on a criterion-referenced test is usually a straightforward count of correct answers or a percentage of answers correct for each individual student. If a student scores poorly on a criterion-referenced test, the teacher can look at which questions were answered incorrectly and reteach those concepts. The test is considered *formative:* it gives the teacher information that allows him or her to take action to improve the student's understanding.

Norm-referenced tests have been developed around a very general curriculum and then normed using large groups of students. That means the test is given to groups of students from different schools around the United States, and the results are examined to see which questions were answered correctly and incorrectly. This is an expensive process, so norm-referenced tests are almost always developed commercially. Questions answered correctly by the majority of students are considered appropriate for the age group taking the test and so are usually retained. When the majority of students answer a question incorrectly, it suggests the wording of the question is confusing or the content of the questions is too difficult for students of that age, so these questions are usually rejected or replaced by questions that are less confusing or easier.

Norm-referenced tests are usually scored by the company that produces them, and scores are usually given for the whole class or grade level, not for individual students. That means these are composite scores, expressed as averages and/or percentiles. Thus if students score poorly on the test, a teacher does not have enough information to know which concepts were poorly understood by the students and need to be retaught. The results for norm-referenced tests are considered *summative:* they give a summary of how students have performed but they do not provide information that helps a teacher intervene and improve a student's understanding.

the end of each week, end-of-unit/chapter quizzes, and constant questions and requests that students demonstrate their skills and knowledge. A teacher only knows that teaching is effective when students can show they have learned, and good teachers reteach or modify their teaching according to the results of such tests.

Federal and state education agencies cannot take such a detailed interest in each individual student's progress, but they do require information from school districts and states on how their students are performing overall. For this reason, at certain points in their education all students are tested using commercially produced norm-referenced tests, with the results expressed as averages and percentiles.

Average scores are a composite score for a group of students and give a general idea of performance for the whole group of students who sat for the test (e.g., a class or year group). Percentile scores indicate how well students scored in comparison with all of the other students of the same age who took the test at the same time. You have no doubt been involved with students who have taken norm-referenced tests, such as the Stanford Achievement Tests, California Test of Basic Skills, or state curriculum tests. These are used as indicators of how well a school district is doing—that is, how well it accomplishes its purpose of providing an education for students.

Let's pause briefly here to define some of the terms used in connection with testing, particularly the terms *norm-referenced* and *criterion-referenced* (see previous page). The differences between the two tests are quite substantial, but they do have different purposes. A teacher usually writes criterion-referenced tests for a particular group of students, so the only resource involved is the teacher's time. Norm-referenced tests, in contrast, have to be purchased from the company that developed them, which can represent a considerable cost to a school or school district.

The Challenge of Tests

Although you are not likely to be involved in writing tests for large groups of students, it is important to understand some of the issues related to testing. Students undergo tests of different sorts many times in their school career, so we have learned to accept them as part of the system. However, testing is quite a controversial subject—and for good reason.

Value Added: How Much Students Have Learned. One of the main problems with using tests for teaching/learning accountability is that none of the scores takes into account the level at which the students began—that is, how much better they are now than they were before the teacher started teaching them. This is sometimes referred to as *value added.* One group of students, for instance, may already be very knowledgeable at the beginning of the school year, so even if their new teacher is not very effective, they may score reasonably well at the end of the first trimester. Another group of students may have very little knowledge and poor skills to begin with, but a superb teacher can help them move ahead to a considerable extent, and these students may also score reasonably well on the same test.

Although both groups of test scores would show the teacher/school seems to be doing a good job of teaching the students, the reality is that the second group received much more value from their time in school than the first group. This issue of value added has been used as one of the justifications for more frequent testing of students. Advocates of annual testing using norm-referenced tests point out that schools will have a much clearer picture of how far students have progressed in a given time span, not just what they know at a particular point in time.

Valid Tests: Matching Tests with Teaching. When tests are written, teachers or curriculum specialists ideally review them carefully to make sure the wording is clear and items are not too difficult for students to read. Then the tests are checked to ensure that they only test concepts included in the chapter or material they were written for. But they also need to be checked to make sure they cover everything in the chapter, so teachers can check students' understanding of all of the concepts, not just some of them. This process takes a long time and can involve a lot of people. That means it is expensive. Textbook publishers are not always willing to invest large amounts of time and money developing the tests they include in their textbooks, and as a result, those tests may not meet the same high standard as the rest of the textbook. But this is an important concept for all tests, including the simple tests you give your students. You would not generally include items on a spelling test, for example, that you have not asked the students to learn, but you also need to be sure a test of math or history facts relates directly to the content of your teaching, and you neither test more nor less than what you taught. This is the concept of test validity.

Look at the example of part of an end-of-chapter test from an imaginary curriculum in the nearby box. Can you spot the test items that do not match the curriculum content of the chapter? Can you understand how frustrating it would be for students to be tested on concepts they had not been taught? How frustrating it would be for the teacher to have students perform poorly on a test, when she thought they had learned the concepts thoroughly?

Sample Chapter Summary and Test Items

Content of Chapter 5: Fractions
Variety of ways of expressing fractions, including decimals
Addition and subtraction of fractions, including decimal notation

Test
1. $1/4 + 1/4 =$
2. $1/2 + 3/4 =$
3. $3/8 + 3/8 =$
4. $1/4 \times 3/8 =$
5. $7/8 - 3/8 =$
6. $1 - 1/4 =$
7. $6/8 - 1/2 =$
8. $0.75 + 0.25 =$
9. $1 + 0.4 =$
10. $0.5 + 0.6 =$

When students fail an end-of-unit test, teachers do not always realize it is because the test is invalid. That is, it does not match the chapter content, so it does not test what it should (and what the teacher has taught). If any of your students perform very poorly on a test, check the test to make sure it matches what you have been teaching. This is also true of tests that you or the teacher write, not just tests included in textbooks, so be very careful if you are asked to write test items for students. Test development is not as simple as it looks, and the effect of a poorly written test on student morale can be disastrous!

Testing and Management of the Learning Environment

If you already work as a paraprofessional, or have spent much time in learning environments, you will already be aware that testing of student achievement happens regularly. Testing, like teaching, takes time. That means it has to be allowed for in managing the learning environment. This is an important part of the teaching process—not only because it holds teachers and schools accountable, but also because it enables teachers and paraprofessionals to know whether students are being successful. Students who are successful (whether that success is academic or social) are generally much more motivated and content to be in the classroom than those who are not successful. A successful student is an indication of a successful teacher, and successful teachers are also more motivated in their work. So although we sometimes consider tests to be an afterthought and a necessary evil, they are actually part of the instructional process. As such, they must be scheduled and planned for as you manage your time and workplace.

C-H-A-P-T-E-R S-U-M-M-A-R-Y

In this chapter, we looked at the structure of the learning environment and what influences the management of that structure: curriculum, instructional techniques, and testing of student achievement. However, the first and most important point is that a professional educator has overall responsibility for the learning environment you work in and you therefore work under the supervision of that professional. This is a legal requirement, as described in Section I. Thus, even if you spend a part of your day without direct supervision, remember that decisions about curriculum, instructional techniques, testing, and management should be referred to your supervising professional, who decides how much responsibility for any of these factors is delegated to you as a paraprofessional.

One result of prescribed curriculum content and standards for student achievement is that classrooms must be very busy, focused workplaces. In the lower elementary grades, educators recognize the need for activities that develop creativity and social skills and can usually allow time for them. In the secondary grades, however, students are expected to acquire enormous amounts of new information in every subject each trimester, so a student's time is very structured, and little time seems to be left for "play" or informal activities. Whichever type of environment you work in, be aware of the important role that curriculum selection plays in driving the activities of your workplace, as well as testing requirements that give an indication of the success of your endeavors.

By reading this chapter and completing the activities, you have learned:

- To identify the appropriate role for the teacher as a classroom manager.
- Your supporting role as a paraprofessional in the classroom.
- How curriculum requirements affect the organization of the classroom.
- The ways in which achievement standards and testing impact classroom organization.
- How testing of a student's achievement influences the ways in which the learning environment is managed.

Now you should be able to answer the questions posed at the beginning of the chapter, and you have an enhanced view of the reasons behind the how and the why of the teacher's organization of the classroom. The school curriculum and standards, student testing, and student achievement all have an influence on what goes on in the classroom.

E-X-T-E-N-D-I-N-G—Y-O-U-R—L-E-A-R-N-I-N-G

Identifying Your Responsibilities for the Learning Environment

Before you begin the next section of the book, which details techniques you can use as you work with students, be clear in your mind about your responsibilities for managing the learning environment in which you work. Use the form provided to map your responsibilities in relation to curriculum, management of the physical environment, and testing of student achievement. If you work with several different groups of students, you can complete this exercise for each of them; if your responsibilities are similar for each of those groups, you need only complete the exercise once. If you find you are unsure about any of these responsibilities, ask your supervisor to clarify the situation for you.

Student/Instructional Group:
CURRICULUM
My responsibilities include: **My responsibilities do not include:**
MANAGEMENT OF THE PHYSICAL ENVIRONMENT
My responsibilities include: **My responsibilities do not include:**
TESTING OF STUDENT ACHIEVEMENT
My responsibilities include: **My responsibilities do not include:**

CHAPTER

6 Learner Characteristics

In Chapter 5 we considered several important factors that influence the management and organization of the learning environment. One more aspect of your working environment you have to consider when planning your work is the characteristics of the students you teach. As you well know, students come in all shapes and sizes, both literally, in a physical sense, and metaphorically, in that each student is an individual. Even the youngest students are already subject to a wide variety of influences when they first come to school, and these influences continue to operate in their lives. This includes their racial and ethnic background, the makeup of their families, and their gender. Some of these influences may be more positive than others, but the education you offer will always interact with these influences and different students will receive it differently. By the end of the chapter, you will be able to answer these questions:

- What cognitive and metacognitive processes are involved in student learning?
- What learner characteristics and events enhance or detract from learning?
- What are some of the social influences on students' capacity to learn?
- What are some of the important differences or exceptionalities that students exhibit?
- What learning styles assist in information processing?
- What are some appropriate instructional aids that I can use to help students process information in light of these learning styles and characteristics?
- What strategies will assist me in my job as a paraprofessional who supports student learning?

With the knowledge you gain in this chapter, you will understand the effects of exceptional conditions on an individual's learning, which will enhance both your personal learning and the learning processes of the students you are helping.

Learner Characteristics: Cognition

The word *cognition,* often used in talking about the process of learning, or gaining knowledge, is essentially a synonym for *thinking.* Cognitive abilities include the sensing and processing of information, recall of information, comprehension, problem solving, and the synthesis of information (see nearby box). In many ways, the mind can be compared to a computer, and we often use similar words to describe the processes involved in thinking and computer use. When students receive infor-

Words to Describe Cognition

Recall: The ability to remember or produce a piece of information from memory.

Comprehension: The ability to see, read, or hear a statement and understand its meaning. Comprehension is particularly important when students need to follow instructions or extract meaning from a text.

Problem Solving: The ability to provide a solution to a problem. For example, when asked to multiply 32 × 7, the student must be able to select a process that will provide the correct answer of 224; in a story problem such as "If two friends were walking down the street and each picked up 30 pieces of litter, how many pieces of litter did they pick up altogether?" the student must understand the process involved is multiplication of the number of people (2) by the number of pieces of litter (30), or 60 pieces of litter.

Synthesis: The process of putting together known facts and arriving at an answer or drawing a conclusion. Synthesis is similar to putting together a jigsaw puzzle. Individually we see small cardboard pieces, usually in interesting and unique shapes, but when we put them together, the individual pieces collectively make a large picture. The individual small pieces are like the facts that students learn, and the larger picture is what students can see when they put all the facts together and arrive at an answer.

mation and try to learn it, it is like saving information on the computer: they store it for later retrieval. A good deal of classroom time is taken up with teachers presenting information and students working to store that information for later use.

Some cognitive tasks are obviously easier than others, and as you ask students to show their knowledge and understanding, you need to be aware of the comparative difficulty of the task. For example, a recall item on a test would require the student to supply the correct answer from his or her own memory, by filling in a blank. By contrast, an easier activity is a recognition item: the student is required to select or identify the correct answer from a short list of items (commonly called multiple-choice tests). The recall item has no built-in prompt for the student to provide the correct answer, whereas the recognition item contains the correct answer: the student only has to identify it from the list.

We cannot see what students are thinking. Although they are always thinking about something, we certainly cannot be sure they are thinking about the lesson! We only see the product, or results, of cognition, for example, the answer the student gives to a question, orally or in writing. If the student gives a correct answer, you assume there are no problems with the cognitive process. However, if the answer is incorrect, you have to try and figure out what went wrong in the student's thinking—or cognitive—processes, one of the major challenges of working with students.

A variety of ways are available to assess the results or product of thinking. Some of these are formal tests. Others may be informal, such as simply giving the student a problem and watching how he completes it, or even having him tell you how he is working through the problem to complete it. We discuss how to assess a student's cognitive processes in greater detail further on in the book, where we also explore teaching strategies that are most effective for promoting learning.

Later in this chapter, as we talk about metacognition, you will learn how to help students identify the strategies and learning styles that help them learn best. Meanwhile, here are a few effective strategies that assist the learning process:

Rehearsal Strategies

For basic tasks, such as memorizing a list of words, have students recite the list, repeating it over and over (rehearsing it). For short pieces of information, such as a telephone number, a spelling list, or multiplication tables, rehearsal can be very effective. However, a more complex task, such as learning key facts or points in a text, requires more complex strategies, such as copying the material, taking detailed notes, or underlining the key points.

Organizational Strategies

Clustering techniques are a useful strategy for the basic task of memorizing a list. For example, to learn a spelling list, try these:

- Group together any words that rhyme.
- Group words that have the same first letter.
- Group words that have common characteristics (e.g., that end with *-tion* or begin with *dis-*).
- Put the spellings to music.

Organizational strategies for more complex tasks may include outlining the content, diagramming, or mapping:

- Charts and matrices are helpful for organizing large amounts of information into meaningful patterns or groups.
- Models can be built to represent relationships that cannot be observed. The solar system and each planet's relationship to the others can be represented with a model.
- Outlines are also helpful in showing organizational structure. Textbooks often use an outline at the beginning of the chapter to give learners advance notice of the contents of the chapter.

Mnemonic Strategies

Another organizational strategy is to use *mnemonics:* assign a word or phrase to the concept you are trying to teach. These strategies help form associations that facilitate recall of information. You may recognize some of these mnemonics from your elementary and high school days:

- Never Eat Shredded Wheat (N, E, S, W—the order of the points of the compass, clockwise from the top).
- Sammy's Old Horse Carries Aunt Hannah To Old Alabama. This one is for trigonometry: SOH: sine = opposite/hypotenuse; CAH: cosine= adjacent/hypotenuse; TOA: tangent = opposite/adjacent.

- HOME = names of the Great Lakes (Huron, Ontario, Michigan, Erie).
- FACE = the names of the musical notes that correspond with the spaces on the staff.
- King Philip Came Over From Greece Singing (in biology: kingdom, phylum, class, order, family, genus, species).
- Grammar spelling rules (e.g., "*I* before *e* except after *c*" has a useful rhyme and rhythm to aid memory).

Elaboration Strategies

Elaboration is the process of taking information and making it meaningful by linking it to existing knowledge. Thus an image of something that is already known can be used to prompt recall of new information. For example, to remember the difference in spelling between *desert* and *dessert,* ask yourself which you would rather have more of (there's only one *s* in desert, but two in dessert). More complex tasks can utilize elaboration strategies such as paraphrasing, summarizing, or creating analogies.

Hands-On Activities

Active participation in the learning activity facilitates learning. Elementary school teachers often teach students hand movements to help them remember the words of songs, but even adults can benefit from adding hand or body movements when they are trying to memorize information, particularly sequences of facts or movements. Some researchers believe hands-on learning is at the heart of cognition, and for some students it is essential, as we discuss next.

Metacognition and Learning Styles

Metacognition is the awareness of your own learning: knowing how you learn best, what seems to inhibit learning for you as an individual, and the ability to regulate these processes. These skills help you assess a learning problem, determine the learning strategies needed to solve the problem, evaluate the effectiveness of the chosen strategy, and, when needed, change or improve the learning strategy for better learning effectiveness. We often talk of learning styles, meaning the ways or methods by which a student learns best. Some students are *visual learners* and learn best by seeing or visualizing the activity, which is sometimes called *observational learning* because the learner is often watching other people to see how something is done. You may worry that students are copying each other if you see one student observing another, yet observation is a valid part of a visual learner's style.

Another preferred learning style is *aural,* which means students need to hear what they are to learn. You may have seen aural learning when a student hears a tune and then is immediately able to sing or play it, but this learning style also applies to students who do not need to see information written down in order to remember it.

Another learning style is *kinesthetic,* which means the student learns most efficiently through a combination of touch and movement. This type of learning is related to the moving sense and the positioning of the learner, and it is most often associated with physical skills such as dance or sports. It also can be applied to learning less concrete concepts, however, such as shape and time, as long as the student is engaged in a physical learning activity and not just expected to absorb information while sitting still.

These are just a sampling of preferred learning styles, but they are not the only ways in which people learn. Some students may need a combination of styles, and different circumstances or material may lend themselves better to one approach than another. Remember the old Chinese proverb: "Tell me and I forget, show me and I remember, involve me and I understand."

Some students will remember if you just tell them, but some will prefer to be shown, and others will need to be physically involved in the learning activity in order to absorb new information. Think too of the story of Helen Keller. When 19 months old, she was stricken with an acute illness that left her deaf and blind. She had no way to get information through those senses that most of us depend on. No method could be found to educate her until the age of seven, when she began her special education in reading and writing. With the help of a skilled and dedicated teacher, she was able to learn. She ultimately became a lecturer, published fourteen books, met with several U.S. presidents, and visited thirty-five countries.

It is essential that a teacher—and you as a paraprofessional—know how best to support students' learning. Careful observation of how your students react to different teaching approaches will help you support their learning in the most effective way, but using a multistyle approach, you will be able to help many more students. Insisting on using only one method of teaching is ineffective because it limits access to the information you are trying to impart for some students. For example, if you always use a lecture approach or read information to students without adding visuals, you can cause a great deal of anxiety in students who are visual or kinesthetic learners (see box on next page). In future chapters, we identify a wide variety of teaching methods you can use to make the teaching and learning process more effective. However, at this stage the important concept to remember is that each student has a preferred learning style, so your teaching style needs to be very flexible and varied to reach all of the students.

Helping Students with Metacognition

Students need to understand their own individual learning style so that they know which learning strategies will be most helpful to them and can determine better the learning strategies they need to use to solve a problem. This also helps students advocate for their own needs in the classroom. For example, a student who needs to *hear* the explanations and problems (aural learner) may ask permission to record the class lecture so he can listen to it again before completing the assignment. Another student may ask the teacher for a copy of the lecture notes so she can *read* them (visual learner) before the test. Still another student may ask you to *demonstrate or walk him or her through* a procedure (kinesthetic learner). Once students know their own preferred learning style, they are more able to choose an effective strategy for learning, and when they feel they are not learning, they have a better idea of what to do about it. This is a planning strategy because the student is planning how he will approach the problem. The student may also evaluate the amount of time available for completion of the problem or problems and plan how many minutes can be devoted to each. For example, a 30-minute test with 20 problems may allow the student 1.5 minutes per test question. Or the student may evaluate the questions and see they get progressively more difficult, so the student allows herself progressively more time for the last few problems—7 minutes for the first 10 questions, but as much as 13 minutes for the last 10 problems.

Using a monitoring strategy, the students check, or monitor, their performance on a test, making sure they are keeping to the predecided strategy. In the example of allocating differing amounts of time to questions according to their relative difficulty, on completion of the test, a student may decide a better strategy would have been to allow the same amount of time for each problem. Armed with this type of information, students can go into the next test with a better strategy.

Another monitoring strategy involves students checking on themselves and the learning that is taking place. A good example is reading comprehension. A student

Techniques I Can Use to Accommodate a Variety of Learning Styles

Example: Use drawings (not just text) for students who need the visual support.

1. _____

   _____

2. _____

   _____

3. _____

   _____

4. _____

   _____

5. _____

   _____

6. _____

   _____

who knows his mind wanders when he is reading may develop a strategy to self-check at the end of each paragraph. As he completes the last line of the paragraph he says to himself, "So what was the meaning of that paragraph?" He decides what the meaning was (and may write it down), verifies his answer by rereading key sentences in the paragraph, and then moves on to the next paragraph.

Educators need to know how best to support students' learning. Look at methods used by the teachers around you. See if you can develop a list of strategies you could also use in your assignments to help your students. Add to the list as you recognize strategies that have been used effectively to enhance your own learning.

What About Adult Learners?

It is as important for adult learners to understand their own learning styles and needs as is it for students. Without this awareness, it is difficult to take charge of your own learning. Once you are aware of your own preferred learning style and needs, you too can use metacognitive strategies to take steps to assist yourself and your students. If you ask a group of adults to say how they learn best, they may not be able to tell you. However, if you ask them to remember an important number or an address, they may say, "I'll have to write that down to remember it" or "Number 54? Oh, that's easy to remember—same as my mother's house." What about you? How do you learn and recall information best? The short activity in the box will help you identify your preferred learning style.

Other teaching and learning ideas are covered in Section III, but the important thing to focus on here is that both adults and students have preferred learning styles. Being aware of your own learning processes (metacognition) and how you learn best (learning style) will help you appreciate that students learn differently too. The extra steps you take to help students will pay huge benefits in learning.

You have read about cognition, metacognition, and individual learning styles, but there are many other factors related to student achievement. In the next sections of this chapter, we cover some of the most important areas that affect learning: intelligence, culture and ethnicity, gender, and social influences.

Degrees of Intelligence or Exceptionalities

Most people have a sense of what *intelligence* is. In your social groups, you probably have a friend or two whom everyone considers bright, sharp, or gifted, and others who seem less so. In our classrooms are students who have a whole range of abilities and intelligences. Intelligence has been defined as three dimensional: (1) the capacity to acquire knowledge, (2) the ability to think and reason in the abstract, and (3) the capability for solving problems. *Aptitude* is another word often associated with intelligence, defined as the ability to acquire knowledge. However, remember that intelligence is not only associated with abilities in academic subjects or formal school-based study; intelligence is a much more general concept

Many skill inventories can help you discover how you learn best. Try this activity to gain more insight into your own learning style. Complete each sentence by checking either A, B, or C. There is no best answer. Just choose the one you feel suits you best.

I feel as if I learn the most when I

A. _____ see the information written down.

B. _____ hear the information read aloud.

C. _____ get involved in a hands-on activity.

When I want to relax, I love to

A. _____ read.

B. _____ listen to music on a tape or a CD.

C. _____ cook, garden, or exercise.

I am usually

A. _____ a thinker who contemplates often.

B. _____ a talker.

C. _____ actively involved. People call me a doer.

When in a classroom as a student I learn best when

A. _____ I have pictures and written information such as a textbook.

B. _____ the instructor has us answer many questions, give reports, and talk about the material.

C. _____ I am involved in giving presentations and sharing the material with peers.

When learning to use new equipment such as a computer I learn best when

A. _____ I read the information from the operating manual.

B. _____ someone talks me through how to use it.

C. _____ I get involved by trying it.

Now calculate your score: Total number of A choices _____

Total number of B choices _____

Total number of C choices _____

This fun little test gives you an idea of how you prefer to learn. If most of your answers were "A" you probably are a visual learner. If you answered "B" the most, you are an auditory learner and like to hear things when learning. If you marked "C" most of the time, you are a kinesthetic learner and like to be actively involved in the learning process.

relating to many different types of ability. In your work with students you will see many facets of their intelligence, but there may be many additional areas in which they excel. Student abilities are on a continuum: they may have high or low abilities in any given skill, or they may be somewhere in between. They may have high abilities in one area and lower abilities in another area. In the educational system, students on the very able end of the continuum of ability are often considered gifted or talented, whereas those on the limited end have entitlement to special education and related services.

Special Education

Educational services for students on the low end of the abilities continuum may look very different from the services provided for the majority of students. Their services may constitute education in the broad sense but strongly emphasize training in basic life skills, such as eating, dressing, and toileting. The law is clear that these children have a right to a free, appropriate education regardless of the severity of their disabilities, but appropriate in this case may mean training in life skills rather than academic subjects.

As we discussed earlier, students with disabilities are entitled to receive related or supportive services to the extent these services are necessary for them to benefit from their special education program. Occasionally people view special education services as only services to students who have lower intelligence. This is inaccurate. The range of abilities among students eligible for special education services is very broad. Even some students who are gifted in intelligence may be eligible for special education services. Consider again Helen Keller who was blind and deaf but obviously highly intelligent. In our current educational system she would have received services because of her deaf-blindness, not because of limited cognitive abilities.

In Chapter 2, we outlined the requirements of the Individuals with Disabilities Education Act (IDEA), which provides students who have disabilities with access to public education and requires all school systems in the United States to provide each child with a free, appropriate public education in the least restrictive environment. IDEA defines special education as "specially designed instruction, adapting, as appropriate, the content, methodology, or delivery of instruction to address the unique needs of the child that result from the disability and to ensure that child access to the general curriculum." A number of rights are offered to parents and students with disabilities under the IDEA '97 and 2004 (see Figure 6.1). All of these rights are designed to mitigate the possible effects of low ability in certain areas, so students can develop in areas of higher ability.

Categories of Disability Used in Special Education When the law states that students are eligible to receive special education services, it is referring to thirteen categories of disability recognized by IDEA: autism, communication disorder or speech or language impairments, deaf-blindness, developmental delay, emotional disturbance, hearing impairment/deafness, intellectual disability, multiple disabilities, orthopedic impairment, other health impairments, specific learning disabili-

---

Rights of Students and Parents Under IDEA

A free, appropriate, public education tailored to the needs of the individual

Nondiscriminatory assessment, using more than one test or measure, in the child's native language, and administered by a professional trained in assessment

An IEP (Individualized Educational Program) including the provision of supplementary aids and services to ensure the success of the educational program

Placement in the least restrictive environment with emphasis on participation in the general curriculum

Procedural safeguards that include parent involvement in all steps

Due process—parents are notified of all decisions, procedures are followed, and parents have legal recourse if they are unhappy with services

---

Figure 6.1

ties, traumatic brain injury, and visual impairments (including blindness). These are the only categories of disability under which students can be considered eligible for special education. Although many students are identified by their medical doctors or by parents as having attention deficit disorder (ADD) or attention deficit hyperactivity disorder (ADHD), as of yet these are not a recognized disability category under IDEA. Such students may be served under the category of "other health impairments" or under a 504 plan if they meet eligibility requirements.

Of the thirteen special education disabilities accepted under IDEA, some are more prevalent than others; that is, greater numbers of students are considered eligible for services under these categories. These are therefore known as *high-incidence disabilities* and include specific learning disabilities, speech or language impairments, intellectual disabilities, and serious emotional disturbance. *Low-incidence disabilities*, or those occurring less frequently in the population, are autism, hearing impairments, deafness, visual impairments (including blindness), deaf-blindness, multiple disabilities, orthopedic impairments, traumatic brain injury, and other health impairments.

The law requires each local education agency (usually a school district) to develop policies and procedures to ensure that all students with disabilities, birth through twenty-one years of age, who are in need of special education and related services are identified, evaluated, and provided with appropriate services. Each disability has specific identification and evaluation rules outlined by the law. Colleges, universities, and local school districts offer courses that study the characteristics of each of these disabilities and the identification procedures, teaching techniques, and programs that provide the best help to students with each one of them.

As a paraprofessional, you may be assigned to provide education or related services—under the direction of a teacher—to a student receiving special education services. The assignment may be to provide basic health care, such as toileting or suctioning (for cystic fibrosis), or it may be taking notes for a secondary student with physical disabilities or specific learning difficulties in an advanced history class. A great deal of information is now available to teachers and paraprofessionals who work with students with disabilities. If you take the time to conduct an Internet search on a specific disability, you will find multiple sources of information, including websites set up by parenting or support groups, as well as national organizations representing a particular disability. An example of one such organization is the National PTA, which is the largest volunteer child advocacy organization in the United States. This not-for-profit association of parents, educators, students, and other citizens active in their schools and communities boasts six million members. You can learn more about the National PTA and the information it provides at **www.pta.org**.

Gifted Education

Students on the higher end of the intelligence and ability continuum are not considered eligible for additional education services under IDEA, which caters specifically for students with *dis*abilities. No law mandates entitlement to education that matches giftedness. However, many U.S. school districts have recognized the need for an enriched curricular program for these students and have developed gifted and talented programs. In the past, many schools responded to differences in learner abilities by ability grouping. This arrangement was most common at the high school level. Students with high ability were usually assigned to college preparation courses. Thus this was also called *tracking* because some students were on the fast track, as it were, to a college education.

In theory, tracking supports effective practice by grouping students so instruction can more easily meet their common needs and abilities. However, in practice, tracking often meant that all special education students were grouped together, regardless of type of disability, which is totally inappropriate. Obviously a student with a hearing impairment has quite different needs from a student with serious emotional disturbance, for example.

In addition, teachers' expectations of students with disabilities were too often universally low, although many students eligible for special education are cognitively able. Thus all students with special needs were not only inappropriately grouped together, but they were provided with an oversimplified curriculum. Similarly, students learning English as a second language were often grouped together without regard for the fact that some of them were gifted and talented but others of them had special educational needs other than their need to learn English. For these reasons, the use of ability grouping is quite controversial and many educators have called for changes in the way school systems program for student grouping.

Culture, Ethnicity, and Diversity

Culture refers to values, customs, attitudes, and behavior patterns that characterize a social group. There are many aspects to a person's culture, including the way we dress, the kinds of food we eat, and what we do in our spare time. Culture also includes family structure, religion, and values we cherish. Culture has an influence on a student's success in school through the attitudes, values, and ways of viewing the world that are held and transmitted by that culture. Ethnicity is an important part of culture because it is the person's background. *Ethnicity* refers to a person's ancestry and may reflect the ways individuals identify themselves with the nation from which they or their ancestors originally came. Members of an ethnic group generally have a common history, set of customs and traditions, value system, and language (although not every member of the group may speak it).

The term *diversity* generally refers to students with different types of backgrounds. Although language is the most obvious form, diversity can also refer to differences in philosophy, religion, and lifestyles within any given cultural or linguistic group. Diversity is a fact of life and should be seen as a plus, not a minus, for the classroom and students. Adults in the classroom should draw on it and see it as a resource. Later in the chapter, we suggest how best to take advantage of diversity.

Although certain ethnic groups have historically been dominant in different parts of the United States, many states are experiencing significant growth in ethnic minority populations, particularly those of Hispanic origin. Another aspect of this shift in population is that in many rural communities, these ethnic groups have traditionally been itinerant or seasonal workers and may have received supplementary educational services through local summer school programs. They are now settling permanently in the community, and their children face the challenges of regular education classes. These are some of the issues raised by these changes:

- A lack of infrastructure to support them in the school system—for example, an English as a Second Language (ESL) program that may not be able to expand rapidly enough to accommodate all of the new ESL students.
- Low numbers of ethnically diverse teachers, particularly special educators and those representing the major ethnic groups. Although students from minority backgrounds do not have to be taught by teachers from the same background, it is much more helpful if they can have role models from their own cultural background as well as additional linguistic support.
- Lack of training in teacher preparation programs to prepare teachers and paraprofessionals to meet the needs of multicultural students.
- Few teachers who speak enough of the students' home language to be able to communicate effectively with parents or even with the students themselves.
- Curriculum that is offered only in English, with very few materials available in other languages.

Because many of the parents of these students do not speak English, their children may often miss school to act as interpreters for medical appointments and other official business. This reduced attendance contributes to lack of achievement, but it is also often misinterpreted as a lack of motivation or ability on the part of the students. When parents do not attend meetings with teachers because of economic struggles and lack of English, it is too often assumed they have no interest in their children's education. In short, many students from minority cultures perform well below their educational potential, and many of the difficulties can be attributed to a school system that does not provide adequate support for their success. Thus too many minority students end up in special education programs and alternative schooling arrangements because of low achievement and inappropriate behavior.

We know that one of the most critical components of school success—and subsequent lifelong achievement, career prospects, and social integration—is learning to read in the early elementary grades. For young minority students, literacy skills must be acquired in two languages simultaneously, which research indicates is possible. This is not easy, but many children do succeed and become literate in both English and their first language. However, success usually occurs when both languages are used at home. Many minority students also enter the U.S. educational system during their middle and high school years, with varying levels of English. These students face the challenge of switching instructional language during a phase in the education system when they are expected to absorb large amounts of subject matter in a wide variety of curriculum areas. These are high demands to place on students during vulnerable points in their cognitive and social development.

Implications for Educators. Fortunately, the same techniques apply to enhancing the success of minority students as students with other abilities and characteristics. First, we must identify strengths, finding the learning styles and intelligences of the individual student. Then, to accommodate learning effectively, the student must be comfortable in the learning environment—the classroom and the school. Students need to feel valued and included and that they are in a safe environment. This is not just a question of physical safety, but instructional safety. When students fear ridicule, for example, they are not as likely to risk making a mistake, so we need to foster an atmosphere in which students know that mistakes are part of learning and are acceptable. *Inclusion* is a term often used in relation to students with disabilities, but it also applies in a much broader sense. Inclusion of all children in learning is a comprehensive concept of teaching all students that they have value and abilities. In this context, diversity can be used to enrich the curriculum, and different cultural perspectives can enhance the learning of all students. Simply put, all means all. All students, including those from minority backgrounds, need opportunities to learn and display their skills.

Take a moment to review an activity, discussion, or explanation you recently completed with students. Identify examples or illustrations that you used that were drawn from minority cultures. If you have not used any such examples, try to think now of some you could have used. Share your ideas with colleagues to see if together you can identify other activities or illustrations that could be included the next time you complete this type of activity or discussion.

Description of activity or discussion:

_____

_____

_____

_____

Multicultural perspectives or illustrations that apply to the activity:

_____

_____

_____

_____

_____

_____

_____

Paraprofessionals: An Insider View. Paraprofessionals most often are members of the local community and live within the school district where they work. As a paraprofessional, you are more likely than teachers to speak the language of the local ethnic minority group. You probably already recognize that students and their parents may speak a language other than the dominant language spoken at school. You may know the students who come to the United States in the later grades and of course recognize that these students already have substantial knowledge and skills in their own language, even if they are unable to communicate that in English.

If you are hired to work with culturally diverse students, be sure to establish your teacher's preferences in relation to the use of a student's home language. Although it is useful to encourage students to read and speak in their first/home language so their general language, social skills, and concept development can continue, identify with the teacher under what circumstances you should speak English versus the first language of the student. Different states also have different requirements regarding the provision of information to parents in minority languages. Find out what your state requires, and determine what you can do to support the school in offering frequent, clear, and positive communication with the home and family.

Diversity: Gender

It is generally accepted that there are some basic differences between the learning styles of boys and girls, and many cultures have different beliefs about educational outcomes for girls versus boys. The notion that males excel in mathematics, science, and technology but females excel in the arts is one of many prevalent beliefs and cultural influences that have been passed down through generations and still persists today. This notion is not only unfounded but also potentially damaging for both girls and boys. Subtle and unintended messages can create the idea among students that certain careers are closed to them because of their gender. Classroom research has shown that teachers frequently give boys more opportunities to answer the more difficult questions, encourage them to enroll in more science and math classes, and generally have higher expectations of them than of girls. When interviewed, the teachers involved had not realized they held these beliefs and acted on them subconsciously. They were usually unaware of the biased behaviors they exhibited through verbal interactions, eye contact, and body language, making it very difficult to correct themselves. Civil rights laws such as Title IX of the Education Amendments of 1972 support the national agenda to end sex discrimination in all federally assisted education programs. Under these laws, every individual has the right to develop his or her individual talents and strengths.

Implications for Educators An awareness of this problem can go a long way toward improving your teaching practices. Educators must work to build a world in which girls and boys are treated, and treat each other, with respect and equity. No one should have limits placed on their abilities, and all students must be urged and expected to fulfill their potential, without restriction. *All* students must be encouraged to achieve mastery of knowledge and skills so they have the tools they need to pursue their personal education goals and preferred careers. You may feel you do not discriminate between the boys and girls you work with, but such discrimination is usually very subtle, and as suggested by the research just reported, often subconscious on the part of the educator. You can cultivate behaviors and knowledge that will permit you to recognize inequality in educational opportunities, to carry out specific interventions that constitute equal educational treatment, and to ensure equal educational outcomes.

When you are in the classroom working with students, for example, you may wish to ask an observer to take note of the number of boys you call on versus the number of girls. Then also ask the observer to identify which are high-level questions and which are merely responses to facts (low-level questions), to check you are not inadvertently directing the more difficult questions to boys and the easier ones to girls. In Chapter 8 we discuss high- and low-level questions and stress the importance of giving all students opportunities to use their imagination, to problem-solve, and to develop analytical thinking through the use of high-level questions. Carefully evaluate the data the observer provides to you, to see how well you are doing in relation to discrimination based on gender. If you find you have been making a distinction between boys and girls in this way, make a plan to change. Ask each student a question in turn, so all students have a chance to respond, or tell your students, "This question is for the girls. The next one will be for the boys," and make sure the questions are equally difficult.

At the end of this chapter are examples of seating charts that can be used by an observer. Ask your observer to put a tally on the shape representing each student every time you call on a student to respond. At the end of the lesson, you can count how many boys you called on and how many girls. If you are also interested in whether you are asking high- or low-level questions of boys and girls, your observer can mark an *H* or *L* rather than a tally. Reflect on the data collected and see how you can improve.

Social Influences

Psychologists have studied the social development of students at different ages and developed theories of how students' social development varies with age. We know, of course, that younger students think, feel, and act in ways that are very different from those of adults. Many courses have been developed on this subject, but for the purposes of this chapter, we touch on two major social influences that have a significant impact on student learning: socioeconomic status and abuse.

Socioeconomic Status

One of the most alarming factors affecting student performance is socioeconomic status, or SES. We say alarming because researchers have found that the combination of parent income, occupation, and level of education consistently impacts students' learning. When SES is low, student achievement is almost always extremely poor; test scores, grades, dropout rates, and truancy are worst among these students. If you consider the previous comments about students from minority backgrounds, you will appreciate that those who are both from minority backgrounds and low SES are doubly at risk of school failure. As an example of some of the effects of SES on school success, the box provides details of school dropout rates.

Why Is Socioeconomic Status So Influential?

SES is one of the most powerful influences on learning—or inhibiting learning. Students who are hungry or need medical attention but are unable to get help have difficulty concentrating on their studies. Poverty can also influence the quality of family interactions. When parents are frustrated because they cannot pay the bills or because their children are hungry, the frustrations can lead to marital conflict, anger, depression, and even abuse. Parents who are preoccupied with financial

Dropout Rates in the United States (from the National Center for Education Statistics)

- Five out of every 100 students enrolled in high school in October 1999 left before October 2000 without successfully completing a high school program.
- More than 50 percent of students from poor families typically drop out of school—that is, twice as many as the general population.
- In 2000 young adults living in families with incomes in the lowest 20 percent of family income were six times as likely as their peers from families in the top 20 percent of the income distribution to drop out of high school.
- In 2000 about two-fifths (42 percent) of dropouts were under age seventeen.
- In the decade from 1990 to 2000, between 347,000 and 544,000 tenth- through twelfth-grade students left school each year without successfully completing a high school program.
- Hispanic students in the United States have a higher dropout rate than Asian/Pacific Islander students, whites, or African Americans. In 2000 the rates were Hispanics, 27.8 percent; Asian/Pacific Islanders, 3.8 percent; Whites, 6.9 percent; and African Americans, 13.1 percent.

concerns and who work long hours to make ends meet are also unlikely to have time to help their children with homework. Working long hours often prohibits attendance at parent-teacher conferences to keep abreast of their child's progress (or problems) at school, or even to keep track of where their children go and what they do after school and at weekends.

Note that high SES is not a guarantee that students will succeed in school. There are many students whose families would be considered to be of high SES with well-educated parents and a substantial household income. These students may be very well provided for in terms of physical necessities, but if their parents also work long hours, with no time to help with homework, and leave the child unsupervised after school, many of the same negative effects will be seen in these students as in those who live in poverty.

Implications for Educators. As a paraprofessional, you cannot change a student's SES. Much as you may want to, you cannot alter family circumstances or income, and you cannot compel parents to change their priorities, occupations, or work schedules. What you can do is to be aware of these issues and pay close attention to students and their needs. Thus to the extent it is possible for you to do so, you can make a difference. A student who is hungry or has a toothache will have trouble concentrating on academics. Be aware. Wherever possible, attend to the most immediate physical need so you and the student can then attend to the instructional need. Notify the teacher or administrator if you see student needs are not being met. It is inadvisable to intervene directly with the family, unless you are closely associated with them outside school. Schools have resources and contacts with other agencies to assist students and their families. You can make a difference if you are vigilant and use the appropriate channels to meet those needs.

Abuse and Neglect

Abuse and neglect is a huge topic, so only some basic points can be discussed here. As you already know, child abuse can be physical, sexual, or emotional, and each of these can take many forms. There are usually visible signs of physical abuse, such as bruising, although children usually hide the signs whenever possible or make up an explanation for how they acquired the marks. Visible signs of sexual abuse are less frequent, except under medical examination. Deliberate emotional abuse typically leaves no visible marks on a child's body, but all forms of abuse mark a child emotionally. No child is unaffected by abuse or neglect, although some children seem to survive better than others. Like cognition, these marks cannot be seen, but we do see the effects on a child's behavior.

The signs of possible abuse include the following:

Physical marks (e.g., bruising)

Anxiety and depression (without an academic explanation)

Withdrawal

Talking about abuse

Poor relationships with peers

Fears of going home

Cutting or burning self

Threatening or attempting suicide

Inappropriate clothing for weather or situation

Excessive absences or tardiness

Incidents involving cruelty to animals

Students who suffer abuse may react by internalizing behavior (e.g., withdrawal and refusal to participate in class) or externalizing (acting out) behaviors. Most students who suffer abuse or neglect are affected in their ability to participate fully in the learning process. There are legal requirements for reporting suspected abuse or neglect. Check with your supervising teacher to make sure you know the proper procedures. The other way in which you can help students who have suffered abuse of any kind is to help them succeed in school. It is not advisable to excuse them from doing their work because you think (or know) they are being abused. If they can apply themselves to their schoolwork, make it a priority to help them do it. Success in school will provide them with at least one positive area in their lives, and schoolwork can often be a mental refuge for them if they are given the support they need to succeed. In the nearby box are some statistics on child abuse, and basic guidance on how you should deal with students who have been (or you suspect to have been) abused. Remember: you should *always* talk to your supervisor if you have any questions or concerns about one of the students you work with.

Abuse and Neglect

Every day in America, almost eight thousand incidents of child abuse or neglect are reported. These are not children who are occasionally cuffed or spanked for extremely inappropriate behavior. Forms of discipline differ among cultures, and some families consider mild physical punishment such as spanking to be acceptable. The abuse referred to in this statistic is much more severe. Also, for every reported case, many more incidents go unreported.

Research shows that one person can make a difference in protecting children and youth who are experiencing crisis. Experts advise: be supportive of the student and say, "The teacher and I are here for you and you are not alone." If a student discloses abuse, do not promise to keep it a secret. Tell the student, "When you care about someone, you get them help. I have to tell my supervisor so we can help you." Then report to your supervisor immediately.

In some states *suspected* abuse must be reported to local law enforcement authorities or the Division of Child and Family Services (DCFS) in the Department of Human Services. You do not have to know that the abuse has taken place. Even if you only suspect it, you must report it.

Remember that emotional abuse, sexual abuse, and neglect are all forms of child abuse and should be taken very seriously.

Implications for Educators. Requirements to report suspected abuse differ by state, but most have a legal requirement that *suspected* abuse or neglect must be reported to the proper authorities. You may be committing a misdemeanor if you fail to do so, but also in the long run, it is not in the student's best interests for abuse to be ignored or allowed to continue. We must strongly emphasize that under no circumstances should you, as a paraprofessional, try to provide counseling to students. A professional with the appropriate training should do this so it is carried out properly and can be supported with any therapy that may be needed to help the student work through the emotions that surface when sensitive issues are disclosed and discussed. We use the phrase *provide counseling* in its broadest sense. If a student begins a conversation with you about abuse he or she may be experiencing, you may listen, but do not prolong the conversation or try to provide advice. Early in the conversation, tell the student you cannot promise to keep secrets on such a serious matter as abuse and that by law you have to tell someone about it. Do not encourage a student to start a conversation about abuse in order to disclose information, even if you strongly suspect abuse exists. See the nearby box for a summary of how to deal with abuse.

As a paraprofessional who works closely with students, you may be the first one to notice the warning signs of abuse of any kind. Speak to your supervisor about this issue and request guidelines on how you should proceed if you have concerns about a particular student. Ask your teacher supervisor, school counselor, or school psychologist what is expected of you if they typically work in a different part of the building. You may wish to ask if you could attend any training that is available from the school district or at the state level.

Dealing with Abuse

What you must do:
Stay calm.
Believe the student.
Listen, but do not press for information.
Explain to the student that everyone has the right to be safe, physically and emotionally.
Tell the student that in order to keep him or her safe, you will need to get some help.
Tell your immediate supervisor or school counselor as soon as possible.
Respect the dignity of the student by not talking about the abuse with people who do not need to know.

What you must not do:
Make promises regarding whom you will or will not tell.

C·H·A·P·T·E·R S·U·M·M·A·R·Y

In this chapter, you learned about some of the critical characteristics of learners and the effects of these characteristics on learning. By now, you can:

■ Describe some of the cognitive and metacognitive process involved in learning.
■ Identify learner characteristics and events that enhance or detract from learning.
■ List some strategies to assist you in your job as a paraprofessional.

This helps you understand the effects of exceptional conditions on a student's life, whether those conditions are intellectual or social. Your awareness of social issues and your knowledge of learning strategies to enhance learning will greatly assist your students in experiencing school success. The two case studies that follow will give you opportunities to apply what you have learned in this chapter to real-life situations with students and their families.

E·X·T·E·N·D·I·N·G Y·O·U·R L·E·A·R·N·I·N·G

Case Study 1: Fun, Discipline, or Misunderstanding?

Read the following paragraph and consider the implications for your work as a paraprofessional.

> A second-grade teacher learned she was charged with battery after she allegedly snapped a rubber band against a student's arm, which raised welts. Students in the class reported to the investigator that the teacher had popped the band on a boy's arm until he wept. The teacher says she snapped the boy's forearm only once as she tried to take the rubber band away from him.

What are your thoughts on this situation? Do you see this as abuse, assault, discipline, or just a terrible misunderstanding? Write your reaction to the situation we have described:

_____

_____

_____

_____

_____

_____

_____

_____

_____

How do you know who to believe in such a situation? If you did not witness the incident, how would you deal with students, staff, or parents who talked to you about it?

_____

_____

_____

_____

_____

_____

If you had witnessed the incident and the students' version of the story was correct (the teacher had done more than she admitted), what would you do about it? Who would you talk to?

_____

_____

_____

_____

_____

_____

_____

List three things you can do to prevent this type of situation from happening:

1. _____

_____

_____

2. _____

_____

_____

3. _____

_____

_____

Consult with your supervisor and learn if legal safeguards are in place in your employment to protect you if similar charges should ever be brought against you or your supervising teacher.

Case Study 2: First Impressions

Read the following case study and write what you would do and say under the circumstances we describe. You may also wish to discuss your reactions with a colleague.

> My name is Rosa Gonzalez, and I've been living in the United States for just over six months. My husband finished his Ph.D. in Mexico and got a faculty position at an American university, so I was finally able to give up work and concentrate on our children. We thought that would be particularly important with them moving from Mexico to the United States. Although we have always spoken both English and Spanish to them in our home, we knew there would be many cultural differences for them to get used to, and I wanted to be available when they came home from school every day.
>
> Once both of the children were in school, I thought I'd like to volunteer some hours at the school, perhaps helping with reading or providing support to some of the other Spanish-speaking children in the school. So I approached the principal, and she seemed very happy to have some extra help. She suggested I talk to Mrs. Nelson, the fifth-grade teacher, because there are already several volunteers in kindergarten and first grade, and Mrs. Nelson had a new girl from Ecuador in her class who was struggling with the language. From what the principal said, I guessed Mrs. Nelson was also struggling, not having had an ESL student before or any ESL training.
>
> The principal told me to just go along and introduce myself to Mrs. Nelson, so when I'd picked up my girls after school we went to the fifth-grade classroom, and I told the girls to wait outside the door while I talked to Mrs. Nelson. She was working at her desk when I knocked on the door, and a student was working at one of the tables nearby—the Ecuadorian girl, I guessed, from her looks.
>
> Mrs. Nelson looked up when I knocked, and as I was crossing the room, before I had time to say anything, she turned to the Ecuadorian girl and said, very loudly and slowly: "LUISA, HERE - IS - YOUR - MOTHER. TELL - HER - SHE - MUST - COME - PARENT-TEACHER - CONFERENCE - NEXT - WEEK."
>
> I looked around, thinking the girl's mother had come into the room behind me, but there was no one there, just my two girls peeking in to see what the shouting was about. It wasn't quite what I was expecting, so when I introduced myself, it must have sounded a bit garbled. And it wasn't helped by the fact that at the same time I was saying, "No, I'm Mrs. Gonzalez," Luisa was also saying, "No my mother" or something like that. So I suppose I shouldn't have been surprised that Mrs. Nelson replied with "YES - TELL - HER - SHE - MUST - COME - TO - MEETING." What a fiasco!

If you were Rosa Gonzalez, what would you say to the teacher?

_____

_____

_____

_____

I told Mrs. Nelson that I wasn't Luisa's mother but had come—with the principal's approval—to offer my time to help out in her class. She wasn't very gracious in her reply. She was obviously out of her depth in trying to help Luisa and frustrated by the situation, but we agreed on a time when it would be convenient for me to attend and she said she'd see me then. She started trying to tell Luisa—again in very loud, slow English—who I was, but I quickly explained to the poor girl in Spanish, and I told her when I was coming back to help.

When I returned on the agreed day, Mrs. Nelson was just about to start a history lesson. She asked me to sit with Luisa—a chair had been placed for me—and help her out, but she gave no indication what she meant by that. I sat down and greeted Luisa very briefly, in Spanish, because that's all I had time for. Mrs. Nelson was starting the lesson and frowned over at me as she heard me speaking. The rest of the class members were already silent.

The whole lesson was conducted as if Luisa and I weren't there. Mrs. Nelson presented the information she had prepared, asked the students (but not Luisa) some questions, and then had the students complete a worksheet in silence. I tried to communicate in whispers and ask Luisa what she had understood about the lesson, but I got a frown from Mrs. Nelson every time. By the end of my agreed time in the classroom, I didn't feel I'd been able to help at all, and Mrs. Nelson just dismissed me with, "Thank you, Mrs. Gonzalez, I'll see you again on Friday," and she escorted her students out to recess.

If you were Rosa Gonzalez, what would you do in this situation? What would you say to Mrs. Nelson?

_____

_____

_____

_____

_____

_____

_____

You may wish to discuss your reactions with a peer and gather ideas for problem-solving strategies. Remember that although Rosa is a parent volunteer, her situation is quite similar to that of paraprofessionals who are assigned to assist a student with limited English proficiency in the regular classroom.

Sample Seating Charts for Data Collection

Write student initials or first names in the boxes, or if the students always sit at the same tables, you can leave the boxes blank. The observer makes tally marks in the appropriate box as a student answers a question.

Sample 1: Student Tables Arranged in Rows

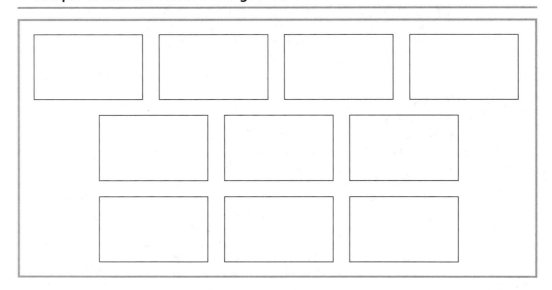

Sample 2: Student Chairs/Tables Arranged in Semicircle Around Your Chair/Table

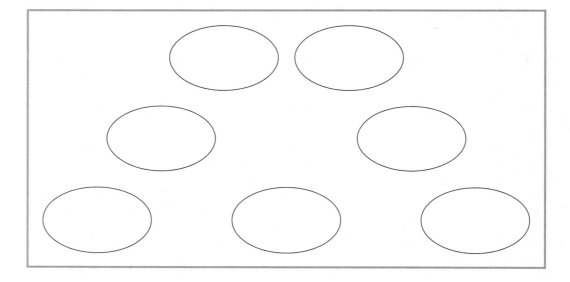

7 Instructional Supervision

This chapter discusses supervision. Being supervised means knowing who your supervisor is, the ability to identify different forms of supervision, and recognizing the importance of seeking supervision, especially in the form of modeling and training. In this chapter you will also learn the importance of documenting the supervision and training you receive.

By the end of the chapter, you should be able to answer these questions:

- Why is it important to receive instructional supervision?
- Who is my supervisor?
- What are the different forms that supervision can take?
- How can I seek supervision?

The Importance of Instructional Supervision

As we discussed in Chapter 5, the learning environment must be ordered and organized so it can run effectively, and it is the teacher's responsibility to be in charge of these dimensions. In Chapter 3 we discussed the roles, responsibilities, and limitations of paraprofessionals as dictated by federal law. Then in Chapter 5 we also looked at the role of the teacher as a classroom manager and discussed how curriculum requirements and achievement standards impact the organization of the learning environment. In this chapter we look at your role in the classroom under the supervision of a professional, the importance of knowing who your supervisor is, and the value in seeking supervision, before we go on to Section III, where we detail instructional and behavior management practices and techniques you can use in your work.

Defining Supervision

The term *supervision* has many different definitions. Some authors emphasize that supervision is control and management, which ensures the effective and economical use of personnel. Others define it as orientation and inservice training. And others see it as guiding and helping staff to improve their performance in an instructional setting. The particular situation in which you work may emphasize one of these views more than another. We believe all of these definitions are valid:

the teacher is responsible for orientation and inservice training of paraprofessionals so the best possible use can be made of their time and skills, in order to help students succeed. You will notice that we use the term *instructional supervision*. This is because—as we already discussed previously—your role as a paraprofessional is to support the instructional process, even if you are not directly involved in providing instruction to students.

Taking the Metaphor to the Next Step

Earlier we introduced a metaphor proposed by David Berliner: *teacher as executive*. We discussed various other metaphors for the teacher's roles that Berliner felt were not comprehensive enough to describe the responsibilities of today's teachers, in particular *teacher as Mother Earth* and *teacher as information giver*. You probably remember that this discussion arose because Berliner was looking at the broader role of teachers, which includes the need to supervise other adults. And, of course, the *teacher as executive* metaphor properly acknowledges the teacher's supervisory role. Now let's focus on your role in the supervision process: that of being supervised. We explore this through another metaphor.

As a child, one of the authors remembers regular summer visits to sheepdog trials in her native Wales. She was fascinated by the skill displayed by the border collie sheepdogs as they gathered up the scattered sheep and herded them into a pen. The shepherd controlled the dogs using just a few words of command or short whistling sounds. On command, the sheepdogs would lie down or dash around the sheep, keeping them in a close group, until they were safely penned. Many years later in New England, the same author attended sheepdog trials that included a demonstration using a young border collie puppy. The shepherd explained that the puppy had had no training in herding sheep but showed a natural inclination to gather the sheep. Indeed, at a gesture from the shepherd, the puppy, who had been sitting quietly beside the shepherd, dashed off toward the sheep, who were quietly grazing on the other side of the field. Although they scattered at the puppy's exuberant approach, the sheep were soon gathered up into a corner of the field, with the puppy standing guard—and looking very pleased with himself.

Why do we tell you this story? It seems to us that the metaphor *paraprofessional as sheepdog* may serve a useful purpose for our discussion of supervision. Do you remember the comments about metaphors in the earlier chapter? You may protest on reading this, "I'm no sheepdog!" Consider some of the insights it provides, however. The metaphor is very complimentary:

- Even the young, untrained sheepdog puppy was able to gather and herd the sheep, in the same way that a newly hired paraprofessional will be able to perform some assigned tasks extremely well even without training.
- A paraprofessional may possess some innate abilities that make a good teacher, or may have experience as a parent, or other experience of children or teaching.
- On the surface, it is often difficult to distinguish between an experienced and an inexperienced paraprofessional, in the same way that both sheepdogs were able to gather and herd the sheep.

The difference between the two sheepdogs would have been evident, however, as soon as something more complicated was required. If, for example, the shepherd had given the puppy a specific instruction—such as which direction to herd the sheep—the puppy's lack of training would have quickly been very obvious. Trained and experienced sheepdogs can not only move sheep around, but they can also respond to a wide variety of commands given by the shepherd, such as separating individual sheep from the herd or working as a team with other sheepdogs. They can also be left on their own to watch sheep. However, all of these skills require lengthy training and a relationship of trust and harmony with the shepherd. In similar fashion, both experience and training make excellent paraprofessionals, who have the skills needed for their assigned responsibilities and know how and when to use them under the supervision of a professional. Even innate skills are improved by training and supervision.

Using the metaphor to draw a parallel between the roles of paraprofessionals and sheepdogs may be all too obvious, but it deserves some discussion. There is nothing negative about the important role that the collie sheepdog serves. The shepherd and the teacher also have important roles. The shepherd could round up the sheep and move them, but it may take him away from other important duties. The teacher can also do many of the same tasks as the paraprofessional, but that, too, takes her away from other important tasks that might be required. Each role is vital to the effective function of the whole.

Supervision as a Requirement of the Law

If you are like many paraprofessionals, you have already worked in education for a number of years (e.g., in the year 2000, the average time a special education paraprofessional had been employed was seven years). You may figure you already know what you are doing, so why would instructional supervision be important? You do not feel like a paraprofessional puppy, as it were, anymore, and you have herded enough sheep to know how it works. However, the teacher is in charge of the classroom, just as the shepherd is in charge of the sheep. It is particularly important to note that much more is involved in shepherding sheep than just rounding them up and moving them from field to field. There is the purchasing of other sheep, marketing, assuring that supplies (grass and fields) are adequate, and many other dimensions that make livestock a viable livelihood.

Teachers also have responsibilities to ensure that the classroom is adequately resourced, sometimes even negotiating with the school administrator for a classroom better suited to the needs of the students (e.g., closer to the playground, closer to the counselor's office, on the main level with no stairs for students in wheelchairs to negotiate, etc.). Teachers also report to parents and complete report cards. In short, their responsibilities go far beyond merely keeping students under control and moving in the right direction. Under the law, the teacher holds the ultimate responsibility for everything that happens in the classroom.

We talked in Section I about federal laws regulating the U.S. school system and how these laws impact the role of the paraprofessional. The No Child Left Behind law specifies that paraprofessionals may not provide instructional support services except under the direct supervision of a teacher. Although this legislation was only enacted in 2001, there have already been investigations and rulings relating to this question of supervision. Some of these are due to the previous enactment of IDEA in 1997. A growing body of case law—court decisions from district and state courts—is influencing the way judges rule in school disputes regarding supervision and training of paraprofessionals. Under the direction of a licensed teacher, paraprofessionals may offer education and related service support to the curricular goals and objectives specified by a student's Individual Education Plan (IEP) or a Section 504 student plan. However, the rulings in these cases strongly support the principle that paraprofessionals do not replace qualified teachers.

In the nearby boxes are summaries of a small selection of such cases that begin with a Section 504 case. (Recall from Chapter 2 that Section 504 of the Rehabilitation Act guarantees equal access to education for all students, including physical access.)

Case 1 illustrates that it is appropriate for paraprofessionals to *assist* teachers in the instructional process, but they cannot *replace* the teacher. Likewise, the teacher cannot abdicate the responsibilities of instruction, curriculum selection, and supervision of noncertified or nonlicensed staff.

The results of case 2 are consistent with case 1. When administrators and teachers leave paraprofessionals on their own to provide instruction to students, without the supervision and direction of a certified teacher, the district is at risk of being sued—and losing. This can be very expensive in terms of time and money but also in the loss of proper educational progress by the student.

Case 1	Section 504 Discrimination Complaint Against a School District (DeKalb County, Georgia)
Complaint	Parents alleged that discrimination had occurred because their children were receiving English as a Second Language (ESL) instruction from a noncertified teacher (paraprofessional).
Case heard by	The Office of Civil Rights (OCR)
Outcome	OCR ruled in favor of the school district.
Discussion	The Office of Civil Rights examined the district's ESL programs and concluded that classes were being taught by certified classroom teachers. Paraprofessionals were assigned to some of the classes, but it was determined that they only assisted the teacher in the instructional process and were supervised by the teacher. Because the paraprofessionals did not have full responsibility for teaching the classes, it was ruled that no violation had occurred. During the investigation of the complaint, the district was able to show that the paraprofessionals were aware of their proper role: providing support to the certified classroom teacher. Consequently, OCR found in favor of the district.

Case 2	Office of Civil Rights (OCR) Complaint Against a School District
Complaint	A Missouri parent filed a complaint alleging that the district had failed to place her daughter (who had a disability) with students without disabilities to the maximum extent appropriate to her needs. Among other things, the parent objected that her daughter was placed in a trailer classroom *with an aide but without a teacher.*
Case heard by	The Office of Civil Rights (OCR)
Outcome	OCR ruled for the parent.
Discussion	The Office of Civil Rights investigated the situation and held for the parent. As a result, the district agreed to place the child in a regular education environment. The district also agreed to compensate the student for her loss of educational benefits while she was not in a regular classroom and receiving educational services without a teacher present.

Case 3	Minnesota State Special Education: Due Process Complaint (2002)
Complaint	An unresolved issue in this hearing was whether the district's paraprofessionals lacked proper training, resulting in a student being deprived of a free and appropriate public education (FAPE).
Case heard by	Due process hearing officer
Outcome	The hearing officer ruled in favor of the school district.
Discussion	Among other things in the case, the hearing officer found the record contained ample evidence that the district had provided sufficient training to the paraprofessionals before they began working with the student and had followed up with additional training when it became available. The hearing officer further found that the district's paraprofessionals were properly trained and supervised and the student was therefore not being deprived of FAPE.

Interestingly, the decision of the hearing officer in case 3 was appealed, but a court judge upheld the decision. This ruling highlights these critical issues:

1. The importance of the district's ability to show evidence of sufficient training of the paraprofessionals before they began to work with the student and that it had followed up with additional training.
2. Neither the state of Minnesota nor IDEA federal regulations determined the type or amount of training that paraprofessionals should receive when providing services for students.

Importance of Legal Rulings

These examples of complaints, investigations, and rulings give insight into some of the attempts to clarify the intent of federal law. They also highlight the significance of the phrase "appropriately trained and supervised" as it applies to school paraprofessionals. Since the reauthorization of IDEA in 1997, there has been a dramatic increase in the attention given to paraprofessionals and the services they offer. Further, the No Child Left Behind Act promises to increase judiciary interest and involvement in the pertinent issues of training and supervision for paraprofessionals. Teachers and paraprofessionals represent service delivery at its most fundamental level—face to face with students on a daily basis—and the effectiveness of this instructional team is therefore most crucial to student success. If you are working in a school, make sure you review your assignment and confirm you are not working outside of the boundaries of the law.

The requirements of the law are the most fundamental reason for instructional supervision. You need a professional to assess your effectiveness as a paraprofessional, to ensure that students are getting the quality of services they deserve and the law requires. But there are also what we would consider professional reasons for that supervision, reasons prompted by professional ethics and a commitment to quality education. We believe students intrinsically deserve to be taught according to high standards, not only because the law requires it. In Chapter 9, you will learn about monitoring student progress and your effectiveness as an educator. These concepts interrelate and are important components of the overall effectiveness of the educational process. In addition, in Section IV, you will learn about the responsibilities of education as a profession which also relates to the overall schemata of giving and receiving supervision.

Let us reiterate here that the law does not actually define supervision. There are no actual definitions of appropriate supervision based on the federal law or on current cases and complaints filed. Yet, as an adult, you have quite a good idea of what appropriate supervision is and is not. A paraprofessional receives supervision in many different ways. Keeping the teacher informed, requesting and receiving training and modeling from the teacher, and meetings discussing ways in which the teaching team can assist student learning are all forms of supervision.

The nearby box lists activities that are often a part of the supervisory process. Check those that you believe apply to your situation by marking yes or no. If you have been a paraprofessional for more than a year, you have likely been exposed to various types of supervision from different teachers and therefore could mark all

Supervisory Activities	Applies to my situation?	
	Yes	No
The teacher gives me a list of tasks to do each day.		
The teacher has me keep a log or record of my work.		
We discuss students' progress or needs.		
We (paraprofessional and supervisor) keep a record of training I receive, including informal training and meetings.		
The teacher asks for my input on students' progress.		
My supervisor allows me to observe his or her teaching.		
My supervisor and I discuss my observations of his or her teaching.		
The teacher observes what I do and grades or scores it.		
The teacher discusses her observations with me.		
The school administrator (principal or assistant principal) evaluates me once each year.		
My supervisor conducts a formal evaluation of my work once each year.		
My supervisor recommends training I could attend.		

of the items. However, for this activity, only think of your current situation and mark the form according to how you are supervised now. Add any additional ways in which you feel you receive supervision.

Note that we do not ask how often some of these activities occur. They constitute supervision whether they occur frequently or not. However, your daily work obviously needs more frequent supervision than just annual evaluation and feedback from your supervisor. Having completed the checklist, identify in the space provided the areas in which you would like to receive more help or support from your supervisor. This may include the need for more frequent supervision activities, or it may be you feel the need for additional activities that your supervisor currently does not provide.

These are the areas in which I would like more active supervision from my supervising teacher:

1. _____
   _____

2. _____
   _____

3. _____
   _____

4. _____
   _____

If you find yourself in a position where you supervise other paraprofessionals, complete the form twice, first in relation to the supervision you receive (i.e., activities your supervisor provides for you) and then in relation to supervisory activities you provide for those you supervise. We reprint the form for this purpose. If you do not find yourself in any supervisory capacity, you may skip this second form.

These are the ways in which I think I could offer better supervision to those I supervise as a paraprofessional:

1. _____
   _____
   _____

2. _____
   _____
   _____

3. _____
   _____
   _____

Seeking Supervision

Now that you have identified areas in which you feel you could use additional supervision, you may want some ideas to help you gain that support. Here is a brief list of things you can consider to increase the supervision you receive from your supervisor and other professionals:

- When paraprofessionals are assigned to different teachers each year, often at short notice, opportunities for training and supervision or for meeting together to give or receive feedback are limited. Training may only be offered at the start of the school year or it may be offered whenever a new paraprofessional begins employment. If training is not offered to you, it is appropriate for you to request it. Call your supervisor or the staff development director, write them a letter or brief note, or make the request in a personal conversation.

■ A helpful proactive strategy was developed in a rural school district where some twenty-five to thirty paraprofessionals got together to discuss their own training and supervision needs. They informally chose representatives of the group who approached their school building administrator and requested the formation of a study group to review paraprofessional training material, discuss training issues, and develop training objectives. The administrator and superintendent were especially pleased with their proactive attitudes and offered to provide the training in the areas they had identified. Thus the administrative infrastructure needed to provide regular ongoing training was developed in the district because these paraprofessionals took the initiative.

■ Training is most often delivered to paraprofessionals alone, without including supervising teachers or informing the teachers of the content and nature of the training. Teachers also typically attend training without their paraprofessionals, even when the course content would also be suitable for the latter. This is not the ideal situation because teachers and paraprofessionals must then find time to exchange the information. If you are not receiving training alongside the teacher (or teachers) with whom you work, ask your supervisor for time to discuss the information you have gained. You and your supervisor could also put in a request to attend future courses together. Staff development trainers usually have no difficulty with paraprofessionals requesting training and may be willing to accommodate the request if space is available in the training sessions.

■ In some schools—and usually the school administrator makes this decision—paid planning time is allocated for teachers and paraprofessionals together. They use this time to delineate tasks, discuss student progress, assess instructional skills and performance, and share information in the mode of on-the-job training. Such planning time should not come out of your pay. If the school administration cannot reimburse you for additional time for instructional planning, ask your supervisor to consider arranging a time during working hours when the two of you can meet. This could occur while students are completing activities that do not require your direct input and supervision.

■ Finally, we strongly recommend that you carefully document all activities related to the training and supervision you receive. This is critical. Such documentation need not be extensive or time consuming, but both teachers and paraprofessionals should be encouraged to keep notes of training provided or received. As you have seen in the case described previously, such documentation was used to demonstrate the school was giving proper attention to its responsibilities in providing appropriate education services to students.

Who Is Your Supervisor?

We have discussed the importance of receiving supervision. However, in a number of situations, paraprofessionals may not be able to identify their immediate supervisor. Consider the situation of Maria, who worked in a rural school district in the western United States.

Case Study: Maria the "English Teacher"

Maria is a paraprofessional hired to work with bilingual students in the English Language Learners (ELL) program. Although her title is *English teacher,* she does not have a teaching degree. Her tremendous strength is her ability to speak two languages, in addition to English. These languages are spoken by members of minority groups in the local community. Maria also has tremendous rapport with members of the community and knows most of the ELL students and even their younger siblings who are not yet in school.

Maria is assigned to serve three different elementary schools. Two of the schools are located on the north and south ends, respectively, of the rural town. The third school is about fifteen miles to the west. In the mornings, Maria visits four students at the north-end school and during the afternoons, she works with six south-end school students. These students receive her help on Mondays, Wednesdays, and Fridays. On Tuesdays and Thursdays, she drives out to the third school to work with another eleven students. At each school she regularly meets with the parents of the ELL students, discussing the students' progress and the instructional support the parents can provide at home.

The director of the ELL program at the district level hired Maria for the English teacher position. The director has an office at the administration building, located in the geographical center of the district, more than a hundred miles from Maria's schools. This distance makes it very difficult for the ELL director to visit all of the schools where she has English teachers, so she does not provide on-site supervision, nor does she conduct formal evaluations of their performance.

Each of the elementary schools has its own administration—a school principal and an assistant principal. However, none of these administrators in any of Maria's three schools had a part in hiring Maria, nor do they have a clear picture of her instructional responsibilities. They consider that she comes under the jurisdiction of the district ELL program, so they do not carry out any type of supervision or evaluation activities for her. None of them speaks any language other than English, so they know they would not be able to assess the quality of her interactions with parents.

Given this situation, who do you think is, or should be, Maria's supervisor? Why do you think that person should be her supervisor?

It should be the district ELL program director because

_____

_____

_____

It should be the individual administrators at each of the schools because

_____

_____

_____

It should be one of the teachers whose students Maria works with because

_____

_____

_____

Explain how you feel Maria could benefit from having that person or persons supervise her work:

_____

_____

_____

_____

_____

_____

_____

_____

Authors' Comments

In light of the discussions we have had so far in this chapter, you must first acknowledge the legal requirement for Maria to receive active supervision. If only to meet the demands of the law, Maria should be supervised in some way by someone. Although we discuss this topic at greater length in a later chapter, there is also the professional or ethical need to provide supervision, to ensure that Maria teaches according to acceptable standards, using appropriate instructional and behavior management practices. The school district, not Maria, would ultimately be answerable to the law if a formal complaint should ever be brought about her work, and therefore the district ELL program director should ensure that Maria receives supervision, either from herself or by arrangement with the administration at each school. However, it would also be appropriate for Maria to request some type of supervision, so she can be sure her work meets high professional standards and she receives training and mentoring in areas where she feels inexperienced or weak. It is in the best interests of individual school administrators to provide supervision of some sort for Maria, so if questions arise about her work—from parents or from the school district—they can at least speak with some authority on the type and quality of the work she does.

Whose Responsibility?

Whether supervision and training are provided by district or school administrators or not, it inevitably falls to classroom teachers to provide paraprofessionals with, at the very least, an orientation to assigned tasks and students. But in the absence of further training opportunities provided for you at the school district or state level, your teacher or other direct supervisor also often becomes your *only* source of training and information. To a large extent, your supervisor is the most logical and useful source of training specific to your assignments, rather than the generic training that the school district or the state might offer. However, be aware of the challenges and concerns that teachers face when they find themselves in this situation:

1. How to find time to train a paraprofessional in classroom duties while continuing to provide effective instruction to students. Planning time is a rare commodity among teachers and paraprofessionals, especially at the elementary level, and even less often allocated to teachers and paraprofessionals together. Teachers face the dilemma of giving up valuable instructional time during the paraprofessional's working hours to provide training or asking the paraprofessional to stay on after the paid working time to discuss instructional practices. However we believe the investment of time for training paraprofessionals is worthwhile. A teacher can assign independent seatwork to students on a weekly basis to allow time to train the paraprofessional, who will then be better equipped to support the teacher's work.

2. How to deliver training in such a way that the paraprofessional can be immediately productive. Paraprofessionals are often hired for the first day of school, so teachers may not have a clear idea of a newly assigned paraprofessional's skills. They can therefore initially assign only the most basic tasks, despite the fact that the need for support is immediate and often complex. We believe this is the natural dynamic of hiring paraprofessionals at short notice, but the situation also occurs when a new paraprofessional is hired during the school year. Teachers need to plan for this eventuality and expect to assign only basic tasks at first to a paraprofessional. If you are assigned only basic tasks to begin with, do not be offended. The teacher is exercising proper caution until he or she can determine the true extent of your skills.

3. How to ensure that a paraprofessional continues to increase in skills (and therefore in the extent of her usefulness), and how to develop and implement a systematic plan for assessing and enhancing the paraprofessional's skills through the school year. In the same way that teachers plan and work toward increasing students' skills and understanding during the school year, they should also plan how a paraprofessional's skills and knowledge can be increased, so she becomes more useful in supporting student learning.

This gives you a view of the complexity of the supervisory role from the teacher's perspective and the difficulties that face teachers when they must find time to supervise other adults in addition to carrying out their responsibilities to teach and supervise students. In defense of teachers, very little training is provided at either the preservice or inservice level in how to supervise other adults effectively or how to provide appropriate training for paraprofessionals.

Actively Seeking Supervision

So what happens when you find yourself in a situation in which you have been left alone, without supervision? You must know who your supervisor is and what type of supervision you may expect. At first glance, this may appear too obvious. Yet we surveyed more than four hundred school administrators and found that although they often hired paraprofessionals, they did not supervise or evaluate them. That responsibility fell to someone else. According to the setting in which you work, it may not be immediately obvious who your supervisor is, so the best way to find out is to ask. We have already noted that some paraprofessionals do actually serve as supervisors to other paraprofessionals and may be given the title of *teacher* even if they are hired as paraprofessionals. But whatever your precise assignments (including that of a supervisor of other paraprofessionals) or title, you need to know who your supervisor is, and you should seek guidance and supervision from that individual if it is not already provided. Whenever there is a question, ask!

C-H-A-P-T-E-R—S-U-M-M-A-R-Y

Receiving supervision is an important part of your job. The No Child Left Behind Act and other laws place limits on your job. NCLB specifies that "paraprofessionals may not provide instructional support services except under the direct supervision of a teacher" (U.S. Department of Education, 2002), and the IDEA only allows paraprofessionals who are appropriately supervised to assist with special education and related services. In this chapter, you have learned the following aspects of instructional supervision:

- Why it is important to receive instructional supervision.
- What is meant by instructional supervision.
- The different forms that supervision can take, depending on the supervisor and the circumstances.
- How to identify your supervisor, and the different forms supervision may take.
- Ways in which you can obtain greater supervision.

The importance of supervision cannot be underestimated. The law requires every paraprofessional to receive adequate supervision. Now that you have read the chapter and participated in the activities, you should be able to identify your supervisor and how (and when) you receive supervision. You should be able to state this information clearly, even in a court of law, if needed. As an adult who is seeking to learn and improve, make a habit of accessing the supervision that is available so your concerns and questions can be addressed.

E-X-T-E-N-D-I-N-G—Y-O-U-R—L-E-A-R-N-I-N-G

We present two case studies here relating to paraprofessionals and professional supervision. Read each section of the case studies carefully and then answer the questions that follow. You will find a brief summary of the issues after the presentation of each case study.

Case Study 1: Old Enough to Be Her Mother

Tanja is a new teacher who just graduated from the local university. She had close to a 4.0 grade-point average, and her student teaching supervisor rated her in the top 5 percent of all observed student teachers. She interviewed well and was one of the first chosen for a premier school district.

Tanja enters her new classroom with a great deal of confidence but is a bit surprised to find a woman already sitting at the teacher's desk. She learns this woman is Charlotte, a paraprofessional assigned to the class. Charlotte is old enough to be Tanja's mother and has been working in the school district for more than twenty-five years. Charlotte knows all of the children except the two who moved in just this week. She knows most of their parents, too. In fact, she was a paraprofessional when the principal was a student in this same school. Clearly this paraprofessional and the principal are on very good terms and the principal respects Charlotte's opinions.

What benefits do you feel that Tanja (the teacher) would get from supervising this experienced paraprofessional?

_____

_____

_____

_____

_____

_____

_____

_____

_____

Let's dissect this situation a bit more. Charlotte is an experienced paraprofessional, but Tanja is new to teaching, to the school, and to the community. How could Charlotte, a veteran of the classroom, possibly benefit from receiving supervision from a newly qualified and inexperienced teacher such as Tanja?

_____

_____

_____

_____

_____

_____

_____

What possible negative consequences could there be if Tanja did not take steps to provide proper supervision for Charlotte?

_____

_____

_____

_____

_____

_____

_____

_____

_____

_____

The Facts

Looking at federal law and legal rulings, the answers are clear. As a paraprofessional, Charlotte must be supervised. From a professional and ethical perspective, that does not mean she has to be bossed around. It means Tanja and Charlotte need to meet together and carefully define their respective roles, responsibilities, and limitations (as discussed in Section I). It means Tanja, as the teacher and supervising professional, should be observing Charlotte's work and providing honest feedback: suggestions for improvement as well as praise for work well done.

Case Study 2: William's Story

My name is William and I am a certified teacher enrolled in a university graduate program. The university program has a requirement to serve an internship, so I decided to pursue my interest in paraprofessional training. I interviewed and began serving an internship as a computer lab specialist in a middle school. Although certified, I was employed as a paraprofessional, paid less than $8 per hour, and worked just under thirty hours per week (although as an intern and paraprofessional I was ineligible for health-care benefits).

The week before school started, I was entrusted with the key to a brand-new computer lab with thirty PCs, a couple of laser printers, and a good selection of software that includes a word processing program. The computers are fully networked to local and wide-area networks. The first day of school, I had a full class load of about thirty students per session for six sessions. So during the week, almost 180 students would rotate through my lab as part of their Technology, Life, and Careers (TLC) curriculum. The two other classes in the TLC curriculum, home economics and industrial shop, are both taught by professional teachers. As part of my assignment, I have one preparation period each day. This helps because I have no students during that period and I can prepare for the next classes.

After a few weeks of working at the school, some questions begin to arise. I have not had a supervisor or any other teacher in the classroom with me. The class teachers get their planning time while their students are in my lab. I feel like I am running the whole show by myself. I have quite a few questions that need answering.

Imagine you are William. What are some of the questions you would ask, and who would you ask?

Question 1: _____

_____

_____

_____

I would address this question to _____

Question 2:_____

_____

_____

_____

I would address this question to _____

Question 3:_____

_____

_____

_____

I would address this question to _____

What if you ask, "Who is my supervisor?" and you are told you do not have one. You were hired because you said you could work independently and had informational technology (IT) skills. How would you justify your need for a supervisor in light of what you have learned about the potential pitfalls for paraprofessionals and for students when no instructional supervision is provided?

_____

_____

_____

_____

_____

_____

_____

List some of the safeguards that William and the school administration could put in place to protect William, the students, and the school. For example, what are some ways William and the school can demonstrate there has been "appropriate supervision"?

_____

_____

_____

_____

_____

_____

_____

_____

_____

_____

The Questions

In William's position, we would have many questions: What if I have problems with the computers? Where do I find a technician to solve hardware problems? What if I have behavior problems with the students? What is the school's discipline policy? What if the students visit inappropriate Internet sites? Who is the proper person to refer those students? How do I know what I am doing is really helpful to the students, and how can I coordinate their IT experiences in the lab with their needs in other curriculum areas? What if parents come to speak to me about their children? Should I talk to them or refer them to one of the teachers? What about the paraprofessionals who come into the lab to support individual students? How much responsibility do I have for them or for the students they support?

Some of these questions relate to instruction (coordinating curriculum and solving technical problems) and others to management issues (student behavior problems, inappropriate Internet usage, other paraprofessionals, and communication with parents), but because William is a paraprofessional, they are all also questions relating to supervision. William should not have to make these decisions himself. He should have a mentor and advocate supervising his work.

No Supervisor

If William is told he has no supervisor in the school, he can protest that he needs one—for all of the reasons we have already discussed—and he should be able to request support from district IT program staff, particularly for addressing his technical needs. If the school administration continues to insist he has no supervisor, he can approach individual class teachers to discuss whether there are specific ways he can support their curriculum through the IT lab work, as well as requesting their support with students in their class who behave inappropriately.

Safeguards

Here are some reasonable safeguards that the school could put in place:

- Information: providing William with the school discipline policy and the contact information for technical support.
- Training: as appropriate and where available William could attend training, or at the very least be allowed to consult with one of the teachers or a district adviser for behavior management and, of course, IT.
- Supervision: designating one member of the staff as William's direct supervisor or requiring class teachers whose students attend William's lab to remain with their students occasionally and observe his teaching on a rotating basis.

III

Instruction

In Section III we address the techniques and strategies associated with your role in supporting the instructional process. Each of the four chapters in this section deals with an important aspect of instructional effectiveness.

Chapter 8 looks at the teaching process itself and the strategies that have proved effective when delivering instruction. This is a huge topic that you will study, no doubt, in greater depth through other courses or training. However, the chapter gives you an overview of the elements of instruction, as well as many practical suggestions on how to enhance your teaching skills.

The whole of Chapter 9 is devoted to monitoring instructional effectiveness because it is such a critical element of the instructional process. Teaching and learning are inseparable activities. Good teachers—and good paraprofessionals—monitor the effects of their teaching continually to ensure that students are learning, and they adjust their teaching accordingly.

Chapter 10 looks at time management. A portion of the chapter examines how you can best use your time as an adult, but the majority of the chapter addresses the effective use of student time. We discuss how you can maximize the time available to ensure it is spent on meaningful learning activities, with students fully engaged and experiencing success. We also focus on transition time as a valuable source of additional learning time and suggest many ways in which you can reduce unnecessary transitions and engage students more quickly and effectively.

Finally, in Chapter 11, we discuss behavior management not only in terms of dealing with individual student behaviors, but also how you establish and enforce rules, reward positive student actions, and support the schoolwide learning environment.

8 Effective Instruction

The basic principles of effective instruction apply to a wide variety of settings, not only to paraprofessionals who work in a standard classroom setting in a formal instructional role. They are appropriate for anyone who is assisting students to gain new knowledge and skills.

Many books have been written on this topic, and your program of study may require you to examine effective instruction in much greater depth. However, in this chapter you will begin to understand the teaching and learning process more fully and to assess your current levels of effectiveness in supporting student learning.

By the end of this chapter you should be able to answer these questions:

- How does effective instruction relate to the prescribed curriculum and to student abilities and levels of performance?
- How can I determine whether my students are learning?
- What are the basic components of the cycle of effective instruction?

We make no distinction between the effective instructional practices that teachers should use and those that paraprofessionals should use. They are the same. A teacher may choose to have a paraprofessional support only a part of the teaching process (such as through the use of guided practice, which you will read about later on), but anyone who is supporting the teaching and learning process can use these principles to improve their instructional skills and enhance student learning.

Effective Instruction, Curriculum, and Student Abilities

If your teaching is to be effective, you must take into account your students' abilities and the current levels of their performance and the requirements of the curriculum. You must present material at an appropriate level for students to succeed: challenging enough to show your high expectations and to keep your students interested, but not so far above—or below—their abilities that they become frustrated or bored.

Figure 8.1 shows the relationship among prescribed curriculum, student abilities, and levels of student performance. Notice that the arrows face in both direc-

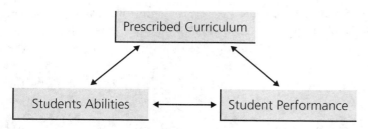

Figure 8.1

The Relationship Among Curriculum, Student Abilities, and Student Performance Levels

tions: the curriculum prescribes what a student should learn, but student abilities and current levels of performance dictate how much of that curriculum you can expect to cover; current levels of student performance are measured against the prescribed curriculum but are partly determined by a student's abilities.

We discussed earlier how curriculum is selected. Of the three items in Figure 8.1, curriculum is the one you will have little influence over as a paraprofessional: curriculum requirements will already have been set for your students. Students also come to you with innate abilities: they have a certain capacity for learning that you cannot change. Your role is to assist students in accessing as much of the prescribed curriculum as possible and in performing to their maximum potential, according to their abilities. Effective instruction is the tool you use to do this. Your challenge as an educator is to present the curriculum in such a way that your students will be able to demonstrate their true abilities: to teach in such a way that your students learn.

This last point is a very important one and carries a heavy responsibility: if your students are not learning, you really are not teaching. Logically, none of us can claim we are teaching, if no learning is evident. All children *can* learn, even those who have very limited abilities. So if any of your students do not appear to be learning (that is, the levels of their performance are worryingly low or they seem unable to grasp the ideas you are trying to convey), you need to examine carefully the difficulty of the curriculum you are trying to cover and the students' abilities, as well as your teaching methods, to find the cause of the problem. But this is good news. It suggests that when a problem arises, you can tackle it systematically by examining all the elements that impact student success and making the necessary changes. Obviously, you are not alone in dealing with this issue of student learning. You work in collaboration with a professional educator, who can assist you in improving both your teaching and your students' performance. When you have concerns about whether the students assigned to you are learning or not, your first resource is your supervising teacher.

How Do I Know If My Students Are Learning?

Each student has unique abilities and skills and reacts in a different way to what you teach. This makes the task of meeting all students' needs a complicated one. But there are many ways in which you can determine whether students understand what you have taught, that is, whether they are learning, because you have matched your teaching to their abilities. Take a moment to list here some of the ways you currently use to determine whether a student has understood what you have taught.

Methods I use to determine whether a student understands what is being taught:

1. _____
2. _____
3. _____
4. _____
5. _____
6. _____
7. _____
8. _____

You may have listed asking questions, giving short tests and quizzes, and asking a student to repeat what he heard or demonstrate what you have shown him. These are all excellent ways of deciding whether a student is learning.

But you may also have included watching facial expressions and body language and how the students react to questions, tests, and quizzes. These are often the best and most immediate indicators that students do *not* understand or are *not* keeping pace with the lesson. Students are often reluctant to admit they do not understand, but they will often show us by their reactions. According to their age, they may look puzzled, ask their neighbor for help, cry, or misbehave. These are all possible signals that students are out of their depth and need further explanations and learning support. But they can also be signals that students already know the material you are covering and are bored. We talk more about specific ways of monitoring student understanding in this chapter as we discuss teaching new concepts and guided practice. Chapter 9 is also devoted to monitoring instructional effectiveness.

The Effective Instructional Cycle

Many methods are available for delivering instruction. However, in order for instruction to be effective, certain key elements should be included, whatever method you choose. In your previous experience, or in future discussions on effective instruction, you may find that different terms are used for these elements, but essentially they are (1) a check for prerequisite skills, (2) the presentation of new content in small steps, integrated with (3) guided practice, (4) independent practice, and (5) reviews (see Figure 8.2).

We explain what is meant by each of these terms and provide examples of the most effective ways to address each one. You may be one of the many paraprofessionals assigned to provide guided practice (often in the form of drill and practice

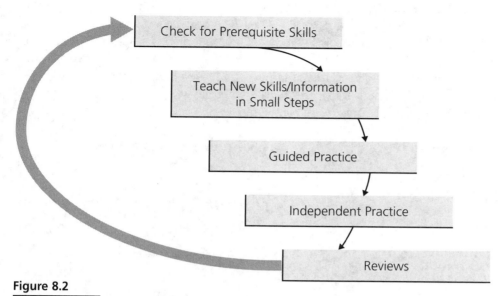

Figure 8.2

The Cycle of Effective Instructional Practices

activities) rather than teaching new content. However, understanding the whole instructional cycle is important so you can see where your assignment fits into the larger picture. You will use the same principles even if you are only focusing on a part of the cycle.

A typical 40-minute lesson might be divided up among each of these steps as illustrated in the nearby box.

Notice that teaching new skills is interspersed with guided practice in small steps because guided practice is given after each small teaching step. That is, we teach, give guided practice, teach, give guided practice, and so on. When paraprofessionals are assigned to provide only guided practice, typically this separate activity supplements the guided practice that the teacher directs during the teaching of new content.

Check for Prerequisite Skills

Before teaching new material, teachers must be sure students have the necessary skills and knowledge base on which to build new concepts and ideas. A prerequisite

Step in the Cycle of Effective Instructional Practices	Time Allocated
Check for prerequisite skills	Five minutes
Teach new content in small steps interspersed with guided practice,	Twenty minutes
Independent practice,	Ten minutes
Review.	Five minutes

is something that must be in place before something else can be added. If you attempt to teach facts or skills prematurely—that is, before students have a sound understanding of more basic principles—you will set students up to fail. When you present new ideas, you are leading students onto unfamiliar ground. If you verify they have the prerequisite skills, you at least know they have a base on which to build.

Think of some skills that are prerequisites (that is, what students have to know beforehand) if you want to teach the following:

If you want to teach . . .	**a prerequisite skill would be . . .**
Example: calculus	algebra
spelling	_____
map reading	_____
mixing paint colors	_____
how to tie shoelaces	_____
the future tense of Spanish verbs	_____
prime numbers	_____

There is often more than one prerequisite skill for each new skill or knowledge you teach. For example, some of the many skills or knowledge that children need before they begin to read include knowing the letters of the alphabet, understanding that reading is from left to right (in English), and knowing that the marks on the page (i.e., the letters and words) represent sounds. Remember that some prerequisite skills are cognitive and some are physical. For example, the ability to mix paint colors accurately depends on both knowledge and understanding of colors and their components (a cognitive skill) and dexterity in handling a paintbrush or palette knife (a physical skill). Students may be more skilled in the cognitive aspect or in the physical aspect, so if a student is not able to mix paint colors well, it may be because of a lack of skill in either the cognitive aspect of understanding the components of colors or the physical aspect of handling a paintbrush—or both. Check your students' competence in both areas, so you know which prerequisite skills they have and which ones they lack.

The further that students progress through school and the more complex the skills they need to learn, the more prerequisites there are. You can assume students have mastered certain skills by the time they reach a certain age, but it is always better, for you and the students, if you check what students already know before you try to build on those skills. Much of the failure that students in secondary education experience is due to low levels of basic skills (reading, writing, and numeracy) that prevent them from engaging with the new material at an appropriate level. Although you believe a student should have acquired certain basic skills by the end of elementary school, you cannot assume that.

So how do you conduct a check for prerequisite skills? Here are some examples:

■ Tell students what new topic you are about to cover, and ask them what they can already tell you about it.

- Give students a pretest (written or oral) on the new topic.
- Ask students to provide a demonstration if the new skill is physical.

If the check for prerequisite skills shows your students already have a sound basic understanding of the prerequisites needed for the topic or skill you are about to teach, you can move on to teaching the new content. But you must be sure students have a thorough understanding of the prerequisites so you do not move on prematurely. Otherwise, students are likely to get bored or frustrated and may misbehave.

Present New Content in Small Steps

As a paraprofessional, you may not be responsible for presenting new curriculum content: your teacher or supervisor may not feel this is an appropriate role for you. However, even if this is true, do not skip this section of the chapter because you almost certainly will be required to teach new knowledge or skills of some sort during the course of your responsibilities. Or you may need to reteach something the student is already supposed to know, so you should be aware of the most effective way to do it. Or you can apply the concept to your own children.

Always present new material or instructional content in small steps, one or two related concepts at a time. Even if you begin a lesson with an overview of all the points to be covered, proceed through the material in small steps. Because the material is unfamiliar to your students, their confidence levels will be low and you will need to support them in acquiring the new knowledge or skills. This is true whether you are teaching factual information or the application of facts: you should always teach in this way.

If you are assigned to teach new content, your teacher or supervisor will decide what new content you present to the students. Make sure you have a clear understanding of what aspects of a topic you are supposed to cover before you begin to teach. The amount of content that is appropriate will depend partly on the students' age. Generally, we teach new material to younger students in very small chunks, whereas older students can usually handle larger amounts of new information at one time. This is partly because older students already have a fairly large store of knowledge and skills that they can relate and link to the new content. But a student's capacity to accept new information is also based on ability. This means you will need to present new concepts in smaller chunks to older students who are less able, just as you would for younger students.

Earlier in the chapter we discussed how we know whether students are learning. The same principles apply to how we know whether we are presenting new content in small enough steps: we must pay attention not only to what students say but also to how they react or what their behavior tells us. This helps us answer this question: How small is a small step? The answer will differ for each student, but a small step might best be defined as the amount a student can easily understand and absorb: enough to be challenging and interesting, but not so much that it causes frustration. As you teach, time and experience help you become more competent at determining whether you are teaching in small enough steps. You learn what is typical for students of a particular age and ability level, you get to know individual students and their abilities, and you come to recognize their behavior and the signals they give that show whether they understand or not.

Guided Practice

Guided practice is supported practice, giving students the opportunity to practice new skills and knowledge under direct supervision and with immediate feedback. The critical aspect of guided practice is immediate feedback. There are three important reasons for guided practice:

1. It tells you whether students have understood what has been taught.
2. You can immediately correct student errors.
3. The students know whether they have understood, and can therefore keep track of their own learning.

If you teach new content, provide guided practice after each small step of instruction. While they are acquiring new knowledge and skills, students need many opportunities to practice so they can increase in confidence and accuracy. Also, as students acquire new knowledge, their ability to apply it to a variety of situations will be limited. First, they have to master the facts, and then they will also need to be guided through the process of learning to apply those facts.

Although there are many ways of giving guided practice, we look next at one commonly used technique you can work on with your students: asking questions. It is something we all do frequently, but two aspects of questioning will make it more effective: (1) increasing the number of questions you ask, and (2) varying the type of questions you ask.

Asking More Questions. Think for a moment why you ask questions. Write down three reasons why you ask students questions.

1. _____

2. _____

3. _____

If you ask a large number of questions:

■ More students should have a chance to respond and practice using their new knowledge and skills.
■ You get more information about whether students understand what you have taught.
■ More students receive confirmation about whether they have understood the concepts being taught.

Although it takes more time to ask more questions and get responses from students, it is well worth the investment because you help fix the new knowledge and skills in the minds of your students and gain a clearer understanding of whether your teaching efforts have been successful. Both of these are important. In this process, you need to monitor the students' understanding, so you know whether your teaching has been effective or not. But students also need to know whether they have remembered facts and grasped concepts accurately. They need to know if they are right and may lack confidence if they are left in doubt.

Here is a challenge for you. Suppose you are working through a long multiplication problem with your students, for example, 37 × 42. Write down the questions you could ask them as you work through the appropriate procedures to find the answer to the problem. List as many as you can.

_____

_____

_____

_____

_____

_____

_____

_____

How many questions did you manage to list? _____

The following list contains twenty-nine questions you could ask in relation to this math problem. See how many of them you thought of or whether there are any you thought of that we missed.

1. What's this number?
2. What does this sign (×) mean?
3. How do we set the numbers out on the page for multiplication?
4. Why do we do that?
5. Which numbers do we multiply first?
6. Are these the hundreds, tens, or units?
7. What's 7 × 2?
8. Where do we write that answer?
9. Can we write the whole number under the line or do we have to split it?
10. What's the rule about how many numbers you can write in a column?
11. What's 3 × 2?
12. Where do we write that answer?
13. What about the 1 from our previous answer? What do we do with that?
14. Have we finished?
15. What do we do next?
16. Why do we put a zero before we multiply any more numbers?
17. What numbers do we multiply next?
18. What's 7 × 4?
19. Where do we put the answer?
20. What do we multiply next?
21. What's 3 × 4?
22. Where do we write the answer?
23. What's the next thing we have to do to finish the problem?
24. What's 4 + 0?

25. What's 7 + 8?
26. What's 4 + nothing?
27. What's 1 + nothing?
28. Now have we finished?
29. So what's 37 × 42?

Obviously you would not ask this many questions every time you worked through a math problem. It would not be appropriate to all teaching situations or student age groups, and some students might be intimidated by having so many questions fired at them. But ideally you see the point: it is possible to increase the number of questions you ask while you are teaching. In fact, it takes no more time to ask a question than to make a statement, but the value of asking questions greatly exceeds the value of making statements if you are checking students' understanding because the answers you receive from students provide you with a picture of what they understand. In a case such as this long multiplication problem, you do not need to cover large numbers of problems because the same procedures apply to all similar problems. By asking many questions about one or two problems, you can probe students' understanding of procedures more deeply. If your aim is to test students' knowledge of multiplication facts, you can do that separately, by giving an oral or written test on math facts.

Asking Different Types of Questions. Types of questions can be classified in many ways, but here we discuss low-level versus high-level questions.

Low-level questions require a factual answer. They usually begin with *What*, *Who*, or *How many* and generally only have one right answer.

High-level questions require students to analyze facts, express an opinion, or make predictions. They usually begin with *Why*, *What do you think*, or *How* and may have many correct answers.

Low-level questions are important because they allow you to determine if students have a grasp of facts. But high-level questions are also crucial because they make students think, analyze facts, and make predictions or express opinions. As you monitor student understanding through asking questions, ask both low- and high-level questions, even if you are working with very young students. The content we teach young students is obviously less difficult than the curriculum content for older students, so the low-level questions we ask young students relate to simpler facts (although they may not seem simple to the young students). But even very young students can speculate, and they are usually very willing to give their opinion. Even if their ideas often seem wild and illogical, we need to give young children opportunities to use their imagination and creativity to make sense of the world. We do this by asking high-level questions, not just requiring the factual responses of low-level questions.

One of the real advantages of high-level questions is that they can have many right answers. When you ask students to express their opinion with a question such as "What do you think will happen next?" it allows them to use their imagination (no matter what their age and ability) to come up with creative ideas. But it also means they can all be right because there are no wrong answers to such a question. The same is true for a question such as "Why do you think that happened?" Although there may be official explanations for the Civil War or nuclear fusion, students can be asked to speculate on all kinds of events, and they often come up with a variety of creative explanations that reveal their understanding and ways of thinking. This is particularly important for students of lower ability, who often cannot provide the right answer when it comes to facts but who can express an opinion and may offer novel ways of looking at topics when they are encouraged to use their imagination.

This idea—a question can have many right answers—is one that students may not be familiar or comfortable with. Students are used to being required to find the one right answer to questions that teachers ask, and they can be quite cruel and derisive toward less knowledgeable students who do not know that magical right answer. You may have to teach them that they will all be right, whatever their answer, when you ask a question such as "What do you think will happen next?" or "Why do you think that happened?" You might sometimes encourage them to be as wild and outrageous as possible in their speculation, with a "What if anything were possible?" approach.

Preparing to Use Both High- and Low-Level Questions. A useful exercise you can include in your lesson preparation is to plan the questions you might ask your students. This is helpful whether you are working with an individual student or conducting a group discussion. In the nearby box, write down some of the questions you might ask, and then mark beside each one whether it is a low-level or high-level question. Add up the number of high- and low-level questions you have written down and record the totals. There is no ideal ratio for low- or high-level questions, but be sure to ask some of both. First you establish whether students know the facts, and then give them an opportunity to use those facts to speculate, predict, and analyze. So if you find you have only written down low-level questions as you plan your lesson, go back and add some high-level questions that will allow students to use their imagination.

Independent Practice

The purpose of independent practice is to help students build fluency in a particular skill or area of knowledge. *Fluency* means that students have facts at their fingertips and no longer have to expend much effort finding the answer to a particular question. Fluency in prerequisite skills allows students to spend more of their time and effort on new skills and knowledge. For example, if a student is learning long multiplication, one item of prerequisite knowledge would be basic math facts, in this case the times tables. If the student is fluent in that prerequisite knowledge, she will not have to waste a lot of time trying to find the math facts in her head before being able to use them for the long multiplication. Fluency can be acquired during independent practice, which differs from guided practice in that *no immediate feedback* is given to student responses.

Here are some of the typical ways we offer independent practice:

- Written assignments, in class or for homework
- Written drill and practice
- Timed exercises or tests
- Student demonstrations or performances

Planning to Use Both High- and Low-Level Questions

Proposed lesson segment:		
Possible questions I could ask:	**Is this a high- or low-level question? (Circle one)**	
	Low	High
	Low	High
	Low	High
	Low	High
	Low	High
	Low	High
	Low	High
	Low	High
	Low	High
	Low	High
	Low	High
Total number of each type of question:		

Because no immediate feedback is given to students during independent practice, students must have reached a reasonable level of skill and competence before we allow them to practice unsupervised. This is fairly obvious if it is a physical skill, such as using shop or laboratory equipment. You would not allow students to use such equipment at all until they could demonstrate in your presence that they knew how to use it appropriately and safely.

If a student cannot spell ten words correctly, there is no physical danger in letting that student use the words in an essay. However, in an educational sense, we are putting students at risk of failure if we have them practice skills they have not mastered. So we must make sure the student knows the correct spellings before we ask him to use the words in his essay. We give students practice so they learn material more thoroughly. If they practice on material they have not mastered, they practice—and learn—errors. If our student has not learned how to spell a word correctly and we ask him to write an essay that requires the use of that word, he will write the word incorrectly many times during the essay, which will fix the incorrect spelling in his head. Better to make sure he can spell it correctly because using it will then help fix the *correct* spelling in his head. During guided practice we can determine whether a student has sufficient mastery of a skill or knowledge to be allowed to continue practicing unsupervised, that is, whether he is ready for independent practice.

A Special Case: Homework. Homework is one of the most common forms of independent practice. Unfortunately, students are often assigned relatively unfamiliar material for homework, which is not good educational practice. Homework assignments should only include material the students are familiar with or can work

Steps in the Teaching and Learning Cycle

Steps in the Instructional Cycle	Delivery Methods	Steps in the Student Learning Cycle
Check for prerequisite skills	Quizzes; asking for a summary of a previous lesson; asking for as many facts on the new topic as possible	Students need a context for new material. They need to feel secure in approaching new material without criticism or fear of failure.
Teach new material in small steps	Demonstration; direct instruction; lecture	Students lack confidence in new material. They may not have a good grasp of concepts. They need to know they can express their lack of confidence without repercussions.
Guided practice	Choral responses; individual responses; peer tutoring; physical guidance; timings	Students may be hesitant. They need a lot of encouragement. They may be able to repeat facts but only apply new knowledge to a limited extent. They need to know if their responses are correct.
Independent practice	Drills; games; enrichment activities; application tasks; homework	Student responses become more fluent and spontaneous. Students acquire greater depth of understanding. Confidence grows as they demonstrate growing expertise.
Reviews	Student demonstrations; quizzes; cumulative assignments; reports	Students may still have a better grasp of facts than the application of those facts. They should be able to show a reasonable level of mastery.

Advantages and Disadvantages of Various Methods for Monitoring Student Understanding

Method of Monitoring Student Understanding	Advantages	Disadvantages	Most Appropriate For
Paraprofessional asks individual student a question, in front of the rest of the group, and the student gives an oral response.	As each individual student responds (and is given feedback on the correctness of the response), other students in the group also hear what the correct response is.	Students who lack confidence may be unwilling to perform so publicly. Can be very time consuming in a group setting.	Guided practice
Paraprofessional asks an individual student a question, and the student gives a written response.	Students who are unsure of the correctness of their response may be more willing to respond in writing.	More difficult to provide immediate feedback if working with a group. Students who experience difficulty with writing and spelling may be unable to give a true picture of the extent of their understanding.	Independent practice
Paraprofessional asks a whole group of students a question, and students give a choral response.	Those who are less confident may be more willing to respond because an incorrect response will be partly masked by other students' answers. More material can be covered in a shorter time.	Individual understanding is more difficult to monitor.	Reviews
Paraprofessional asks a whole group of students a question, and students each give a written response.	Students who are unsure of the correctness of their response may be more willing to respond.	More difficult to provide immediate feedback to all members of the group. Students who experience difficulty with writing and spelling may be unable to give a true picture of the extent of their understanding.	Independent practice

on confidently and accurately without supervision (such as learning spelling words). When students are given independent practice on materials they do not understand, they practice errors rather than building fluency.

Reviews

Reviews may be conducted daily, weekly, or monthly, at the end of a curriculum unit or at the end of the trimester. They may take the form of a quiz or more formal written test, a class discussion, or an individual assignment. The purpose of reviews is to see whether students have retained the material you have taught, but they can also serve as a check for the prerequisite skills for the new material you are about to teach. Reviews complete the instructional cycle and begin a new round of teaching and learning for you and your students.

The effective instructional cycle discussed in this chapter describes what the teacher or paraprofessional does. The nearby boxes list some of the methods you can use during each phase of the cycle, as well as the type of behaviors you might expect from students as they acquire both new knowledge and skills and confidence in their learning.

CHAPTER SUMMARY

In this chapter we looked at the cycle of effective instruction. You have learned:

- How effective instruction relates to the prescribed curriculum and to student abilities and levels of performance.
- How you as a teacher or paraprofessional can determine whether your students are learning.
- The basic components of the effective instructional cycle.

This chapter provided a brief overview as a reminder of some of the ways in which your approach to teaching affects student learning. As a paraprofessional, you may not be involved in every phase of this teaching and learning process: your assignments may cover only some of the phases. But it is important for you to have a context for what you do and understand where your work fits into the instructional cycle and how important each phase is to the success of your students.

In the Extending Your Learning sections, you will explore some of the monitoring techniques you can use with your students and learn about some commonly used and well-researched teaching tools: peer tutoring, group responding, and teacher-directed instruction.

Monitoring Student Understanding

Consider what you would do in this fairly typical elementary school teaching situation. A paraprofessional is working with a group of elementary school students who are practicing spelling words. The six students are studying ten spelling words.

Question: If the paraprofessional asks, "How do you spell . . . ?" how many questions would he or she have to ask in order to determine whether each student could spell each of the assigned words correctly?

Answer: Sixty questions. The paraprofessional would have to ask each of the six students "How do you spell . . . ?" for each of the ten words.

Earlier in the chapter we recommended you ask as many questions as possible, so would this be a good way to give guided practice for the spelling words? No doubt you said no, and you would be right. Even if the students gave fast and accurate responses, with no corrections needed, it would take about fifteen minutes of nonstop questioning to ask all sixty questions. So the students would have to sit for fifteen minutes, listening to the ten questions being repeated six times each while only being required to answer ten times. That is only a little more than two minutes out of the fifteen that each student would spend on task or directly engaged in learning. Even though the repetition would help some of the students learn the words, you probably would not choose to work this way because it would produce a very bored group of students. You would know whether each student could spell each of the words, but you would have to deal with major behavior problems.

More often in such a situation, we ask each student to spell perhaps two words, which only gives a partial picture of how well the students know the words. Alternatively, we might ask students to answer in writing, which can be done quickly, keeps them all on task, and provides an easy way of checking what they know. However, remember that the critical aspect of guided practice is immediate feedback. As soon as a student answers a question, he or she needs to know if the answer is right or not. In true guided practice, as students write each spelling word, they need to know whether it is right or wrong as soon as they write it, not when everyone has finished writing the whole list of words.

Here are some possible alternatives that are more effective:

▪ You can circulate around the group to check each student answer individually and give immediate feedback, which works well if the group is small.
▪ The students can write the words on a small lap-size whiteboard as you say them. As soon as the word is written, each student turns the whiteboard so you can see which students have spelled the word correctly. If you then write the word and show it to the students, they get immediate feedback on their response, without the possible embarrassment of being told publicly that they gave a wrong answer.

Here is a secondary school example. The paraprofessional is assigned to a high school health classroom with thirty students, four of whom have learning disabilities. The teacher is in charge of teaching the whole group, lecturing on chapters, giving assignments, and assuring that the students are learning the material. The paraprofessional has the responsibility of circulating among the students, checking work and paying special attention to the four students with learning disabilities. List as many methods as you can think of to check for students' understanding, including some addressed to individuals and other addressed to the whole group:

1. _____

2. _____

3. _____

4. _____

5. _____

6. _____

Look back at the beginning of the chapter and check your answers against the suggestions listed there.

Peer Tutoring

Peer tutoring involves students tutoring, or teaching, each other. Research indicates that peer tutoring, properly used, can be a very helpful tool, especially for drill-and-practice skills such as math facts, spellings, or paint color combinations, which have short and indisputable answers. Pairs of students or the whole class/group simultaneously can use peer tutoring.

Here is a simple example. Mr. Jones schedules a peer tutoring session for his fourth-grade class every day for fifteen minutes after recess. Students are in pairs and stay in the same pairs for four weeks. Mr. Jones uses the peer tutoring sessions for spelling practice. The students are assigned ten spelling words every week. Each pair of students has a set of the ten spelling words written on index cards. For half of the session one of the students acts as the tutor. The tutor reads the word on the first card; the other student writes the word on a piece of paper and shows it to the tutor. If the word is spelled correctly, the tutor says, "That's correct," sets the card aside, and moves on to the next word. If the word is spelled incorrectly, the tutor says, "No, the word is spelled . . . and spells out the word; the other student writes the word down as the tutor spells it. The card for that word is placed at the back of the set of cards, so it can be used again when all ten words have been covered. After seven to eight minutes, Mr. Jones gives the signal for the roles to change, and the other student becomes the tutor.

Here are some additional ways to set up peer tutoring:

- Sessions can be longer (although twenty minutes is usually a good maximum).
- Responses can be given orally; they do not have to be written.
- Pairs or individual students can be assigned different spelling lists or sets of math facts, to match their abilities, but take care to ensure the reading level is not too difficult for the tutor.

- Students can keep a tally of their correct responses, so they can chart their own progress through the week.
- Pairs can be assigned to one of two classroom teams and their scores can be added together for a weekly competition.

Peer tutoring procedures must be taught carefully to students so sessions run smoothly and students are not distracted from its primary purpose of providing guided practice.

Group Responding

To check for student understanding with a whole group, try using group responding: you ask a question and all students answer simultaneously. If students are giving an oral response, it can be quite noisy, but it is also possible to have them respond silently using signals or response cards. As with other classroom procedures, students need to be taught how to give appropriate group responses or use response cards correctly, so the procedure runs smoothly and does not interfere with its purpose: allowing you to monitor students' understanding.

Here are some guidelines for using group responding:

- Use group responding for questions that only have one right answer (i.e., for low-level questions). You obviously cannot ask students to respond as a group to a question such as "What do you think will happen next?"
- Always signal clearly when the students should respond: allow a few seconds of thinking time, and then cue the response by clapping your hands or saying something like "Answer"; this allows all students to join in, not just the fastest responders.
- Although there is only one right answer to how a word is spelled, spelling a word is essentially several responses one after the other. So be sure to provide a cue or signal so students can simultaneously give each of the responses (i.e., the letters of the word).
- If the response to any question is ragged, review the correct answer and then ask the question again later in the session.
- Responses can be silent. Students can use signals (e.g., thumbs up for "Yes/True," thumbs down for "No/False," thumb horizontal for "Don't know," or they can hold up the number of fingers corresponding to the correct response (with fingers under the chin and close to the chest to prevent cheating) for math problems when the answer is less than ten.
- Oral responses may be easier for students with good aural memory (they can hear the answer in their heads rather than see it); provide opportunities for both written and oral responses.

Response Cards

Response cards allow you to see written responses from many students very quickly and from the front of the class or group, without having to circulate. Many of the same principles apply to response cards: questions must have short answers; allow students time to think before cueing a response; and review questions when responses are poor. Here are some of the possibilities for response cards:

- Students write their responses with a dry-erase marker on a laminated card and hold up their cards when you cue them.
- Cards printed with "True" (or "Yes") on one side and "False" (or "No") on the other. For "Don't know" or "Undecided," students can hold the card horizontally.
- Three response cards can be provided for each student: one for "Yes," one for "No," and one for "Don't know." If these are also different colors, it is easy for you to gauge student understanding in a large group. However, it may be too confusing for students to manage three cards. As an alternative, give each student a cube made of card stock with each side one of three colors and opposite sides having the same colors. The student chooses a response and holds the cube so the color for that response is facing him. That color will also be facing you.

Timings

One of the important aspects of monitoring student understanding is to check progress over time. This may be over the course of the school year or trimester, but for specific skills it is important to show progress over much shorter time periods, from day to day or from one week to the next. For sets of facts (e.g., the names of each of the states in the United States or math facts), give students repeated tests of the same information under timed conditions. Monitor student progress both in terms of amount of material covered (e.g., how many of the states they tried to name) and accuracy of response (i.e., how many of the responses were correct). Students can keep their own records and graph their own progress. Because they are competing against themselves, comparison between students is kept to a minimum, and students are more likely to take up the challenge to improve. Although speed is not always critical, fluency is important because it allows students to retrieve information quickly. This is true of factual information, but it is particularly important in reading: students who have to decode every word will not have enough mental capacity left over to understand the meaning of what they are reading.

Here are two examples of how teachers have used timings. A geography teacher was disappointed in his sixth graders' knowledge of the states in the United States. Although it was not part of the sixth-grade curriculum, and he had little time to spare, he felt the students were at a disadvantage when he talked about regional variations in agriculture, climate, and so on. So at the beginning of each class period, he gave them a two-minute timing. Each student was given an outline map of the United States and asked to write in the names of as many states as possible within the time limit. Students checked their own work using an answer sheet and recorded the number of correct responses in the back of their notebooks. The teacher gave points to all students who made progress from one day to the next.

In the second example, the resource teacher in an elementary school gave each of her students a one-minute timed reading every day. She, or one of the paraprofessionals who assisted her, listened to each child individually as they read a printed passage. The child was encouraged to read as quickly and accurately as possible; the teacher noted any incorrect words but did not point them out to the child until the end. At the end of the minute, the teacher told the student to stop reading, calculated the total number of words read, and reviewed the words read incorrectly. The student recorded both the number of words read and the number read correctly on a chart and graph provided by the teacher. The teacher praised students who increased the number of words read and/or increased the number of correct words. The teacher changed the reading passage each week, unless the student specifically asked to be allowed to continue working on the same passage.

Teacher-Directed Instruction

Teacher-directed instruction, or direct instruction (DI), is a comprehensive system that integrates the principles of effective teaching with curriculum design, classroom organization and management, and monitoring student progress. The developers of DI identified five important aspects of teaching. The one we focus on here is teaching critical skills using the principles of effective instruction by coaching, guiding, and giving continual feedback to students as they learn. Teacher or paraprofessional support is gradually reduced as students learn to complete tasks independently. Students are assisted in applying the new knowledge and skills by connecting them to skills/knowledge they already have gained, and they are given frequent reviews to make sure they remember.

DI materials are often scripted, which has provoked criticism from those who see them delivered in a mechanical and robotic manner. However, when they are used appropriately, DI materials can provide much needed drill and practice to increase students' skills and fluency whether in a secondary or an elementary classroom. In its most basic terms, DI includes all of the principles of effective instruction you have read about in this chapter:

■ Getting the attention of your students.
■ Motivating students to want to learn.
■ Showing students the skill or concept.
■ Using precise language.
■ Asking frequent questions.
■ Providing feedback.
■ Reviewing the material regularly with your students.

Here is an example of a short DI sequence:

1. (Get attention) Teacher says, "Students, look at me."
2. (Motivate) "You will now learn to read a very important word."
3. (Show skill/concepts). Show students a card with the word written on it.
4. (Use precise language). Teacher says, "This word is _____."
5. (Ask questions). Teacher asks, "What word is this?"
6. (Provide feedback). Teacher says, "You read this word correctly, it is _____."
7. (Review). Teacher asks individual student or signals for a whole group answer: "Students, what word is this?" The teacher also returns to this word and asks students to read it again later in the lesson.

CHAPTER

9 Monitoring Instructional Effectiveness

Students encounter many people in their daily lives who could be considered teachers or who function in the capacity of a teacher, for example, soccer, basketball, and other athletic coaches who teach sports; piano, voice, and other music coaches or tutors; or Sunday school teachers. Yet few of these teachers actually know and apply the most vital concept of teaching, that is, how to monitor the effectiveness of teaching and learning. Without the application of this knowledge, a teacher cannot be maximally effective. In this chapter we talk about the relationship between teaching and learning (i.e., teacher behavior and student outcomes) and look at ways in which you can effectively monitor both. This chapter covers skills you can use in your paraprofessional role, but again—as the law states—under the direction of the teacher. By the end of the chapter, you will be able to demonstrate your knowledge by answering questions in each of the following areas:

- What teacher behaviors can positively influence students' motivation to learn?
- What other factors influence student motivation?
- What are some effective ways to monitor student progress?
- How can I support the development of goals and objectives for learning?
- How can I provide appropriate feedback to students?

The Relationship Between Teacher Behavior and Student Outcomes

In Chapter 8 we discussed how you can make your teaching—and student learning—more effective. Before we talk about the relationship between *teaching* and *learning,* take a moment to write your definition of these two terms. What do they mean to you?

1. *Teaching* is _____

_____

_____

2. *Learning* is _____

_____

_____

We sometimes talk about teaching and learning as if they were two distinct activities—the teacher (or paraprofessional) teaches and the student learns—whereas they are in fact inseparably connected. An educator can present a concept or demonstrate a skill, but this is not the same as teaching the concept or the skill. Nor does the presentation guarantee the student will learn the concept or skill. *True teaching really only happens if a student learns.*

That *teaching equals learning* is not an easy concept. It is not difficult to understand, but it can seem harsh in the demands it makes of teachers. As a paraprofessional, you must also give it serious consideration. If you present a lesson and your students do not seem to learn the information or skills you are presenting, have you really taught anything? If you accept the direct relationship between teaching and learning, logically you cannot say, "Well, I taught them fractions, but they don't seem to have learned anything." If your students have not learned something, you have not truly taught it: you cannot separate the two. You could say it is a question of semantics and what we mean by the word *teach*. If teaching means merely presenting information, you can teach without students learning anything. However, the concept of "teaching means student learning" places overall responsibility for student learning where it belongs—with the educator.

This is a heavy responsibility and one reason why teachers are required to study and acquire qualifications. Teaching is not a casual endeavor. The work you do with students is enormously important and indispensable to the educational system. You need and deserve to understand the complex processes of teaching and learning, so you can carry out your responsibilities with greater confidence and efficacy. This chapter deals with one of the important processes involved in teaching: assessing the extent to which you and your students are successful in the teaching-learning partnership.

Whose Responsibility: Teacher or Learner?

Many possible obstacles can get in the way of learning. Some relate to the responsibilities of the teacher, and some to the learner's responsibilities in the process. Consider the analogy of radio or television. The programs are broadcast but they are received only if a set is switched on and tuned in to the right channel. Teachers may fulfill their responsibilities to broadcast information to students, but students also have to be "switched on" and "tuned in," so to speak. They have some responsibility to be alert and receptive to the information sent their way. You know that all students are not always tuned in to the content of a lesson, and even the most diligent student is sometimes distracted. However, if a student is not switched on and tuned in, this does not absolve you, the teacher, from any further responsibility. This is perhaps the difference between teaching a lesson and teaching a student.

Influences on Student Motivation. In addition to imparting information, teachers have the responsibility to motivate and interest the student in the content of the lesson. Although some teachers say students should come to them already motivated to learn, in reality, that does not always happen. Teachers encounter many types of student motivational problems. For example,

- Students do not want to be in school.
- The material may be too hard or too easy.
- Students cannot see the relevance of the material to their lives.
- Some students are afraid to try because they fear failure and embarrassment.
- Students are bored.
- Some students have a limited ability to succeed.
- Other students lack the self-confidence to believe they can succeed.

To compound matters further (as discussed in Chapter 6), students who are hungry or emotionally/physically abused are not necessarily ready or able to focus on learning.

In spite of what may appear to be insurmountable odds against teaching, much can be done to influence students' motivation to learn. The teacher or paraprofessional can try the following:

- Present the information in a way that shows the relevance and value of the material for the student.
- Make it accessible by ensuring that the level of content is right for the student's ability and understanding. Review Chapter 5 where we discussed the balance between curriculum requirements and standards of achievement.
- Make the material engaging by using visuals and role playing.
- Work with parents and other school personnel to help students believe they are capable of completing a task successfully.
- Celebrate small successes and shape students to move toward greater successes.
- Encourage students to set goals for their learning; students who are involved in setting their own goals are more likely to be motivated to achieve.
- Use extrinsic motivators to assist students who are unable to see the value of learning "for learning's sake." *Extrinsic motivation* is a reward (such as free time or extra bonus points toward a grade) for completing a task, whereas *intrinsic motivation* refers to completing an activity for the personal satisfaction or enjoyment of it.

The relationship between teaching and learning is at once simple and complex. At its simplest, if learning is not taking place, teaching is not present either. However, so many factors influence the relationship, it truly is a complex process. As we discuss why and how we monitor student progress, you will see how you can tackle the challenge of ensuring that you and your students experience success.

Monitoring Learning? Or Monitoring Teaching?

We talk about monitoring—or checking—student progress, but because of the direct connection between teaching and learning, when you monitor a student's learning you are also monitoring the effectiveness of your teaching. In the next section, we discuss self-evaluation and the importance of continually monitoring your work, so we do not go into the topic in any detail here. Nevertheless, keep this principle in mind: student success is also teacher success, and lack of student success may be a reflection of poor teaching methods. It is far too simplistic to say that if your students are learning, your teaching methods are effective, and vice versa. However, if your students are not learning, the good news is that you can almost always do something about it and begin to identify the cause by carefully examining your teaching.

As a paraprofessional your role usually will not include teaching new content (see Chapter 8), but if you are assigned to drill-and-practice duties (i.e., guided practice) with your students, you may identify areas in which their understanding is weak and you therefore need to reteach concepts the teacher has already presented. Thus this principle of *teaching equals learning* or conversely *no learning equals no teaching* also applies directly to your work. You may also be in a situation to support students in a work environment or listen to students read, situations in which you may feel you are more of a support and helper than a teacher. But even these situations require good practices and are a version of teaching. They are certainly situations in which you need to monitor student learning and take steps to enhance learning opportunities for the student.

Remember that the professional in charge of the learning environment is the person to consult for advice if you find your students do not seem to be learning or mastering the material you are assigned to cover with them. You are not alone in your responsibility for student learning. You can monitor or evaluate your own teaching skills according to the principles you have been taught in this book and elsewhere to make sure you are using effective instructional practices, but always seek guidance from your supervisor also about how you can better meet the learning needs of individual students who are struggling.

As part of a teacher licensure program, your supervisor has received training in effective techniques and teaching practices. This places the teacher in an ideal position to discuss your concerns about the students with whom you work. Your supervisor also needs to know if students are struggling and seem to need additional support. If you monitor a student's progress and difficulties carefully, you can provide feedback to your supervisor on specific aspects of the student's understanding. If you document what you do and the methods you have used to teach and to monitor student learning, you will have the basis for a useful discussion with your supervisor. Use the vocabulary you learned in Chapter 8 to be specific about the activities you have engaged students in, so your supervisor has a clear picture of what you have done and what might need to be changed.

Monitoring Progress Toward Student Goals

When we talk about monitoring student progress, we are talking about monitoring progress toward the learning goals that have been set along with the prescribed curriculum. In this section we first take a look at goals and then consider the different ways in which we monitor student progress and give feedback to students on that progress.

Whose Goals?

Teachers set learning goals and objectives for students, but essentially these are also your teaching goals: you can only achieve your teaching goals as students achieve their learning goals. As a paraprofessional, you probably were not involved in the process of setting student learning goals because they are directly related to and built into the prescribed curriculum and the responsibility of the teacher. In a general education class, the learning goals are typically the same for all students—calculated to give adequate yearly progress, with only small modifications required for students who are considered gifted or for those who are less able. In special education, as mentioned previously, the law requires an individual set of learning goals (an individualized educational plan, or IEP) for each student eligible to receive services. These are crafted to match closely the student's specific abilities and challenges. The student's IEP team determines these goals, and as a paraprofessional you may be included on that team and have some part in the decision-making process. Other team members include the classroom teacher, parents, and often the student.

No matter whether a student is in general education classes or following a modified curriculum, students must be informed of the goals that have been set for their learning. They need to know where they are supposed to be headed and why. This is part of the metacognition discussed earlier. Students need to become more aware of their own learning so they can have some sense of ownership. If they know what is expected of them in terms of learning, they can track and help plan their own progress toward learning goals.

Long- and Short-Term Goals

This is a good point to pause and examine goals in greater detail, so you have a clearer understanding of the terms used as well as the part that goals play in guiding your work. We might say that the long-term goal of the U.S. public educational system is to produce well-educated citizens who are reasonably knowledgeable in specified curricular areas (math, English, science, etc.) and who have the skills and motivation to be independent, productive citizens, who will continue to learn once they have left the public educational system. This is obviously a very broad, all-encompassing goal, and we discussed earlier how the curriculum is set for each grade level and subject area to allow students to progress steadily toward this ultimate citizenship goal.

The broad, long-term goal of productive citizenship is divided into shorter term goals for each year of the student's education. Most likely, this is the point at which you come in, as you deal with students at the classroom level. Shorter term goals for the U.S. system become long-term goals at the classroom level because you provide educational support for students one school year at a time. Thus a long-term goal from your perspective may be for the school year, and short-term goals may only encompass weeks or, in some cases, days.

Goals or Objectives?

We often talk about *goals* and *objectives* and sometimes use the terms interchangeably, but the two are different. *Objectives* are the smaller steps you take to achieve a goal. As a simple mental image, think of a goal as getting up a flight of steps and the objectives as each of the steps in the flight, taken one or two at a time. These are the short-term, or smaller, objectives that lead to the long-term or final goal: getting to the top! We look now at writing goals and objectives. Although this is not your responsibility as a paraprofessional, it is important for you to understand the process that teachers follow in developing the student goals that determine your assignments.

Supporting the Development of Goals and Objectives

Sometimes people have difficulty developing goals and writing them in a way that can be measured. The notion of a *measurable* goal is critical because unless you can measure progress toward a goal, the goal has no practical use. Earlier you learned about the national laws and the requirements of the No Child Left Behind (NCLB) law in making schools accountable for student growth in learning. Writing measurable goals relates specifically to the NCLB law, *and* to shaping student learning, *and* to providing the teacher with the direction needed to provide instruction, *and* to assisting the student to understand what he or she needs to learn in order to be successful (graduate with a diploma, pass to the next grade, achieve the goals on the IEP, etc.). Success is defined in different ways, but a measurable goal is the only way to determine whether progress is being made toward success. (See box below for the rationales for measurable goals.)

Present Level of Educational Performance

When teachers set goals, their purpose is to effect a change in the student's behavior. We talk about changing behavior shortly, but before we can do that, we first need to think about our starting point. The best and most logical place to begin when setting goals for students' achievement is to look at their present level of educational performance.

Measurable Goals

- Satisfy the requirements of No Child Left Behind.
- Make schools accountable for student learning.
- Allow teachers and paraprofessionals to shape student learning.
- Provide direction for teaching.
- Help students understand what they need to learn to be successful.

Here is a sample description of Miguel's present level of educational performance: Miguel is working at the fourth-grade level in reading, language arts, and mathematics. He has remarkable talent in art, which surpasses his current sixth-grade placement.

Based on the information in this example, Miguel is currently in the sixth grade, but he is reading and doing math on a fourth-grade level. He is above grade level in art. In very broad terms, this is his present level of educational performance. Obviously his teacher needs to pay particular attention to instructional goals that would help him improve his skills in reading and mathematics. As the teacher writes instructional goals for Miguel, he is essentially answering a set of questions like these:

- What are the student's strengths in the curriculum areas for which you are writing the goals? (For example, in reading, does Miguel have a good sight vocabulary? Does he have good comprehension skills? In math, what level of difficulty can he manage in the basic operations of adding, subtracting, multiplication, and division?)

- What are the particular areas of weakness? (Is there one aspect of math or reading that Miguel struggles with, such as multiplication or comprehension? And within that area of difficulty, what exactly needs to be improved—understanding of concepts or speed/accuracy of working?)

- Is the goal intended to keep the student moving at the same pace, or does he or she need an accelerated learning program in order to catch up to grade level? (Miguel is obviously behind grade level in math and reading, so the goals set for him need to push him along faster than the average student; otherwise he will always be behind in his reading and math.)

- How will you measure progress toward the goals you set? (Will you use a particular reading test or list of sight vocabulary to check Miguel's progress? Will he perhaps be given weekly timed tests of math facts or multiplication problems?)

- What is the time period for this goal? (Is this a long- or short-term goal? When will you review progress to determine whether Miguel has indeed reached the goals set for him in math/reading—after a month or at the end of the trimester?)

Questions to Ask When Developing Goals

1. What are the student's strengths in this curriculum area?
2. What are the student's particular areas of weakness?
3. Is the goal intended to keep the student moving at the same pace, or to help the student catch up to grade level?
4. How will you measure progress toward the goal?
5. What is the time period for this goal?

Goals can also relate to behavior, of course, not just to learning. The same questions apply to behavioral goals. Teachers need to determine what the student is currently able to do in terms of compliance with rules and procedures; the area(s) in which the student is experiencing difficulty; the way in which changes in the student's behavior will be measured; and the time period for achieving the goal.

As you can see, it is important to first determine, in some detail, where the student currently stands, and then decide which areas the student needs to focus on next. Thus, once the teacher has established current levels of performance, goals or objectives must address these issues:

- Behavior: the particular skill or knowledge that needs to change (usually increase or add to the student's repertoire).
- Conditions: the circumstances under which the behavior might occur.
- Criteria: the level at which the teacher would like to see the student perform.
- Schedule: the time period during which the change should take place.

We look carefully at each of these components, starting with behavior.

Behavior. The three critical features here are (1) the behavior must be carefully defined; (2) the behavior must be measurable, and therefore (3) the behavior must be observable. A teacher needs to define carefully the expected or desired change in the student's behavior. Take the following examples of student goals:

- Increase study skills for academic success.
- Do better in school.
- Make more friends.
- Control his temper.

Although these may all sound desirable, phrases like "doing better" or "making friends" are very vague and need to be much better defined. Which study skills in particular does the student lack? In which sense should the student be doing better in school—in terms of his math, English, or science or in terms of his work and study habits, or in his compliance with school rules? What do we mean by "make more friends"? What behaviors does the student exhibit that show an uncontrolled temper? We cannot support a student's improvement in any area when the target behavior for improvement is poorly defined. In addition, we may focus on a variety of types of change: we may wish to increase, decrease, maintain, or extend the defined behavior.

The other two aspects of behavior— measurable and observable—go hand in hand. We cannot measure something that we cannot observe. We must ask our-

Say	Read	Measure	Write
Compute	Construct	Draw	Perform
Walk	Explain		

selves what it is that the student will be able to do to *show* changes in skills or knowledge. The nearby table gives some examples of observable behaviors. In the blank boxes in the table, add additional observable behaviors.

Federal laws—the NCLB Act and IDEA 97—specify that students must have measurable goals. Measurable goals help shape student learning by assisting students to understand what they need to learn. Words such as *think, understand,* or *enjoy* do not belong in a list of behaviors that need to change because you cannot observe such behaviors even if someone appears to be thinking, understanding, or enjoying an activity. Students show their thinking or understanding or enjoyment through the things they say and do, and this is the point at which you can measure understanding, thinking, and enjoyment: through observable behaviors that demonstrate the invisible processes occurring in their minds.

Conditions. Now look at the *conditions*, or the situations when the behavior might occur. When teachers write the conditions of a goal, they may use words like these:

When asked, or requested

When prompted

When given a fact sheet

When given the third-grade reading book

When riding on the school bus

In writing

In U.S. History class

Without arguing

We include conditions in a goal or objective because we may not expect to see the behavior in every situation: for example, we do not expect students to respond in writing during a physical education class, and we would not expect a student to be on task during recess. Those are behaviors we would aim for in more academic situations. Similarly, a student may only exhibit certain inappropriate behaviors under certain conditions. For example, bullying may only occur on the playground, so the condition statement in the student's goal does not need to include class time; or a student may find it difficult to cope with changes in routine, so the condition of the goal may only relate to transition times during the school day.

Criteria. The measurement you use to determine that the objective or goal has been met is called a *criterion* (*criteria* in the plural). It is what the teacher considers acceptable performance. For example, is the student expected to achieve 100 percent accuracy on all math problems? Or, if 90 percent of the problems are answered correctly, will it be considered acceptable evidence that the student has made satisfactory progress toward meeting the goal? The question of appropriate criteria takes some consideration on the part of teaching staff. For example, in the National Basketball Association (NBA), it would be unusual for a basketball player to be able to shoot foul shots with 100 percent accuracy. Some of the best foul shooters have a season average of 90 percent. In the majority of cases, it would likewise be quite unreasonable to expect accomplishment of 100 percent accuracy before a player (or student) could move on to the next skill in basketball or in the classroom.

Here are some examples of criteria:

1. Makes correct change four out of five times (80 percent).
2. Responds within five seconds of verbal cue.
3. Kicks four out of six (67 percent) field goals at 25 yards on the soccer/football field.
4. Stays in seat for fifteen minutes.
5. Solves fifteen problems in five minutes.
6. Writes list of spelling words in fifteen minutes.

Notice that not all of the criteria relate to accuracy. Some of the criteria relate only to response time (responds within five seconds) or length of time a behavior should last (stays in seat for fifteen minutes). The criterion for a goal must relate directly to the type of change the goal is designed to produce. If a student is working too slowly and the goal is to help the student work more quickly, the criterion for the goal should relate to the time period for the student's work (e.g., solves fifteen problems in five minutes). Once the student has reached the goal of working more quickly, another goal may be set for increasing the accuracy of the student's responses. A variety of different evaluations can be used to measure whether or not the student learned the material or otherwise reached a goal. Notice that these all produce observable evidence of a student's achievement. Evaluation measures might include the end-of-chapter test, a teacher-made test, observational data, or the Friday spelling test.

Schedule.   As the word *schedule* suggests, here we are concerned with *when* or how soon we expect the student to reach the goal or objective. Here are some examples you might consider:

Each Friday

In six months

Each month

For thirty consecutive days

Quarterly

By December 15

Note that some of these schedule phrases relate to a time by which the student will have achieved the goal (e.g., in six months), and others suggest how long the student will maintain a behavior (for thirty consecutive days).

The nearby box summarizes questions to ask when writing objectives.

Relevance to Students

When you discuss goals with students—or indeed when you consider them for your own lesson planning—be very specific about the expectations that have been set for the students. Students need to know, for example, what an assignment

---

Checklist for Written Objectives

- Is the objective a natural step forward from the student's present levels of performance?
- Is the behavior well defined?
- Is the behavior observable?
- Is each objective measurable?
- Does the objective include conditions for the behavior change?
- Does the objective include criteria for acceptable performance of the objective?
- Does the objective state the time schedule for achieving the objective?
- Does the objective lead the student toward achieving longer term or annual goals?

---

needs to look like in order to demonstrate they have reached a particular goal. Goals need to be expressed in terms of (1) *what* is expected, (2) *when,* (3) *how,* and (4) *how good/accurate.*

Goals are milestones for students, providing a sense of direction and purpose in their learning. Reaching goals gives students a sense of achievement and increases their confidence. Goals are not secrets that only adults can understand and use. When we state goals for students and tell them what those goals are, we are expressing our confidence in their ability and showing them we have direction and purpose in our teaching. Even though paraprofessionals do not typically set goals for student achievement, you are part of the process that helps students achieve those goals, and you must keep the goals in mind as you work, as well as sharing the goals with your students. Stating goals in terms of *what? when? how?* and *how good?* gives you and your students a common sense of purpose and a real sense of team achievement at the end of the time period.

Present assignments in these terms:

When	Due date of the assignment (e.g., Friday morning)
Length	For example it should be three to four pages and cover the following areas: (give examples)
Format	What the assignment should look like or what form it should take (notes, essay, graphics)
Minimum standard	What constitutes a passing grade, that is, what level of work is considered good enough (ideally students will choose to exceed that basic standard)

Similarly, the teacher or IEP team may have set a student goal as illustrated in these examples:

By when?	Christmas/end of the trimester you should know . . .
What?	Your multiplication math facts: 0 through 12x
How?	Demonstrate either in an oral or written test
How good/accuracy	Completed with at least 90 percent correct

Obviously, the way we express these expectations to students and the vocabulary we use varies according to their age and ability, but we must let students know where they are headed in their learning.

Students can be given, or encouraged to write, a checklist of short-term goals and objectives, with a place where they can check off completion (or get your signature) to show when they have achieved that goal or objective. For younger children this can be more of a graphic than a written list, with symbols for the different objectives or short-term goals. Young students enjoy being allowed to color in shapes or simple graphics that indicate progress toward learning goals. For older, more visual learners, the checklist may take the form of a diagram or flowchart on which they can show (through the use of color or highlighting) those areas they have covered successfully.

We know of a teacher and paraprofessional who develop the goal for students based on the required curriculum but leave it flexible enough for students to add in their specific areas of interest. For example, Mrs. Baker and Miss Brown's class will be learning about the human body in the health unit. They make the goals sufficiently general so the students can then personalize the objectives according to their personal areas of interest. The team introduces the human body through a motivating introduction and then gives the students a sentence stem to complete: "I want to know more about . . . "

Completing his sentence stem, Johnny writes that his grandfather is going into the hospital for heart surgery soon and he wants to "learn more about how the heart pumps blood to all the parts of the body; and I want to know how a heart attack happens." This provides the teaching team the opportunity to tailor the instruction to the students' interests.

Always review goals frequently with students. If you have not reached the planned level or place in the curriculum, but there is good justification for it, tell your students. Let them know what you are prepared to do to help them make up the work and what they need to do to help make up lost time. Above all, be reasonable. If you and your students have reached your goals, make time to celebrate your achievements together.

Monitoring Progress

We use the phrase *monitoring student progress* to denote measuring the extent to which a student is achieving short- and long-term goals. The word *monitoring* can be taken as a synonym for *evaluating, assessing, or testing.* Although there may be differences of opinion on whether these terms really are synonymous, we treat them as such here and use them interchangeably. When you monitor student progress you are measuring, evaluating, assessing, or testing in some way whether students are reaching the goals set for them. You have an end point or a target in mind—a skill the student needs to learn or knowledge the student must acquire—and you watch to see whether the student is headed in that direction. You are in effect asking yourself these two questions: (1) Is the student acquiring the prerequisite skills for each step of the learning process? and (2) Is the student moving ahead at a reasonable rate?

Some students may be moving in the right direction: they are acquiring the necessary skills but may be progressing at such a slow rate toward their short-term goals that they may not reach the long-term goals set for them. If the rate of learning is too slow in comparison with their peers, the student may be eligible for additional support under Special Education, Title I, or Section 504, as we discussed in previous chapters, and the curriculum goals for that student will be modified accordingly. Otherwise, we expect a fairly wide range of ability in a regular education classroom, so small accommodations or modifications can be made to meet the varying needs of students, ranging from those who are considered gifted or talented to those who are less able but have no identifiable disability.

There are two ways to measure student progress: one is through comparison of the student's progress with his or her peers; and the other is the student's accomplishment of individual goals and objectives. So how do you and other educators monitor student progress? Take a moment to list some of the ways we can check whether a student has learned something, whether it be a skill or knowledge/information. Look back at the standards for proper goals and objectives and then consider both formal and informal methods.

_____   _____

_____   _____

_____   _____

You may have listed end-of-unit tests, weekly spelling tests, short quizzes, term papers, or requesting that a student demonstrate a skill. Now let's look at an instructional lesson. There are the hourly and daily steps we must take to help students achieve their objectives and goals. A student's goals are an expression of your expectations as the teacher. As we discussed in Chapter 8, good teachers monitor student academic progress and behavior continually and adjust their teaching accordingly. They do this almost automatically and informally even if they do not share their thoughts and impressions with those with whom they work. Teachers and paraprofessionals must check for student understanding all the time.

There are many different ways to check student understanding. You know that if you ask a question and get only blank stares from your group of students, something is amiss. Your question may have been unclear, but it generally means your students have not grasped the concepts you have been trying to teach. Conversely, if you ask a question and all of your students raise their hands enthusiastically to answer, it is generally a good indication and suggests they are willing and able to answer your question. Students show their uncertainty and lack of confidence or knowledge in many different ways. They may try to distract you by asking another question, they may refuse to answer, make a smart answer, declare something is boring or stupid, misbehave, or in the early grades, students may even cry if they know they cannot answer a question or demonstrate a skill as requested.

As an experienced paraprofessional, or even a new paraprofessional with experience of other people, you know we all express our apprehensions and insecurities in a variety of ways, but we rarely want to state openly that we do not know how to do something or cannot give a required piece of information. In the classroom and elsewhere, we instinctively and continually monitor other people's reactions to our questions and requests. Although many of the methods we use are informal, we gather much useful information as we pay close attention to the behavior of those around us. When you talk to your supervisor about a student's progress, you may have the results of tests and papers to offer as evidence, but you are just as likely to find yourself saying, "Well I notice that he . . ." or "It seems to me that she . . ." This anecdotal evidence is very valuable. It cannot be the sole basis for our decisions about student progress, but it plays a vital role in our understanding of the learning that is taking place.

If teachers and paraprofessionals believe in the necessity of monitoring student progress and skills in order to facilitate and enhance learning—teaching them in addition to self-evaluate—the same logic can be applied to their own professional development. Not only is it incumbent on teachers, as professionals, to engage in regular and consistent self-evaluation, but also they must act as models for paraprofessionals as they engage in regular and consistent self-evaluation. We discuss effective ways you can evaluate your progress in Section IV.

Formative versus Summative Evaluation

Another difference in monitoring student progress, apart from the type of evidence we gather, concerns the purpose of the monitoring or evaluation. The two terms we use to make a distinction in purpose are *formative evaluation* and *summative evaluation*.

When we conduct formative evaluation activities, we gather information for the purpose of making improvements in teaching and learning. Examples of formative assessments include all criterion-referenced tests, such as spelling tests, end-of-unit tests, term papers, and so on, that are based on the curriculum the student is currently following.

When we conduct summative evaluation activities, we gather information for the purpose of providing a general statement of knowledge and skills at a given point in time or during a certain time span. Summative evaluation activities include end-of-year reports and all norm-referenced tests (i.e., tests that are not based on a specific curriculum but cover a range of skills and knowledge typically found in any curriculum for students of a particular age or grade).

Notice the differences between the two. A summative assessment tool, such as the Stanford Achievement Test (SAT), provides a broad statement of a student's knowledge at one point in time. The teacher cannot use the results of the SAT to address the shortfalls in the student's knowledge because the level of detail is insufficient. The score is expressed in terms of a norm (a comparison with how well a student of that age might be expected to perform) and as a percentile (which shows how well the student performed in relation to the other students who took the test at the same time). The test will address a curriculum area such as math and may have sections on such items as fractions or money, but each section at best will have an overall score, with no detail about the specific aspects of money or fractions the student was able to answer correctly.

In contrast, the results of a formative assessment, such as an end-of-unit test in math, is usually expressed in terms of a whole score (the total number of items answered correctly) and a percentage, but more importantly the teacher can see which test items were problematic to the student and can then reteach those concepts. The results of the formative assessment provide sufficient detail to inform the teacher's subsequent teaching or reteaching.

Both summative and formative assessments have their place and purpose in the teaching and learning process. In your daily work as a paraprofessional, formative assessment activities will be the most common. Note that formative and summative assessments are not confined to written tests and reports. Look at the examples given in the nearby box, and decide whether each one is formative or summative in nature. The first three have been completed for you.

Notice that the critical feature of formative evaluation is the level of detail provided in the feedback:

	Evaluation or Assessment Activity	Formative or Summative	Justification
1	A student report card reads, "Laura has made excellent progress in reading this trimester."	S	The report sums up Laura's progress but does not help you know what to do next to help her continue to improve because you do not know her particular strengths.
2	A paraprofessional walks around the classroom giving out tokens to students who are on task.	F	If the students know what the tokens are for, they also know what they did right to get the token and what to change if they did not receive one.
3	Teacher to student: "Well Jason, you didn't do a very good job on your math homework."	S	Jason knows that he did not do well, but he is not told exactly what the problem is, so he cannot correct it. He cannot use the information to do better next time.
4	Teacher to student: "This is an excellent assignment: legible writing, questions answered in a full and attractive layout. Well done!"		
5	The principal comes into the classroom to conduct an annual evaluation on the teacher or paraprofessional.		

- In examples 1 and 3, the statements made are factual but very broad and general.
- In example 2, *if the students understand why the tokens are being given* (more about that in Chapter 11), they are formative—the students know what to do to receive more tokens.
- In example 4, the teacher's feedback to the student is very specific, so the student knows exactly why the teacher considers the assignment to be excellent. And any other student overhearing the teacher's comment would also understand what he or she could do to receive the same praise from the teacher. So this would be considered formative.
- Example 5 could be considered either formative or summative. The determining factor will be the type of feedback the principal gives the teacher or paraprofessional after the evaluation is completed. If the feedback provides sufficient detail of what was good and what needs attention, the paraprofessional will know what to change and what not to change. If the feedback is expressed in broad, general terms, similar to the student report card in example 1, it will be of no use to the teacher or paraprofessional in improving classroom practice.

Both formative and summative evaluation measures have their place in the effective classroom. Your role is likely to put you in direct contact with students who need clear indications of whether they have understood what you are trying to teach them or not. Therefore you will most often be making formative assessments, those that give you the type of detail you need to guide your teaching and give students enough detail to give them confidence in their learning. Thus when you provide feedback to students, it will be most helpful to them if you can provide details, not just broad summary statements. This is our next topic.

Providing Appropriate Feedback to Students

Feedback means response. A student responds to a question or request from a teacher or paraprofessional and the latter responds to a student's question or response. We have already stressed the importance of including students in the process of setting and monitoring progress toward goals. In Chapter 8 we also emphasized the need to let students know whether the responses they give to our questions and requests for information are correct or incorrect. We suggested honing your questioning skills as a means of giving students more opportunities to respond: (1) increasing the number of questions you ask so more students can be given opportunities to practice skills and demonstrate understanding; and (2) using both high- and low-level questions, so students can show reasoning and prediction skills as well as knowledge of facts.

Next we go into more detail on how to provide feedback to students and thereby give them critical information on their learning.

Feedback According to Student Response

We have already mentioned the need to teach students not only new academic skills and information, but also how to follow procedures. This came up in the discussion on peer tutoring, for example, where we outlined the need to teach the tutoring procedure very carefully, otherwise the students would not be able to use it for its designated purpose, providing guided practice. You will find this point recurs in Chapter 11 on classroom and behavior management: we must deliberately teach students how to follow classroom rules and procedures. We cannot assume they will pick them up if we are not specific about our expectations. Before we get into the details of how we provide feedback to students, we need to apply this principle of teaching expectations and procedures to student and teacher feedback.

Establishing a Nonthreatening Environment for Student Responses

Students often give incorrect responses. How do you react to those incorrect responses? What do you say or do? Take a moment to note what your typical reactions may be when a student gives a wrong answer.

_____

_____

_____

Do you get angry? Do you call the student stupid? Do you even think the student is stupid? Probably not. You may get frustrated if students give incorrect responses because you may feel they have not been paying attention, but generally you have to accept that students will not always get things right the first time, so wrong answers (or incorrect demonstrations) are just an indication a student is still learning and has not quite mastered the skill or knowledge.

But do your students know that incorrect responses are OK and you consider them part of the learning process? Take a minute to think about a group of students you teach, and write down how they typically react to an incorrect response, whether they have given it themselves or whether it was given by another student in the group.

_____

_____

_____

How do your students react to incorrect answers? Do they poke fun or embarrass the student who has given the incorrect answer? Do they roll their eyes or otherwise show by their body language that they think the student is stupid? What about the students who give incorrect answers? Do they seem ashamed or overly embarrassed? Do they then refuse to participate or respond to another question?

If you find you have to ask students not to tease or if your students seem very discouraged when they give an incorrect response to a question or request, take the time to talk to them about the responses they give and the ways they react to other students' responses. Explain to them that in one sense incorrect answers really do not matter. They need to know that you will not be angry if they give an incorrect answer, nor will you take the incorrect answer as an indication of stupidity or ignorance. Help your students understand that in your classroom it is OK to be wrong some of the time, and they will never be punished for a wrong answer, although there may be negative consequences for those who make fun of other students or embarrass them. This has to be stated very clearly because it is unfortunately not true in all classrooms. You also then have to be very careful to stick by this agreement, which is why we are teaching you how to make appropriate responses to student feedback.

One of the ways in which you can reduce students' anxiety about making incorrect responses is to clarify that the answers they give you are an indication of the effectiveness of your teaching. Explain to them the direct link between teaching and learning that we discussed at the beginning of this chapter. Tell them that as an educator, you need to monitor the effectiveness of your teaching, so when you ask questions and they give a wrong answer, you take at least some of the responsibility for the wrong answer because it could mean your teaching has not been very effective. It can also mean the student has not been paying attention, of course, but sharing the responsibility for the wrong answer may help some students be less anxious and perhaps more willing to pay attention. Teaching and learning then become a joint endeavor: you make a greater effort to teach more effectively, and the students make more of an effort to pay attention and do their best to learn.

Types of Student Response

We can categorize student responses as *correct and confident*, *correct but hesitant*, *incorrect*, or *no response*. Responses are sometimes also partially correct, but that type of response can be treated as two responses, and each part can be dealt with as appropriate and described here. Most student responses are given as an answer to a question, but they can of course be a demonstration of physical skills. The same principles apply in both cases.

Correct and Confident. Correct and confident responses should be acknowledged as correct with a brief word of praise. Then move on to your next question or portion of the lesson. Lengthy statements of praise and encouragement are not necessary and can be embarrassing to students, especially at the secondary level, and they interrupt the flow and pace of the lesson. But do take the time to acknowledge the correctness of the response. It is absolutely critical to let the student know an answer is right because that confirms the fact for the student and increases confidence. In addition, it informs the other students in the group that the response was correct, so they can compare it with the response they would have given and make an assessment of their own understanding as well. If the answer is not the same as the one they would have given, they can adjust their mental database; if the answer is the same, they also increase in confidence about their own knowledge.

We say a quick word of praise is all that is needed, but it is refreshing for the students if you can vary that word. Take a moment to write a list of words or phrases that are short but positive enough to indicate to a student that a response was correct. We have started you off with some of the most commonly used.

Good job!   *Yes!*

_____   _____

_____   _____

_____   _____

Correct But Hesitant. When a response is correct but hesitant, acknowledge the correctness of the response and then quickly repeat the question and answer so students hear them together, stated in a positive and confident manner. They say he who hesitates is lost, but when you ask a question of your students, he who hesitates is usually just uncertain. Part of your job as an educator is to reduce uncertainty for your students. You not only need to help them acquire information and skills, you also need to build their confidence in their knowledge and abilities.

Incorrect. An incorrect answer *must* be identified immediately as incorrect. We have already discussed the need to establish an environment in which your students can make errors and not feel threatened or stupid. Part of this atmosphere is that your students have to get used to being told sometimes in a very straightforward manner that their response is incorrect. They will get used to it more easily if your feedback is impartial and nonemotional and if the answer is treated as wrong, not the student treated as stupid. Indicate that the response was incorrect with a simple "No, it's not . . . Would you like to try again?" Some students will try another response; others will choose not to. Give your students the option. If you get another incorrect answer when you ask the question again, do not keep asking the question. Review the material and ask the question again. If you just keep asking the question without conducting a review, students will soon just produce wild guesses. Make sure the correct answer is repeated more than once so the students hear the *correct* answer! For example, say, "Yes, [repeat the answer] is the correct answer."

When students give an incorrect answer, you have three options:

1. Supply the right answer, ask the question again, and have the group give a choral response, so they all say and hear the correct response.
2. Provide prompts to help students remember or find the correct answer.
3. Reduce the difficulty of the question.

Students must hear the correct answer and not be left guessing, or the next time the question comes up they may just remember that no one could give the correct answer and not even bother trying.

No Response. When your question receives no response, treat this situation as an incorrect answer: provide prompts, reduce the difficulty of the question (and therefore the response), and then reteach or review the information so the students hear the correct answer before you move on.

Whenever students are hesitant or unwilling to respond, also review your question mentally. Ask yourself,

■ Was my question clear? Or was it confusing, so students really did not know what I was asking?

■ Did I only ask one question? Or did I really ask two questions, so the students did not know which one to answer?

■ Did I use vocabulary appropriate for the students' age, ability, and understanding? Or did I use words that were too difficult for the students or that I had not used with them when I was teaching the concepts?

Ask yourself these questions when students are hesitant about answering a question or reticent about demonstrating a skill or practical task. As we discussed in Chapter 8, although we ask questions all the time—it is a natural human instinct—there is a skill to effective questioning, and you may wish to plan your questions ahead of time, rather than always making them up on the spot. Writing the questions in advance of the lesson will give you a chance to anticipate what the students will say. See the Extending Your Learning section for a form that will allow you to examine student responses to the questions you ask

C-H-A-P-T-E-R   S-U-M-M-A-R-Y

This chapter discussed how you can determine student progress. It covered both teaching and learning and how you can measure a student's learning growth. You were encouraged to monitor the effectiveness of students' responses to your questions and thus review student learning. We also suggested that the effectiveness of learning is strongly influenced by the quality of your teaching, the questions you ask, the way you deal with incorrect answers, and the measurements you use to identify how well you are moving students toward their learning goals. You should now feel that you can, with some confidence,

■ List the teacher and paraprofessional behaviors that can positively influence students' motivation to learn.
■ Identify factors influencing student motivation.
■ Use effective monitoring of progress and show (1) methods for monitoring, and (2) that these methods are effective in terms of student progress.
■ Support the development of goals and objectives for learning.
■ Demonstrate how to provide appropriate feedback to students.

E-X-T-E-N-D-I-N-G—Y-O-U-R—L-E-A-R-N-I-N-G

Questions I Ask

This form will help you evaluate the questions you ask students. You can use it in a variety of ways. You could write the questions you plan to ask in advance. Then as you teach the lesson, make a notation of the students' responses. Or you could ask an observer to watch you as you work with the students and have him or her write the questions you ask and the students' responses. If the teacher is able to observe you, it would serve as a great catalyst to a conversation about the achievement of the students' goals and objectives. It could also serve as evidence that you seek—and receive—supervision.

Evaluating Questions and Student Responses

Questions I Will Ask the Students During the Lesson	Student Response			
	Correct and confident	Correct and hesitant	Incorrect	No response

10 Time Management

In this chapter, we look at one of the most important resources available to you as an educator: time. Although it may sometimes seem to be in short supply, time is definitely something you can use to your advantage. The time you are allocated for working with students is usually determined by your supervisor or a predetermined schedule, and you may have to cover very specific activities with each student during any given time period. Or you may have considerable discretion in the way you allocate time to students and activities. Whichever is the case, make good use of this valuable resource.

This chapter provides insights into time allocation and use that will help you maximize the time available to you and your students. By the end of this chapter you will be able to answer the following questions:

- What is academic learning time, and how can I maximize opportunities to increase it in my working environment?
- How can I decrease transition time?
- How can I use observation to monitor student use of time?
- What are some of the methods of observation and recording available to me?
- How can I monitor my own use of time?

Increasing Academic Learning Time

First we consider four concepts of time management—available time, allocated time, engaged time, and academic learning time—and then we focus on the most important of the concepts: academic learning time.

Available Time

Students (and educators) are required to spend a very specific amount of time in school: usually 180 days, for approximately 6 hours per day. That is about 1,080 hours each school year. It is all the time we have for teaching and students have for formal learning. We call it *available time*, the first concept in time management.

Allocated Time

The total time when students are available to us as educators is typically allocated to different curriculum areas. *Allocated time* is the second concept in time man-

> Available time = 1,080 hours per school year
> ↓
> Allocated time → Curriculum + Organizational tasks + Recess

agement. Each subject is scheduled or allocated a certain amount of time during the day and week. School districts provide teachers with a curriculum guide, which tells them how much time they should give to each subject. This guide typically has a breakdown of the curriculum by subject. For example, it may say that mathematics should have 50 minutes daily, reading 65 minutes, and so on. This schedule is sometimes adjusted by the school principal, who may put emphasis on a particular area such as reading and require everyone in the school to read for a certain amount of time during the day. However, the precise amount of time spent on any given curriculum area can vary quite substantially between classes in the same school because the final allocation is made by teachers, who allocate more time to certain subject areas than others.

Not all available time can be allocated to academic work because time also has to be spent on organizational tasks such as taking attendance. Time is also taken up transitioning between activities in the classroom, between classes in different parts of the school, or between class and recess. Thus we do not have full use of the 1,080 hours for teaching and learning. Allocated time may only be as much as 80 percent of available time (see box above).

Engaged Time

The third concept is *engaged time,* when the student is actually working on the curriculum and engaged in the learning process (e.g., listening to the teacher, writing, responding to questions, etc.). Engaged time does *not* include time spent handing out papers or waiting for the teacher's attention, even though these activities may be related to learning and may seem necessary. And obviously time spent socializing or visiting cannot be defined as engaged time, even if students are in the classroom and sitting at their desks. So, like available time, allocated time is partially lost in activities that are not central to learning, even though some of them may be necessary (see box below).

> Available time = 1,080 hours per school year
> ↓
> Allocated time → Curriculum + Organizational tasks + Recess
> ↓
> Engaged time (focused on the curriculum)

Academic Learning Time

It is very satisfying to see a class full of students who are all busy and purposeful, apparently completing assignments and engaged in learning. However, the purpose of the classroom is not just to keep students occupied, but also to help them succeed in the learning process. This is where the concept of *academic learning time* comes in, when students are completely engaged in the learning process. The difference between engaged time and academic learning time is success: the student is not just on task—not just completing formal learning tasks—but is experiencing success in that learning. Academic learning time cannot exist independently of student achievement. In order to ensure success and student achievement, the task the student is engaged in must be relevant to the desired outcome, that is, to the student's academic goals. In Chapter 9 we talked about the need to align curriculum with student abilities in order to facilitate student success. We also discussed earlier the direct link between teaching and learning. Thus, during academic learning time, students are being successful in their learning because effective teaching is happening.

One of the most desired moments in teaching is when a teacher or paraprofessional is teaching a well-prepared lesson and students are engaged in learning. The magic moment occurs when students have questions or are problem solving, teaching is occurring, the student is thinking—and suddenly gets a knowing look and says something like, "Oh, I get it now! Yes, I understand."

The goal of effective time management in the classroom is to increase academic learning time for your students. In the ideal learning environment, no time would be wasted on organizational tasks and transitions. Instead, students would spend as much time as possible engaged with learning materials and experiencing success. This may seem very idealistic, and of course some time has to be spent in organizational tasks and movement around the classroom and the school, but too often classrooms are busy places without the critical component of student success. Even if the majority of student time could be classified as engaged time, not enough of it would be considered academic learning time.

Many paraprofessionals work part time and have a variety of roles in the school, perhaps some lunchtime supervision in addition to classroom support or bus duties before and after school. You may also have some clerical or housekeeping responsibilities while you are in the classroom. So take a moment to think through the time available to you in school and how much of that time you spend engaged in learning tasks with students:

▪ Number of hours per week you spend in school: _____

▪ Number of hours per week you spend on clerical/organizational tasks:

_____

▪ Approximate amount of time spent in transition from one class to

another:_____

▪ Number of hours per week you are engaged with students in learning tasks:

_____

If you have a typical schedule and working pattern, probably quite a substantial portion of your time in school (available time) is lost to transitions and organizational tasks, so the amount of time you have to engage with students in learning tasks (engaged time) is significantly limited. This pattern emphasizes the need to make maximum use of the engaged time and ensure it really is academic learning time. You may find it a useful exercise to actually keep track of how you use your time for a week. Note interruptions and how much time they consume and the transfers you make between one class and another or that your students make between classes or between activities in the same classroom. Include waiting time, when students are not yet engaged in learning because not all students have arrived or have the necessary materials ready. This should help you become more aware of the precise ways in which your time and your students' time is spent.

Note that we are talking about time from both a student's and an educator's perspective. And although we are not talking about time management in the sense of adults carrying and consulting planners, remember that paraprofessionals and teachers also need to be on task to ensure the effectiveness of classroom instruction. When the instructional team is chatting about a movie they saw on the weekend, rather than concentrating on the details of teaching, it is next to impossible for students to be engaged in learning. The same applies to any planning time you may have together as teacher and paraprofessional. If you are fortunate enough to have an administrator who has provided you with teacher-paraprofessional planning time, that time should not be wasted in idle chatter; your administrator quite rightly expects you to use that time wisely.

Transition Time

One of the primary sources of additional academic learning time is transition time, which is spent moving around the school, around the classroom, or between segments of a lesson. Consider these facts about transition time and how they might offer additional academic learning time:

- For students in the secondary grades, a substantial amount of time is spent moving from one classroom to another because each subject is taught by a different teacher and generally in a different physical location.
- In the elementary grades, students spend the majority of the day with the same teacher and in the same physical location, but they often move between activities within the classroom.
- Transition time also exists within lessons, between the different segments or activities that make up the lesson. At both elementary and secondary levels, a teacher may first talk to the whole class and then transition to having students complete an assignment or an activity.
- At the secondary level, a transition may only involve handing out materials or finding a place in a textbook.
- At the elementary level, students may move to work on the activity in different groups or at workstations in different parts of the room.

These are all transitions that can yield valuable extra academic learning time if they are handled effectively.

How Much Time?

You may say that only minutes are taken up in finding a book, distributing a handout, or moving to a different area of the classroom. However, those minutes add up to hours and even days over the course of a student's school life. Just one minute gained during each class period each day in grades 7 through 12 translates into about 6,500 minutes, which is more than 100 hours, or almost a month of school. Imagine how much extra time we could have for teaching and learning if we could save several minutes in each class period! The same figures apply to the elementary grades. If just one wasted minute could be salvaged during each hour of the day, an extra 30 minutes would be available each week for learning.

At the secondary level we cannot just remove transitions between classes because students have to move to the next teacher for each subject. However, once the students are in our charge, we have considerable freedom in directing their use of time and in making more effective transitions into the learning process and between segments of it. At the elementary level it is considered good practice to include practical activities and group work that require movement around the classroom, so again we cannot just decide to eliminate transitions. But as with secondary classes, transitions do not have to take up substantial portions of our valuable time. Transitions that are handled effectively and smoothly can lessen wasted time and increase the amount of time available for learning.

Here's a striking example. We knew of a teacher who *always* called the roll. Each day she took several minutes at the beginning of the class to slowly read the names of each student enrolled in the class, pausing for the student to respond. On one cold winter day when many students were affected with an influenza virus and absent from school, the teacher only had four or five students in attendance. Yet again she slowly read the names of each student on the class list and waited for a response. Time could have been used much more wisely if she had quickly engaged students in learning tasks and then, while they were working, looked around and marked the roll.

You probably already do take steps to reduce wasted time during the day. How do you save time during your day? How do you maximize the time you spend with students? Take a moment to think about the transitions your students make. Use the nearby table to describe each transition (e.g., between different rooms or areas of the classroom) and the time it takes. Note whether you think the transition is really necessary, and then think of ways each transition could be made more effective, either by reducing its length or making it a productive time for the students.

The table gives two examples of transitions and suggests ways in which the time they take can be reduced or made more productive. Add your own thoughts, and then discuss the table with your supervising teacher, so it becomes a resource for reducing wasted time in your learning environment.

Transitions	Amount of Time	Transition Really Necessary?	Ways of Reducing the Time	Ways to Make the Time More Productive
Students sit at their desks waiting for the teacher to take the roll.			Roll can be taken silently.	Students can be given a warm-up assignment for the first five minutes of the lesson, to ensure they are immediately engaged in meaningful activities.
Students travel to and from a work site in a minibus.			If the length of the trip cannot be reduced, look at the transition times between classroom and minibus, minibus and work site, to see if they can be shortened.	

In the first example, you may have noted such ideas as having handouts and other materials close at hand, taking a silent roll call, and preparing activities for students who finish an assignment ahead of other students. These are all time-saving measures that minimize the time students spend waiting, but bear in mind that it is not just a case of providing busywork to keep students from getting bored and getting into mischief. We must not only reduce transition time; we must transform it into academic learning time. Thus you must consider the educational value of what you require your students to do during that time and ask yourself these questions.

- Is the activity relevant to the students' learning goals? Or is it just busywork?
- Is the activity academically useful and necessary? Does it have direct relevance to the current topic or area of study?
- Can the student quickly engage with the activity with minimal direction or supervision? Or will the student waste time puzzling over what to do?

When you increase academic learning time by engaging students quickly in the learning process and reducing unnecessary transitions, you are sending a very definite message to students: learning is what we do in this classroom; it is so important we want to spend as much time on it as possible; let's not waste this valuable resource called time! Classrooms become more dynamic, purposeful places when this message is conveyed through efficient and effective use of time.

Monitoring Student Use of Time

As you spend time with students, you are continually monitoring their behavior and activities, as we discussed in Chapter 9. You verify whether students are following directions, completing assignments, or are otherwise busy in ways that facilitate learning. Educators often make observations about the extent to which one student or another engages in the learning process. "He's always busy," you may say of one student. Or, "She really has trouble staying on task. She only works on her assignments if she knows someone is watching her." These types of statements are generally very subjective, however, and only based on anecdotal evidence. We may not actually have an objective measure of how often either of these students is on task.

Judgments about students can be strongly influenced by the extent to which students catch our attention. We often have more positive comments to make about a student who is quiet and undemanding than about a student who is more noticeable because of fidgeting or noise. "He never sits still!" we say, but we may not know how much work the student is actually doing, which is much more important than whether the student fidgets or not. Some students can fidget and work at the same time, although they are in the minority! Chances are we know even less about the quiet student's levels of productivity because that student rarely catches our attention. The following case study illustrates how a formal observation of two students provided their teacher with a much clearer picture of their behavior than she had from just casually taking note during the course of her work.

Case Study 1

A resource teacher was interested to know how well two of her students coped with the independence expected of them in the regular classroom. Both students were attending the resource room for part of the day, but a good portion of their time was spent in the regular classroom.

The regular class teacher assured her the girl was no trouble, although she produced surprisingly little work for such a well-behaved student; the boy never accomplished much either, but he was mildly and continually disruptive, so that was only to be expected. One of the authors observed the two students at the resource teacher's request. The observation was designed to identify how each of the students spent their time, and the author was called in as an extra pair of eyes, so the class teacher could continue her teaching without interruption.

The observation took place over a ninety-minute period while the class worked on a variety of assignments and the teacher circulated or sat at her desk assisting students who requested her help. The observer recorded what each student was doing during the ninety minutes, using a timeline divided into five-minute segments to help her keep track. A portion of the timeline is reproduced here to show what her recording looked like.

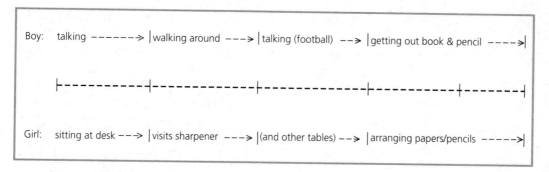

When the teacher talked to the observer at the end of the day and showed her the timeline, she was not surprised to learn the boy had spent a great deal of time at other students' tables, discussing almost anything except the assignment (how they would spend recess, the latest football games, etc.). When the teacher reminded him what he should be doing, he had sat down on the nearest empty chair and appeared to settle to work, but as soon as the teacher's back was turned he had returned to his constant cycle of visiting. As the teacher had suspected, this boy rarely sat still and made no attempt to complete his assignments: his whole focus was on socializing with his peers.

The teacher was also not surprised to find out that the girl talked very little and did not appear to disrupt the other students in any way. As she collected the materials she needed for the assignment, however, the observer had noted she stopped at several tables to see what other students were doing, without actually talking to them. She went to the pencil sharpener several times. Eventually she found a clean page in her workbook and took a considerable amount of time to carefully write the title of the assignment, as requested. She did briefly check with students sitting near her on what they were supposed to be doing, but she did not actually ever begin the assignment. Essentially this girl spent the entire class period in transition, engaged in activities preparing for learning, rather than engaging in learning itself.

On hearing the results of the observation, the teacher found it hard to believe the girl managed to spend so much time doing nothing without her detecting it or without it turning into a disruption for other students. Like many of us, she had the preconceived idea that quiet students are busy students. This is often true, but busy is not the same as engaged in learning with some degree of success, the standard required for academic learning time. In a similar fashion, behavior that is disruptive and difficult to ignore can seem to be much more severe than it really is.

Here are some general rules about observing students, which you will find useful if you are asked to be an observer or if you decide to make some observations yourself:

■ Sit where you can see what the student is doing but not so close that you distract the student.

■ If students approach you for help while you are observing, tell them you have something you must do without interruption for the next fifteen minutes (or however long the observation is to last), and you will help them later if necessary.

■ If students ask what you are doing, tell them the teacher has asked you just to watch what is happening in the classroom for a while and take notes, and the teacher may tell them about it later. Ideally, your teacher should tell the students beforehand that you are doing something important and are not to be disturbed.

■ Formal observation forms are available, but simple checklists that the teacher devises are usually perfectly adequate for this type of classroom observation. The critical feature of a good observation form is simplicity: the form must be easy to use, so it should not have long lists of possible behaviors or unnecessary detail that makes it difficult for the observer to read and record quickly.

■ It is often useful to observe a student in more than one setting, during different activities and at different times of the day, because behavior can vary enormously depending on the activity, the time of day, (e.g., whether it is before or after lunch/recess), and depending on the other students involved.

■ It is also useful to observe two students at the same time, the one causing concern alongside another student who is not, so you can make a comparison and put the behavior in a context. It may be true that a student almost never sits still, but during a preschool class activity, this might be perfectly acceptable and true of all of the students. You would not expect—or accept—the same level of movement in a tenth-grade English class, but nevertheless there can be more of a particular behavior than you realize. You may only be noticing it in one student, but it may be happening with several other students as well.

Methods for Observation and Recording

A variety of acceptable methods for formally observing student behavior and recording those observations is available. In case study 1, the observer watched the students continuously for ninety minutes and used a timeline to mark what the students were doing and how long they were doing it. Most often, however, behavior is sampled during a particular time period. This means we only observe and record a behavior for some of the time, and then we assume the sample is typical of the rest of the time as well. For example, an observer may only briefly watch and record what a student is doing once every minute (rather than for the whole minute). This may not seem very much, but even after ten minutes the observer will have ten small pieces of information about the student's behavior, which provides a fairly good idea of the ways the student is spending his time. Case study 2 provides an example.

Case Study 2

A social studies teacher is concerned that a student is not completing class assignments, even though the student is not disruptive or obviously misbehaving. The teacher asks a paraprofessional to observe the student during the fifteen minutes the students will be working on an assignment in class that day. Students will be asked to read a passage in the text and answer the ten questions that follow it. The teacher thinks that perhaps the student is visiting rather than getting on with the assignment. He does allow students to interact as they complete assignments so there is always talk in the classroom, making it difficult to decide whether that is the problem for this particular student.

The teacher gives the paraprofessional a simple observation form so she only has to make check marks against a list of items of interest, rather than writing notes as she observes the student. The form is marked off in sections, representing thirty-second intervals, and each section has a list of four behaviors: talking to another student, writing on paper or in his notebook, looking at the text, and arranging or playing with materials (such as pencil, paper, etc). The teacher asks the paraprofessional to observe the student for just the first ten minutes of the session. With behaviors recorded every thirty seconds, that will give the teacher twenty pieces of information (two times each minute for ten minutes) about what the student is doing.

The paraprofessional uses a stopwatch, and at the beginning of each thirty-second interval (when the second hand is on the 12 and on the 6), she briefly looks up at the student to see whether he is doing any of the four things the teacher has listed. She puts a check mark next to all of the ones she can see during that brief glimpse, and then she lets the remainder of the thirty seconds pass before looking up at the student again. She only checks what she sees at the beginning of each

Sample Observation Form

Talking to another student	X	X													X			X
Writing on paper or notebook					X													
Looking at the assigned text			X	X	X		X	X	X	X		X	X	X	X		X		X
Arranging materials	X	X								X						X		

interval; she does not add or change anything if the student's behavior changes during the thirty seconds because she is just sampling the student's behavior. In fact, she deliberately keeps her eyes on the stopwatch once she has observed and made the necessary check marks, so she will not be influenced by any changes in the student's behavior. At the end of the ten minutes of observation, the form she has been using looks like the one shown here.

What does the information recorded on the observation form tell the teacher about the student's behavior? What is the student actually doing during the ten minutes of observation? Write your thoughts here about what the observation has taught the teacher about why the student is not completing assignments.

_____

_____

_____

_____

You can see that this short observation was very useful to the teacher. He now knows the student's problem has little to do with visiting or wasting time. The student appears to be spending at least half of the time looking at the text, but only once does he move on to writing something. So when the teacher talks to the student about why he is not completing his assignment, he knows he does not have to reprimand the student for lack of attention to his work. The student may need help with pacing his work (moving on to answering the questions more quickly) or with something more basic such as understanding the assignment or the questions he must answer.

Observable Behaviors

An observation naturally cannot tell us what a student is thinking. Because thinking is not observable, some people would not even call it a behavior. However, an observation does give us a much clearer picture of what a student is *doing*, which gives us a clue to what may be causing a problem and what to focus on if we discuss the problem with the student. Notice that the teacher in case study 2 listed "looking at the text" as one of the behaviors on the observation form, rather than "reading the text," because silent reading is also not an observable behavior. However, the student needs to be looking at the text in order to read it, so the behavior is included that would indicate the student could be reading, rather than talking or fiddling with papers. Notice too that the behaviors listed on the observation form are not all negative. The student is allowed to talk while working and may need to arrange his writing materials. These behaviors only become negative if they get too many check marks on the observation form, showing they are all the student does during the observation, with no check marks beside the behaviors (looking at the text, writing in notebook) that suggest the student is concentrating on his assignment.

Researchers have written a great deal about the various ways we can observe student behavior and record our observations. We have only described two simple methods, but there are many others. Also, for the purposes of formal research it is usual to have two observers for part of the observation time, to verify the accuracy of the information recorded. Most teachers do not engage in such formal observations unless they are pursuing a higher degree and taking classes in research methodology. In the role of a paraprofessional, you are not likely to be asked to use more than the simple methods we have described here. Nevertheless, as you can see, even this simple method can yield useful results because it provides objective evidence, rather than leaving us to rely on subjective impressions.

If you would like to carry out an observation on a student, discuss it first with your supervisor, so you can both get advice on the most useful way of carrying out the observation and ask for your supervisor's approval. Observing a student for the purpose of improving your teaching and the student's learning process is considered acceptable without seeking consent, but parents must give their permission if an observation is to be recorded, videotaped, or seen by anyone outside the normal classroom environment.

Educator Use of Time

Time management is really all about how educators make the best use of the time available to them and their students and how to prevent disruptions. There are many strategies you can use to maximize learning for your students, and you can use the same time management techniques yourself as an adult participant in the learning process. Here are a few ideas that are effective for both students and for adults:

- Plan for planning time. We acknowledge that paraprofessionals are not often given planning time, so you may be faced with the dilemma of whether to use your own unpaid time to do your planning. Talk to your supervising teacher about the possibility of finding even ten minutes two or three times a week when you can meet together regularly to discuss your work. It is usually possible to find this length of time while students work independently on assignments. Ask your teacher if you can plan this time into the schedule, rather than hoping you will be able to find some time during the week.
- Prioritize. Because there are always more things to be done than can possibly be completed in a working day, take time to make a to-do list and clearly mark those items that should have priority. Too often we complete the pleasant tasks first and are left with the ones we enjoy less but have to be done. If you show your to-do list to your teacher and agree on priorities and who is to do what, it will help you be more effective in the many tasks required of you as an instructional team.
- Cut down on repeat tasks. Look at your classroom materials, to see where you can save time. For example, consider laminating frequently used answer sheets to preserve them and save the time it takes to make new copies.
- Think ahead. Be prepared for eventualities such as collecting homework or students who finish their work ahead of time by having a box for homework as students arrive in class or a binder with fun activities students can choose from if they finish assignments quickly.

C·H·A·P·T·E·R S·U·M·M·A·R·Y ————————————

Time is perhaps the most valuable resource you have as an educator, and how you use it can be the most important thing you do to ensure that learning takes place. You can determine how much of the time allocated to you is converted into academic learning time by using some of the techniques and strategies described in this chapter. You can now:

- Identify and show multiple ways you can increase opportunities for optimal academic learning time.
- Discuss and show several ways to decrease transition time, making transitions more smooth and efficient.
- Explain how to monitor student use of time through observation and describe various methods you can use for observation/recording student use of time.
- Demonstrate how you check your own use of time, applying the techniques and ideas that work with students to your own work.

You may be employed in a school district or school that requires paraprofessionals to keep portfolios. Some of the artifacts you may wish to include as evidence of your professional development could be data on the goals and objectives you have set for your work and accomplished. For example, you may show how student academic time was improved as a result of your goal to shorten transition time. If your teacher is able to observe and document this accomplishment, you could include it as part of your evidence. We discuss teacher observations in more detail in Section IV.

E·X·T·E·N·D·I·N·G Y·O·U·R L·E·A·R·N·I·N·G

Ideas for Facilitating Transitions

- Begin and end your teaching sessions with students at agreed times.
- A few minutes before you change to another activity, let students know a transition is about to take place, and make certain students are attending before you give directions for the transition.
- Make it clear to your students that they should only bring essential items with them when they come to work with you. This will save time removing distracting items or reminding students to keep them out of sight.
- To settle students back to work quickly after a break (such as recess), prepare a short activity that you place on their desks during the break and is waiting for them on their return.
- If students are late coming to your sessions, make sure you find out what or who caused the lateness. Be careful not to blame a student for dawdling, for example, if the teacher has kept them behind for some reason.
- Help students understand time in terms of their work. For example, "When you have finished this math worksheet, it will be time for recess," or "If you complete this assignment quickly and accurately, you'll have time to work on your other projects."

■ Students can pace their work if you have a kitchen timer as a signal to begin. Make sure you tell students how long the timer is set for, how much of the assignment needs to be finished when the timer goes off, and what they should do when they hear the timer (e.g., hand in their work or move on to the next part).

■ To get students' attention at the beginning of the class, use index cards with review questions written on them. If you distribute the cards as students are sitting down, it gives them something work oriented to focus on.

11 Student Behavior and Classroom Management

Both the physical environment and the instructional environment can have a direct impact on student behavior. In earlier chapters, we discussed effective techniques for delivering instruction. Many of you, as paraprofessionals, have roles that focus directly on supporting instruction; some of you work in situations that are less directly instructional. Whichever is the case, all of you have responsibilities for managing student behavior. This is inevitable, whatever your role: anyone who works with students is obliged to manage student behavior sooner or later—or else your behavior will be managed by your students!

In this chapter we discuss behavior management not only in terms of dealing with individual student behaviors as they occur, but also in the precedents you set for behavior and the ways in which you can strengthen students' appropriate behavior and help reduce their inappropriate behavior. This relates to the whole learning environment. Within the larger context in which you serve under the direction of your supervisor, you also need to be able to establish behavioral expectations for the groups or individuals with whom you work.

By the end of this chapter, you should be able to answer these questions correctly:

- How can I use instruction as an effective behavior management tool?
- Why are classroom rules important, and how do I teach students to adhere to them?
- What are some ways I can reward and recognize appropriate student behaviors?
- How do I deal with inappropriate behaviors?

First, we talk about the physical and instructional environment and its impact on student behavior. Effective instruction, management of time, and transitions can all influence student behavior.

We have already discussed different aspects of effective instructional techniques at some length in previous chapters, but they also belong here as an important aspect of behavior management. Effective instruction is one of the most proactive measures you can take toward managing behavior in the classroom:

- Setting work that is at an appropriate level for students' age and abilities.
- Presenting content in an engaging way and at an appropriate pace.
- Guiding students carefully through the acquisition and practice of new skills and knowledge.
- Taking all possible measures to ensure that students succeed.

The natural momentum of the effective instructional cycle draws students along with it, if it is followed sensitively and faithfully. Students who are busily engaged in stimulating and interesting lessons have no time or desire to misbehave. It is the students who are bored because the lesson content is not sufficiently challenging or feel threatened because the lesson content is too advanced or challenging who show their boredom or insecurities by misbehaving or acting out. Effective instruction not only ensures learning, it ensures engagement—a critical requirement for learning to take place and a natural controller of behavior.

Time Management and Transitions

In Chapter 10 we discussed time management: the ways in which you can increase academic learning time to its maximum and reduce unnecessary transition time. Again, the use of effective time management techniques is an excellent behavior management technique. As already discussed, not all of the available time when students attend school can be used as academic learning time. But we examined many ways in which the time allocated to learning can be used for that purpose, with students engaged in the learning process at high rates of success and transition time reduced to a necessary minimum. Excessive transition time provides too many opportunities for students to be distracted and misbehave. One of your first tasks with regard to behavior management is to establish a businesslike atmosphere, to make obvious by your focused approach that learning takes priority. Your attitude should show learning is an exciting and challenging activity that you are eager to engage in with your students. Such an attitude also helps keep students on task and reduces the likelihood of inappropriate behavior.

Thus, although effective instruction and time management practices per se are not direct behavior management techniques, they make a critical contribution by setting the stage, creating a purposeful atmosphere, and clearing the path, as it were, for direct intervention with student behavior. Students exhibit a variety of behaviors, some of which are acceptable and others that are not. As someone who works with students,

- You need to know which behaviors are generally considered appropriate within the school context.
- You must know which behaviors your supervising teacher considers appropriate for the classroom.
- You must decide which behaviors you will allow within your particular teaching situation.
- You must determine the ways in which you will communicate this to your students as well as ensure that they comply with these standards of behavior.

Managing Behavior

In some schools there seems to be a belief that behavior management can only have negative connotations because it is only related to inappropriate and negative behaviors. On the contrary, behavior management should be a proactive process of strengthening and encouraging positive behaviors and dealing with negative and in-appropriate behaviors as they arise. You do, of course, have the choice. You can focus on discouraging inappropriate behavior and trying to reduce or eradicate it. Or you can focus on increasing and encouraging appropriate behavior. But the difference is not only in the perspective but also in the results. Effective behavior management takes the positive and proactive stance of recognizing and rewarding good behavior and thus building students' ability and willingness to comply with classroom rules. This is much more effective than only focusing on inappropriate behaviors through criticism and punishment. An increase in positive behaviors naturally reduces nega-tive and inappropriate behaviors. Thus we begin here by looking at ways in which you can strengthen and encourage positive behaviors in your students, before we look at how to deal effectively with negative behaviors when they occur.

Effective teachers develop a classroom structure by

- Establishing classroom rules.
- Limiting the rules to four or five.
- Stating rules clearly and positively.
- Defining both the positive and negative consequences associated with the rules.
- Reviewing rules frequently.
- Taking cultural issues into consideration.
- Developing a risk-free environment where students know the limits.

Behavior Management in the Classroom. With this in mind, before we discuss specific behavior management techniques, take a moment to note the current be-havior management system that has been set for the learning environment in which you work. There may be no formal written plan, but even if you have only worked with teachers for a short time, you will have noticed elements of their approach to behavior management. This would include your supervising teacher's expectations of student behavior as well as the steps taken to encourage positive behaviors and discourage negative, inappropriate behaviors. Make a note of any differences in ex-pectations when the students are working with you, if any. If your supervisor is not on the same premises where you work, or your work is largely independent, write your expectations in the spaces provided that relate to the teacher.

My supervising teacher's expectations regarding student behavior:

_____

_____

_____

_____

_____

_____

_____

Steps my supervising teacher takes to encourage positive behavior and discourage negative, inappropriate behaviors:

_____

_____

_____

_____

_____

_____

_____

Differences in expectations when students are working with me rather than with the teacher:

_____

_____

_____

_____

_____

_____

_____

As you work through this chapter, you may find you have not considered some of the techniques we discuss in the notes you have written in the spaces here. You may wish to add to your notes as you identify, through the chapter, additional strategies you or your teacher use to manage student behavior, even if you have not identified them at this point.

_____

_____

_____

_____

_____

_____

Setting, Teaching, and Adhering to Classroom Rules

All team sports or games have rules of play: rules for which moves are acceptable and which are not and rules about interacting with other players and with the referee and other officials. The rules are there so all the players know what they are expected to do and the game has structure. They also let players know what they are *not* expected to do.

In the same way, the purpose of classroom rules is to let students know what is expected of them and to promote positive interactions in the classroom—student to student and student to adult. Rules also help students know what is not appropriate and thus help prevent behavior that could cause problems for the student or the teacher.

Here are some guidelines for effective classroom rules:

- Establish only four or five rules.
- State rules positively rather than negatively.
- State rules in terms of well-defined observable behaviors.
- Post the rules where all students can see them.
- State the positive and negative consequences for following/not following rules.
- Teach the rules and have students role-play examples of rule-following and rule-breaking behaviors.
- Review rules and consequences frequently—not just at the beginning of the school year or the beginning of each semester.
- Remain consistent in your enforcement of the rules.

The nearby boxes contain samples of classroom rules for younger and for older children.

Sample of Classroom Rules for Younger Children

1. Hands in your lap, feet on the floor.
2. Raise your hand before answering.
3. Be kind to others.

Sample of Classroom Rules for Older Students

1. Be in seat for roll call as the tardy bell rings.
2. Turn in assignments on time.
3. Have paper and pencil for each class.
4. Respect the rights of others to learn.

Your supervisor will already have set rules for the students you work with, even if those rules have not been posted or taught formally to the students. Make sure you know what those rules are and how they should be interpreted. If you wish to change any of those rules when you are working with a group of students, check first with your teacher to be sure there are no objections. Consistency is crucial between yourself and your supervising teacher, and you can only have consistency if each of you has a clear understanding of what is expected and what the other typically does.

Rationale for Rules

Teach students rules by providing a definition and a reason (or rationale) for each rule and then giving them many opportunities to practice role-playing examples of rule-following behavior. Although students must recognize the limits of each rule and understand rule-breaking behavior as well as rule-following behavior, remember to end on a correct example.

Students know that some rules are flexible depending on the situation, so explain to them that some rules (such as raising a hand to respond to a question) may not be necessary when they are working with you in a small group. You may include them in the decision-making process if you think it is appropriate, and do not be afraid to discuss rules and the reasons for them with your students. It is natural for them to question rules. Take the time to discuss the need for rules generally, as well as the need for specific rules if they seem interested. They will be much more willing to abide by the rules if you show you are prepared to entertain their questions and give reasonable explanations when they ask why, rather than just saying, "Because I said so." Also discuss the possible circumstances under which they can safely break a rule. The "What if . . .?" game described in the nearby box is a useful tool for exploring rules with students of any age.

What if . . .?

What if a student needs to break a rule? What will happen?

Play the "What if . . .?" game with your students to explore situations in which they might safely be able to break a rule. Take one of your class rules, for example: You need a hall pass to visit the bathroom. Ask the students to suggest circumstances when they might need to break this rule, starting with the phrase "What if . . .?"

A student may suggest "What if I'm sick and need to leave the room quickly, so I don't have time to ask for the hall pass?" Discuss that circumstance with the class and come to an agreement on whether or not that would be considered a justifiable breaking of the rule. If your students cannot think of suggestions, you can make some and ask for their reactions.

We must catch students being good. We too often focus 90 percent of our attention on the 10 percent of students who are not following the rules and then have little time left for the majority who are. We also tend to focus too often on the negative consequences of not following rules so students only think of consequences as negative. It will help if you develop a proactive plan for managing student behavior. This will guide your thinking through the teaching process in advance of working with the students. It will help you anticipate what might happen, given your knowledge of the curriculum and your knowledge of the students and their behaviors. Refer to the exercise in the Extending Your Learning section for help in developing such a proactive plan.

The ABCs of Behavior

The phrase "the ABCs of behavior" is often used in relation to behavior management. You may already be familiar with the phrase and the concepts it represents. We provide a brief overview here before moving on to behavior management techniques because as an underlying principle it may be useful to you and your students. In this setting, the letters A, B, and C stand for antecedent, behavior, and consequence.

An *antecedent* is a trigger, something that prompts or sets off a behavior. If a student laughs out loud in the middle of a quiet class session, for example, there is usually an explanation for what triggered the laugh. Perhaps another student had whispered something funny, or the student could have been reading a particularly entertaining passage in the class text, or you may have dropped a pile of papers and the student found that funny. There are any number of possible explanations for the student's behavior, any number of possible antecedents or triggers.

A *behavior*, of course, is anything a person says or does. In the strictest sense, thinking could be considered a behavior, but (as we discussed in Chapter 10) we usually only include visible, observable acts as behaviors because this is the level at which we can deal with them. In the example just given, the student's laughter is the behavior of interest, not the fact that he thought something was funny.

A *consequence* is something that follows as a result of a behavior or event. This is where we usually begin with behavior management—meting out the consequences of students' behavior. If you were in charge of a group of students, what would be the consequence associated with one of the students laughing out loud during a quiet study session? You might just give the student a warning look as a reminder to be quiet, or you might quietly investigate the cause of the laughter. Whatever you choose to do, the consequences for the student are not likely to be severe or particularly negative or long lasting.

In a different situation, in which one student provokes another (antecedent) and a fight ensues (behavior), you would of course have to intervene in a much more obvious way, and some sort of punishment or sanction (consequence) would be inevitable. See the nearby box for an example.

Now you try it. Think of a typical classroom situation in terms of the ABCs of behavior. Write the action for the antecedent, the behavior, and the consequence in the nearby box. (Hint: You may find it easiest to think of a behavior first and then decide what you think the antecedent for it might be.)

A = Antecedent	Student reaches over and provokes another student by poking him in the arm with his pencil.
B = Behavior	Students engage in fist fight.
C = Consequence	Students separated and removed from classroom.

Antecedent	(What happens first—before the noticeable behavior?)
Behavior	(The action—what you see or hear)
Consequence	(Punishment or action—usually taken by someone in authority)

Self-Determination of Behavior

Self-determination is a concept used to describe a person's ability to decide the path or action he or she will take. It is an individual's capability to meet goals and carry out personal intentions. As part of self-determination, students must take charge of their own behavior. The notion of antecedent, behavior, and consequences is a very useful one to introduce to students so they can learn to take control over their own behavior.

We talked about metacognition earlier and the importance of students becoming more aware of their learning preferences and strengths so they can begin to take responsibility for their own learning. This is the same principle applied to more general classroom behavior, rather than just learning. It applies to both positive and negative behaviors. Students can learn to identify the trigger or antecedent for a given behavior; they can decide whether they will react to it or ignore it; and they therefore can choose the consequences that will ensue. This idea is a revelation for many students, particularly those who are inclined to inappropriate behavior. We often hear students protest, "He made me do it!" when their poor behavior is questioned, as if they had no choice.

We should also mention here that behavioral differences exist among cultures. The norms of a culture often help dictate the way a student will or should act. This can create problems for students who appear not to be able or willing to retaliate (stand up for themselves), and it can also create problems for those students who feel they must live up to their cultural norms by being—or appearing to be—macho. The adults in the classroom must be aware of these cultural norms and understand that a student's behavior is likely to be influenced by such factors as the loss of status he might face with his peer group or gang. This influence of culture is something you may wish to learn more about, and there are usually classes available that help school personnel gain more in-depth information about cultures. We recommend you seek these out. But you can also learn by observing the students. Understand that many factors influence behavior—culture, family expectations, developmental ages and stages of children and youth, and so on. Although the principle of ABCs can explain a lot, antecedents can differ greatly for individual students because their background and personality make them sensitive to different triggers.

Adults and Behavior

The ABCs apply to you as an adult in the classroom as well as to your students. Your behavior is triggered by things the students say and do. It is also triggered by what other adults, such as the teacher, say and do. And there will be the consequences of your actions—good and bad. However, you too can exercise self-determination and shape events in the classroom by being more aware of what triggers your behavior and then choosing whether to react or ignore.

Consider this situation: a student shouts out an answer instead of raising her hand according to class rules. How do you handle this antecedent provided by the student? And what will be the likely consequences? Fill in your responses in the box below.

Antecedent	What happens first? *Student shouts out an answer to your question instead of raising her hand.*
Behavior	Your typical reaction:
Consequence	The likely result of your reaction:

- Will you rebuke the student, feeling the rebuke is justified because the student has broken a class rule?
- Or will you choose to ignore the shouting out, hoping the student will realize her error and self-correct?
- Or will you remind the student (gently) of the class rule and give her a chance to answer the question in the appropriate manner?

You generally have the choice among all of these alternatives. And your choice can be directed by the potential consequences of each alternative. Like your students, you can choose the outcome. The consequence of your behavior (triggered by the student shouting out) would be quite different in each of these cases:

- If the student is rebuked, she may become less cooperative and you will have more inappropriate behavior to deal with.
- If the student is ignored she may realize her error and self-correct, which would be a very positive consequence.
- If you gently remind the student of the appropriate behavior and then give her a chance to respond appropriately, the consequence should also be a positive interaction between you and the student.

Like the instructional cycle, this sequence of A >> B >> C is cyclical. Consider this situation: A student reads a funny story (A) and laughs out loud in class (B), which leads to criticism (C) from the teacher because the rest of the class is reading quietly. The student feels the criticism (A) is unduly harsh and complains (B) she could not help laughing, so the teacher tells her she must lose her recess (C) for her rudeness.

Notice that the first consequence—criticism from the teacher—becomes the antecedent for the student's next behavior (complaining that she could not help laughing). This behavior then leads to another consequence, and so the cycle continues.

```
        A                B                C
Funny story >> student laughs >> Teacher criticizes
                         Teacher criticizes >> student complains >> Loses recess
                                A                    B                 C
```

This again highlights the role you play as an adult in the constant cycle of antecedents, behaviors, and consequences in the classroom. The consequence you choose to impose in response to a student's behavior has a direct effect on subsequent student behavior. Notice how many opportunities there are for choice in this short sequence of events:

- The student could have chosen not to complain.
- Perhaps she was justified in her complaint, but she could have chosen to express her indignation a little less strongly.
- The teacher could have chosen to address the issues of fairness and rudeness separately.
- The teacher could have chosen to be less harsh in her criticism or in the punishment imposed for rudeness.

Whatever the exact truth of the situation, both the student and the teacher in the example had choices, and generally so do you. Notice that it is usually a choice between adding to the negative aspect of a situation by reacting harshly or critically to a student's poor behavior or minimizing the effects of the poor behavior by using it as a teaching moment and dealing with it fairly, firmly, and reasonably.

We are not suggesting that you tolerate inappropriate student behavior; we are advocating thoughtful consideration of outcomes. There are positive ways of dealing with negative behavior. The challenge you face is to use positive methods so you communicate to the student that the behavior is unacceptable but you are prepared to continue to work with him or her. After all, the way you deal with a student's behavior will help determine how that student behaves subsequently. This is true of negative and positive behaviors, and you set the precedent. Positive outcomes are more likely to lead to positive behaviors and vice versa. You can choose which will predominate in your classroom.

The Truth About Consequences

Let's stop and consider a word we have been using in relation to rules and behavior management: *consequences*. If a student asked you what the word meant, what would you say? And what example could you give of a consequence related to the classroom? Take a moment to write your thoughts here.

The word *consequence* means _____

_____

_____

_____

An example of a consequence in a classroom setting is _____

_____

_____

_____

_____

_____

In the most basic sense, a consequence is the natural result of an action or event: for example, the sun sets and it gets dark. All too often in a classroom context the only examples of consequences that students hear about are negative ones resulting from an infringement of a rule or noncompliance of some sort. However, the word *consequence* is not negative by definition. Consequences can be both positive and negative, and indeed the positive and negative are often two sides of the same coin. If a student infringes a rule, there is almost always a negative consequence, but if a student obeys a rule, there should just as inevitably be an obvious positive consequence.

We have already discussed classroom rules and talk later about the importance of establishing clear procedures for the learning environment in which you work. But this is a good time to remind ourselves of the need to do the following:

■ Establish with students that all rules have both positive and negative consequences associated with them.
■ Help students see they can choose to work for the positive consequences or choose to suffer the negative consequences.
■ Be both willing and determined, as an adult, to apply the consequences that the student chooses, being just as consistent and clear in ensuring positive consequences as negative.

As part of this process of ensuring that students experience both positive and negative consequences according to the choices they make with regard to classroom and school rules and procedures, list here some of the rules you identified in the earlier section, and write beside them the positive consequences associated with compliance with the rule and the negative consequences associated with noncompliance. If you find any difficulties with either the positive or negative consequences, take the time to think the rule through and identify a consequence you think would be appropriate. You may wish to check with your supervisor if you are not sure whether your ideas would be acceptable.

Rule 1 _____

_____

Positive consequence(s) if student complies: _____

_____

_____

Negative consequence(s) if student does not comply: _____

_____

_____

Rule 2 _____

_____

Positive consequence(s) if student complies: _____

_____

_____

Negative consequence(s) if student does not comply: _____

_____

_____

Rule 3 _____

_____

Positive consequence(s) if student complies: _____

_____

_____

Negative consequence(s) if student does not comply: _____

_____

_____

Classroom Routines and Procedures

How can you establish clear routines and procedures for your students? As well as the rules for general behavior, there are routines and procedures that are important for students to follow. This links back to the idea of reducing transition time. If students know classroom procedures, the routine runs more smoothly and efficiently and less time is wasted. As with the rules, you need to check what your supervising teacher considers the appropriate procedure for a variety of different situations (when students finish work, when the bell rings for recess, when they need to visit the bathroom, etc.) and the regular routines the students should follow. As with the rules, there should be consequences for not following proper procedures and routines, but bear in mind the earlier discussion about being fair, firm, and positive in your reactions with your students, so inappropriate behavior is dealt with quickly and without unnecessary fuss.

It is also useful to develop a teaching sequence—a plan of action—that both you and your supervisor use to respond to students who do not follow the rules and procedures. This lets the students know there are consistent consequences if they choose not to follow the rules and procedures and that they cannot play you off against the teacher and vice versa. Notice that the teaching sequence describes a variety of strategies for dealing with inappropriate behavior, starting with the least obtrusive (or most subtle) and leading to more deliberate interventions that can be used if the less obtrusive ones do not seem to work. This underlines an important principle in behavior management: always use the least intrusive or restrictive intervention first. If you come down heavily on a student from the start, you have few options left if that one does not work.

Here is an example of a teaching sequence you can use:

Planned ignoring. The first time a student calls out (or breaks any class rule), it usually makes sense to ignore the behavior. Do not pay attention to the student in any way. Of course, if a student is doing something potentially harmful to himself or someone else, you must take the appropriate action.

Prompt. If the behavior persists, show the student in a subtle way that you have noticed the inappropriate behavior. Teachers are famous for what many students call "The Look" to prompt a student to be quiet or raise her hand; proximity control (moving closer to the misbehaving student) also generally works well to redirect students' attention; and a short verbal cue or physical gesture can also remind a student of the rule.

Praise around. Acknowledging other students who are following rules and who can be recognized or praised is another method of prompting the student who is not following the rules. If you use a statement that specifies the behavior for which the student is being recognized (e.g., "Thanks for raising your hand, Adam. What do you think the answer is?"), you can use the "praise around" as a reminder of appropriate behavior for the student who did not follow the rule or procedure.

Catch students being good. When a student who typically calls out actually raises his hand before responding, be sure to acknowledge this appropriate behavior so you increase the chance of it happening again. Students often misbehave to get attention. If you give students attention for good behavior, you eliminate one of the most powerful reasons why they misbehave.

Teaching interaction. There will always be times when students somehow miss all the cues and prompts you give them. In this situation, look on misbehavior as an opportunity to teach or reteach a rule or expectation. If possible, do this quietly without drawing attention to the student. Describe the problem behavior in nonjudgmental terms, say why it is a problem, and have the student tell you what he should be doing instead. Then give the student an opportunity to do it, and praise him for doing

Checklist

_____ Am I using effective instructional practices in my teaching?

_____ Does the student who is experiencing behavioral difficulties have the skills to do the assignment I have given?

_____ Is the assignment just difficult enough to be challenging to the students, rather than too easy or beyond the students' capabilities?

_____ Have I reviewed the rules recently—either with this student or with the whole group?

_____ Am I reinforcing and providing positive consequences for students who are following the rules?

_____ Am I consistently applying clear consequences when students do not follow the rules?

what he should. If a particular behavior seems to be a problem for several students, it is a good indication you may need to review rules with a group or with the whole class.

Trouble-shooting

Classrooms are very dynamic environments with many things happening—all at the same time. If you have a student who is still acting out, you may want to go through a series of activities from the checklist in the nearby box to help you evaluate the situation.

If you cannot answer yes or check off all of the questions in the list, take the necessary steps to remedy the situation because a lack of attention to any one of these areas could be a trigger for a student's misbehavior. If you feel you can answer yes to all of the questions and you still find yourself frustrated by certain students or certain behaviors, you may want to teach your students a self-management procedure such as the one we describe next.

Student Self-Management

Self-management typically consists of having students monitor and keep a record of their own performance, in order to evaluate and rate that performance against a standard. This (1) helps the student become more aware of his behavior, and (2) provides the student with a yardstick for his behavior as he compares his own perceptions of his behavior with those of someone else. Consider the case of Joe.

Case Study: Joe

Joe constantly interrupted instruction and talked out during class. Whenever anyone tried to prompt him to change his behavior, Joe would get quite upset and insist he or she was picking on him. He usually got so upset that he had to leave class to calm down.

We decided to teach Joe to monitor his own behavior. In a private conversation before class, we told him of our concerns about the number of times he called out in class. He admitted that he sometimes did call out but protested we were just picking on him because it really was not that often. We challenged him to keep track of his behavior by making a tally mark on a piece of paper each time he spoke out in class and making it into a plus sign if he had raised his hand and waited for the teacher to acknowledge him before he spoke. After 30 minutes we looked at the paper together and counted up the tally marks and the pluses. Joe was quite surprised to see there were 54 tally marks—and no pluses!

At this point we talked to Joe about setting a reasonable goal to change his behavior. Joe thought he could reduce the number of times he interrupted by half each day. We agreed that every time he met this goal he could have five minutes of free time at the end of class. By the end of the week, Joe had reduced the number of times he interrupted to two to three per class period, and he was given the agreed five minutes of free time every day. The following week he had no difficulties raising his hand to get the teacher's attention before commenting or responding to a question.

There are other more complex methods of self-management that we cannot cover in this text, but all begin with these basic principles of managing behavior. So if you have a student whose behavior is of concern, you may wish to try this simple method first. You can often accomplish a great deal just by making the student aware of his behavior and allowing him to take responsibility for making the necessary changes, as well as deciding what positive consequences there will be for improvements.

Rewarding/Recognizing Appropriate Behaviors

We have talked about positive consequences for appropriate behavior, which is often couched in terms of rewards or recognition of some sort. Take a moment to note the different types of rewards that you make available to your students for appropriate behavior and the different types of recognition they can receive.

Rewards and recognition that are available to my students:

_____

_____

_____

_____

_____

_____

_____

_____

Rewards and recognition can take many forms. You may have listed points or tokens, free time, choice of activities, or something less tangible, such as praise or other forms of verbal approval. What do you consider to be the purpose of such rewards and recognition?

I give rewards to my students for good behavior because:

_____

_____

_____

_____

_____

The purpose of rewarding and recognizing positive and appropriate behavior is to strengthen or reinforce that behavior and increase the chances of it happening again. We want students to behave appropriately, so we give them positive feedback or consequences when they do. Nevertheless, no one thing is guaranteed to be rewarding. Remember: *rewards and recognition are not appreciated equally by all students.*

Consider your own preferences. At the end of a tiring and busy week, if you have the time and means to reward yourself, what is your choice of reward?

A long soak in the bath and an early night?

A movie?

A solitary walk?

A night out with friends?

You may work with colleagues who have similar tastes, but it would not be unusual to find quite different ideas of what is rewarding, even among a family group or friends. Similarly, there is likely to be quite a range of ideas about what would be a welcome reward for good behavior or completion of assignments among your students. Rewards also differ in appropriateness according to the age, ability, and culture of students. So you may choose something you think would be rewarding to students, but unless they see it the same way, it will not serve its intended purpose and strengthen positive behavior. Beware of giving more work as a reward for completed assignments. For many students it will be a discourager and deterrent to work. It will certainly slow them down and likely get them into the bad habit of stretching out assignments to the allotted time rather than finishing as quickly as possible.

Here are some basic principles to remember and apply in relation to rewards:

■ Rewards should be *simple and nondisruptive.* If the giving of rewards or recognition of appropriate behavior interrupts the teaching/learning process, you need to simplify. Like the quick response to a correct answer, which we discussed earlier, a brief word of recognition is all that is required. Even rewards that are cumulative and delayed are usually most effective if they are simple and to the point.

■ Rewards should be *realistic.* Promises of trips to Disneyland (or even to a more modest local attraction) are worthless if you cannot realistically organize, schedule, and finance them. Such promises quickly become counterproductive as students realize you cannot deliver. Your time commitment must be worth it, too.

■ Rewards should be *on an appropriate scale.* Do not teach your students to expect huge rewards for regular completion of daily assignments.

■ Rewards must be *equitable, fair, and consistent.* Specific behaviors should generate specific rewards in a consistent manner. If distinctions must be made between what one student has to do to receive a particular reward and what another student has to do to receive the same reward, both students must understand why there is a difference in the requirements. It is perfectly feasible to make distinctions, as long as students understand that *equal* does not always mean *same.*

In summary, rewards should be simple and nondisruptive, realistic, on an appropriate scale, and equitable, fair, and consistent. Ideally, success should be its own reward. This is one of our aims as educators: to help students reach a point where they experience the intrinsic motivation of learning for its own sake. The purpose of using rewards (extrinsic motivators) with students is to encourage them to engage in the learning process, until they experience success and want to continue (intrinsic motivation), even without extrinsic motivators or rewards.

Private or Public Recognition?

Another decision, in relation to rewards and recognition of positive behavior, is the extent to which you publicize individual student achievement. Some students are comfortable with public recognition of achievement; others may be acutely embarrassed by it, and you must consider this when you recognize individual students and their achievements.

Recognition given during the course of instruction may well have a public element to it because the classroom is not generally a private place. However, if the recognition is brief, as recommended in order not to disrupt learning, the degree to which it is publicized is minimal. After all, we can reward or recognize students discreetly via a token or points system, or those same systems can have a very public aspect if we post points or introduce competition and team participation. Perhaps it is not so much that the words *reward* and *recognize* mean different things—they are essentially synonymous—but that you need to decide the extent to which your reward or recognition system is to be public or private.

- Check with your supervisor to be sure the reward system you are going to use is acceptable.
- Be aware of possible objections by parents to certain types of rewards (e.g., if a child who has diabetes or is overweight is not allowed candy, candy should not be used as a reward for any child in the class).
- Be aware of cultural differences when considering the appropriateness of rewards.

Take time to think through the details of your reward system, and write what you currently use as a reward or recognition system. Then ask yourself the questions that follow.

The reward (or recognition) system I currently use is

_____

_____

_____

_____

_____

_____

How do I ensure it is equitable?

_____

_____

_____

_____

How do I ensure it is reasonable?

_____

_____

_____

_____

In what ways is it realistic?

_____

_____

_____

_____

How have I adjusted for students with cultural issues (e.g., a student who does not want to be recognized publicly for good work)?

_____

_____

_____

_____

_____

CHAPTER SUMMARY

Instruction and the classroom environment can have a direct impact on student behavior. In this chapter we discussed some effective strategies you can use in your job as a paraprofessional who supports instruction and managing student behavior.

After reading and completing the activities in this chapter you have learned the following:

- To use instruction to assist in managing student behavior.
- To set classroom rules and teach students to adhere to them.
- To reward and recognize appropriate student behaviors.
- To deal with inappropriate behaviors.
- To have a culturally sensitive, nonthreatening classroom environment.

The Extending Your Learning sections will give you: a brief overview of applied behavior analysis (ABA), a formal system for changing behavior that is often used in special education settings; a quick quiz to test the knowledge you have gained from the chapter; and a method for taking a proactive approach to managing the setting in which you work.

E-X-T-E-N-D-I-N-G—Y-O-U-R—L-E-A-R-N-I-N-G

Applied Behavior Analysis

Applied behavior analysis (or ABA) is an approach to behavior management you may have heard of, particularly if you have worked in special education settings. A very systematic and scientific approach to behavior change, it is often called *behavior modification* when used in the classroom. Although ABA is used most frequently in a special education setting rather than in the regular classroom, it can have useful applications in many settings and can be used with an individual, with a group, or with a whole class of students. In essence, ABA carefully documents a specific student behavior and then documents the effects (if any) of intervening to change that behavior—either to reduce a negative behavior or to increase a positive behavior. The underlying principle is that all student behavior is triggered by something in the classroom environment, and the behavior can be changed by modifying some aspect of the environment. That aspect may be something in the physical arrangement, a classroom procedure, something that the teacher says or does, or something another student says or does.

In its pure form, ABA is complex and therefore usually only used with fairly severe behaviors. It is not an approach you are likely to use yourself, but you may work with a teacher who is using some of its principles or you may be required to collect data on a student who has a behavior change plan that is using ABA. These are some of the salient features of applied behavior analysis:

- The focus is on a specific student behavior, such as violent outbreaks in class or noncompletion of assignments; the behavior must be carefully defined and specific (e.g., "acting out" would be considered too vague).
- Frequent collection and graphing of data is characteristic: first to establish a baseline of the current level of the behavior of interest and then on an ongoing basis to document any changes in behavior.
- Desirable changes in behavior can include a decrease in a negative behavior (e.g., swearing), an increase in a positive behavior (e.g., attendance at

school), or greater consistency of a behavior (which is essentially a simultaneous increase in a positive behavior and decrease in a negative behavior).

▪ Interventions selected should be simple and easy to implement without disrupting other students or the learning environment (e.g., a simple token reward system). A package consisting of several interventions is not advisable because if the student's behavior changes, there is no way of knowing which part of the package produced the change; the complexity of the package may be totally unnecessary—one simple aspect of it may have been enough, but it is impossible to tell which was the critical element.

▪ The selected student behavior must be easily observed and measurable as well as frequent; observations can take place in a variety of settings, but the same recording system should be used each time so comparisons can be made (see Chapter 10 on observation of student behavior).

▪ The environment in which the intervention takes place must be very carefully controlled to ensure no other changes are made along with the selected intervention, so if the student's behavior changes, it will be reasonable to assume the effect is due to the deliberate intervention.

▪ There are mechanisms used in research to increase confidence in the efficacy of the intervention. One of these is the use of a reversal technique. If an inappropriate behavior decreases with the introduction of an intervention (say, a reward system), the researcher may withdraw the reward system for a few days to see if the behavior reverts to previous unacceptable levels and then reinstate the reward system to see if the behavior improves again. This type of manipulation is only justifiable if the inappropriate behavior presents no danger to the student or others, and it is generally only considered necessary in a controlled research setting.

Proactive Planning

Students need to learn many behavioral skills. You can be proactive and develop instructional strategies to teach these to your students. Here are some behavioral skills to consider:

▪ Using free time wisely
▪ Solving problems
▪ Accepting responsibility
▪ Working cooperatively in a group
▪ Requesting information or directions
▪ Following directions
▪ Following rules
▪ Learning to live with "wrong answers"

We discussed the last two points in this chapter and earlier. Use the form provided to help you develop plans for teaching these or other skills. The example we have given addresses the skill of taking risks without fear of ridicule.

Proactive Planning for Effective Management of Student Behavior

Before: What strategies will I use?	During: How do the students react to the strategy?	After: What changes should I make, in light of what happened?
Example: I will develop a classroom in which students can take risks and make mistakes without feeling stupid, by telling the students it is better to answer a question and learn whether the answer is wrong than it is to avoid answering the question and not knowing if you were right or wrong.	I told the students that everyone makes mistakes and it is better to answer a question and learn than to avoid answering a question. Later, Bobbie answered a math question wrong and Jose laughed. After giving the right answer, I reminded Jose that everyone should try, and no one is to laugh at a mistake. Cami pointed out to Jose that at least Bobbie had had the courage to try. Jose apologized!	I think I'll still need to remind them that it's OK to give a wrong answer, before I start asking questions. And then I'll praise them for their courage if they do get an answer wrong (they seemed to like it when Cami suggested it took courage).

Application Activity

Here's a chance for you to check and see how much of the information you remember from this chapter. The answers are provided, but try to respond to the questions without looking at the answers until you are finished.

Information Check

1. Sometimes students misbehave because the curriculum supplied to them is:
   a. too difficult
   b. too easy
   c. does not seem to apply to their lives
   d. all of the above
2. A child sees candy in the grocery store checkout line. The child starts screaming and crying for her mother to give her the candy. The mother gives the candy to the child. She stops crying. If the consequence is what the mother

   does (gives the child candy), the behavior is ＿＿＿＿＿＿＿＿＿＿＿＿＿

   and the antecedent event is ＿＿＿＿＿＿＿＿＿＿＿＿＿

   ＿＿＿＿＿＿＿＿＿＿＿＿＿＿＿＿＿＿＿＿＿＿＿＿＿＿

3. True/False? One of the ways that teachers can build positive relationships with their students is to attend more frequently to positive behaviors than negative.
4. A teacher reminds students of the class rules. She explains to them that the purpose of the rules is to maintain order in the classroom and those who do not follow the rules will be sent to the office. In this case, being sent to the office is
   a. a consequence
   b. an antecedent event
   c. a behavior

Answers

1. D
2. A = Seeing the candy; B = screaming and crying; C = giving the child candy. Discussion: In evaluating this set of actions, you may find you do not agree with the consequence. You may believe the mother should not have given the child candy because the next time she sees candy she may scream and cry until the mother gives her candy again. It may be easy to see that the mother is giving the child a positive consequence for bad (or negative) behavior. This happens when people do not take time to think carefully about what they are doing. You may see this in a classroom. Students who need or want attention frequently get out of their seats or use behavior to get the teacher's attention. This may be negative attention; that is, the teacher tells the student to get back in his seat, but it is still attention—and that is what the student wants.
3. True
4. A

Do you have questions about what triggers the students' behavior? We suggest you ask the students: Why do they complain? Why do they comply? Also, ask them to identify possible triggers for their compliance/good work. The more they understand why they do what they do, the more in control they will be of their behavior.

Dealing with Inappropriate Behaviors

■ Some students misbehave (for a variety of reasons) despite the proactive measures you take of establishing a positive classroom climate and using effective instructional techniques. These behaviors may be limited to individuals or they may be more widespread in the class.

■ One of the important aspects of behavior change is to make students more aware of their own behavior and get them to take responsibility for it. Many students who misbehave are really not aware of how inappropriate their behavior is or how frequently it is inappropriate. They may need frequent reminders, but the intervals of appropriate behavior should lengthen as they become more aware of their behavior.

■ Refer back to the beginning of this chapter. It is more effective to focus on increasing positive behaviors than reducing negative behaviors. This principle of focusing on positive behavior applies not just as a proactive preventive measure to reduce the likelihood of negative behaviors ever occurring but also as a remedial approach to reduce these behaviors if they do occur. The appropriate behavior you choose to focus on and the inappropriate behavior you are trying to eradicate need to be mutually exclusive—the student is unlikely or unable to do both at the same time—so in building the positive opposite of the undesirable behavior, you naturally reduce the undesirable. Refer to the nearby box for an example.

Reducing or Eliminating a Behavior

Rubin shouts out the answer to a math problem without raising his hand (the behavior to reduce or eliminate).

Teacher/Paraprofessional says, "Remember to raise your hand before answering" and then calls on a student (Miguel), who is raising his hand. Teacher says, "Yes, Miguel, that's correct, and thank you for raising your hand."

Teacher offers more opportunities for students to answer math problems while watching for Rubin to raise his hand. As soon as Rubin's hand goes up, the teacher calls on him and says, "Thank you for raising your hand. What's the answer, Rubin?" Thus the teacher catches Rubin doing what he is supposed to, and she praises him for doing it.

■ Suggest that students be involved in keeping track of their own behavior and devise a recording system that is simple enough for the student to use without disrupting engagement in learning. Absolute accuracy is not critical in this recording and students have to be trusted to be honest, but the fact that you are asking students to record and report increasingly positive behavior will be much more motivating than asking them to record and report a negative behavior, even if it is decreasing.

■ Add other ideas you glean from your teacher, other teachers, or paraprofessionals.

IV

Professionalism

In this section of the book, we look at a number of issues relating to professionalism. Chapter 12, "Professional and Ethical Behavior," considers aspects of professionalism you should be aware of as a paraprofessional, including confidentiality as a legal requirement, dress and appearance, health and safety, and communications with other adults, including parents. As you ensure you are conducting yourself in a professional manner, you not only improve your efficacy as a paraprofessional but also represent the school system in an appropriate way.

Chapter 13 discusses reflection and self-evaluation. The notion of the reflective practitioner is not entirely new to teachers, but it has not been used extensively with paraprofessionals. As part of a professional approach to your work, we suggest you reflect regularly on what you do, whether it seems to work well, and what you should change to enhance effectiveness. We also offer suggestions on how you can conduct objective evaluations of your own work, as well as seeking advice from your supervising teacher on how you can improve your practice.

CHAPTER

12 Professional and Ethical Behavior

Other paraprofessionals (such as paramedics and paralegals) are expected to adhere to the standards of their profession. You are considered a *para*professional, or paraeducator, rather than a professional educator, but you must still behave in a professional way. We first consider who or what defines professional behavior and then look at some specific examples of the standards of behavior that might govern your chosen profession.

By the end of this chapter, you should be able to answer these questions:

- Professionalism includes many aspects. Who decides what professional behavior is?
- What are the dress and appearance requirements for my work?
- What are the confidentiality requirements?
- When I work with teachers and parents, what must I do to be a professional team member?
- Do I know my role and responsibilities?
- What can I do to communicate effectively with my teacher(s) and others?
- What are the steps I can take to resolve conflict?
- Do I know my responsibilities regarding health and safety issues?

Who Decides What Constitutes Professional Behavior?

It is often assumed that paraprofessionals know how they are expected to behave and the standards they are expected to meet, even though training may not have been offered to identify those behaviors and standards. One of the difficulties lies in the lack of explicit standards for paraprofessionals. Differences of opinion among professional educators regarding what constitutes professional behavior for paraprofessionals is another source of potential difficulty.

Professional Associations and Standards

Many professionals belong to associations, such as the American Medical Association (AMA) for doctors or the American Psychological Association (APA) for psychologists. Some of the teachers you work with probably belong to the American Federation of Teachers (AFT) or the National Education Association (NEA), the

Council for Exceptional Children Performance-Based Standards for Paraeducators (1998)

Standard 1: Foundations

Knowledge: Purposes of programs for individuals with exceptional learning needs.

Basic educational terminology.

Standard 2: Development and characteristics of learners

Knowledge: Effects an exceptional condition(s) can have on an individual's life.

Standard 3: Individual learning differences

Knowledge: Rights and responsibilities of families and children.

Indicators of abuse and neglect.

Standard 4: Instructional strategies

Knowledge: Basic instructional and remedial strategies and materials.

Basic technologies appropriate to exceptional learning needs.

Standard 5: Learning environments/social interactions

Knowledge: Demands of various learning environments.

Rules and procedural safeguards regarding the management of behaviors.

Standard 6: Language

Knowledge: Characteristics of appropriate communication with stakeholders.

Standard 7: Instructional planning

Standard 8: Assessment

Knowledge: Rationale for assessment.

Standard 9: Professional and ethical practice

Knowledge: Ethical practices for confidential communication about individuals with exceptional learning needs.

Personal cultural biases and differences that affect one's ability to work with others.

Skills: Perform responsibilities as directed in a manner consistent with laws and policies.

Follow instructions of the professional.

Demonstrate problem-solving, flexible thinking, and conflict management techniques, and analysis of personal strengths and preferences.

Act as a role model for individuals with exceptional learning needs.

(continued)

> Demonstrate commitment to assisting learners in achieving their highest potential.
>
> Demonstrate the ability to separate personal issues from one's responsibilities as a paraeducator.
>
> Maintain a high level of competence and integrity.
>
> Exercise objective and prudent judgment.
>
> Demonstrate proficiency in academic skills, including oral and written communication.
>
> Engage in activities to increase personal knowledge and skills.
>
> Engage in self-assessment.
>
> Accept and use constructive feedback.
>
> Demonstrate ethical practices as guided by the CEC Code of Ethics and other standards and policies.
>
> **Standard 10: Collaboration**
>
> Knowledge: Common concerns of families of individuals with exceptional learning needs.
>
>   Roles of stakeholders in planning an individualized program.

two largest professional associations for teachers and other education personnel in the United States. Each of these professional associations has a set of written standards to which members are expected to adhere. They are essentially codes of conduct that describes how members should and should not behave in a variety of situations. When a member contravenes the professional standards of conduct, the organization representing the profession may impose disciplinary action, and in extreme cases the professional who breaks the code of conduct may even lose membership in the organization.

No corresponding professional association or set of required professional behaviors exists for paraprofessionals working in education, although as we discussed earlier, several organizations have suggested standards for paraprofessionals' work. In Chapter 3 we referred you to the Council for Exceptional Children (CEC), which has published standards for paraprofessionals working in special education, and the National Resource Center for Paraprofessionals (NRCP), which has also suggested standards for paraprofessionals working in a variety of different settings. The nearby box provides a brief review of the CEC performance-based standards and the knowledge that paraprofessionals are expected to have if they work in special education programs. Notice that Standard 9 directly addresses professional and ethical practice, so we have also included the skills, or application portion, of this standard in the box.

In the absence of a single professional association for paraprofessionals, standards such as those proposed by the CEC or the NRCP are voluntary, and no outside organization exists to bring disciplinary action for unprofessional behavior, although school administrators can do that if a paraprofessional acts in a way considered inappropriate by school district standards.

Ethics

An important part of professionalism is that we act in an appropriate manner because we know it is right, not just because someone is policing our behavior. We behave in a particular way because we have certain beliefs, and integrity requires us to act according to those beliefs. This is what is meant by ethical behavior or ethics: behavior governed by principles. Individuals can have considerable differences of opinion about what is right or wrong behavior, and some of those differences are cultural, but everyone's behavior is governed—consciously or subconsciously—by inner beliefs.

Take a moment to consider your basic beliefs regarding how you should behave as a paraprofessional. We asked you earlier in the book to think about your basic beliefs regarding students and why they come to school, as well as your beliefs about how your work helps carry out the purposes of the educational system. Here consider how you feel a paraprofessional should behave toward students and also toward other adults who work in the school or participate in school activities (such as parents, school and district administrators, etc.).

I believe that paraprofessionals should

1. _____

_____

_____

2. _____

_____

_____

3. _____

_____

_____

In your statement of beliefs you may have listed a set of principles that govern your behavior (such as having respect, showing courtesy, or being trustworthy) or you may have listed examples of how you feel you should behave in particular situations (e.g., I believe a paraprofessional should always be willing to do what a supervising teacher asks). If you have listed principles, try to give an example of how a paraprofessional who believed in that principle should behave in a given situation. If you have done the latter and listed situations and how you should react to them, rather than principles, try and attach a principle to each one.

Although this exercise can be quite difficult, it will help deepen your thinking. In the nearby box are some examples of principles and situations that may help you with the exercise. Some of the spaces have been left blank for you to fill in, and you can add items from your own statement of beliefs at the bottom. Your examples may be quite different from the ones we have included, which is quite natural because your own working situation and personal set of beliefs will dictate what is most important to you at the moment.

What principles should govern a paraprofessional's behavior?	What would that principle look like in action?
Example: *Trust*	*Doing what I say I will, or keeping information confidential.*
Example: *Showing respect*	*Treating all students fairly.*
Example: *Being responsible*	*Knowing what my duties are and carrying them out promptly.*
	Asking the supervising teacher's advice on how to help a particular student.
Keeping confidentiality	
Respecting diversity	

When you read our examples you may not quite agree with the principle we chose as represented in the situation. But that, too, is part of your own individual perspective. For the example of showing respect, we wrote "Treat all students fairly," but you may have written, "Listen carefully when a student talks to me." You may feel a paraprofessional who promptly carries out her duties is demonstrating trust or dependability, rather than being responsible. You may have described quite a different example of respect. Sometimes the words we have used will be synonyms for the ones you have chosen; sometimes quite a different principle will emerge from the situation for you than it did for us. However, the purpose of the exercise is not to give the one absolute right answer; it is to have you think more carefully about some of the principles you believe should govern your behavior as a paraprofessional and how those principles would be acted out in everyday workplace situations.

As a matter of interest, take another look at the list of principles you listed. Are some of them the same as those adopted by teachers you work with when they set classroom rules for the students? Often teachers will share with you the reasons why they do the things they do; it may sound reasonable to you and match your principles—so you adopt it. This is just another great way to enhance your actions on the job.

Situations Requiring Professionalism

Now that we have considered who or what determines professional behavior, we need to consider specific examples of situations in which you may find yourself and how truly professional paraprofessionals might conduct themselves. Professionalism covers all of the following:

- Dress and appearance
- Confidentiality and the use of information
- Working relationships with other adults
- Communication and conflict resolution
- Health and safety issues

We cover each of these areas separately and emphasize the proactive measures you can take to demonstrate professionalism. All of the suggestions we make for proactive measures are appropriate and should not offend professionals or other adults you work with. You can plan your actions ahead of time, rather than always having to react or make a series of instant decisions throughout the day. As a paraprofessional working with students, you already make hundreds of decisions during your working day, but many things can be decided ahead of time, which makes it much easier to make reasonable decisions.

Dress and Appearance

Your appearance and the way you present yourself say a great deal about you. Although we can be very mistaken about a person's character if we only judge him or her by looks, taking care with your dress and appearance will make a positive visual impression on those who you work with and those who may visit your workplace. Your school or school district may have a dress code to which you are expected to adhere, but it is probably expressed in very general terms.

Be proactive:

■ Find a copy of your school and/or school district dress code or guidelines for how paraprofessionals should present themselves; then
■ Consider your own appearance in the light of the dress code or guidelines, and make any necessary changes so you meet the required standard.

If no guidelines are available for how a paraprofessional should dress:

■ Check for guidelines on teacher/professional dress and appearance; then
■ Seek the advice of your supervising teacher about whether you should adopt the teacher's dress code, and make any necessary changes to your dress and/or appearance.

As in many areas, there are no absolute standards for what would be considered appropriate dress because of local cultural and social influences, but common sense dictates you should dress in a way that allows you to carry out your responsibilities easily, with clothes that are practical enough to permit you to do your job efficiently. Modest clothing is generally preferred, as is slogan-free clothing. In the absence of any guidelines relating to dress for teachers or paraprofessionals, most schools and districts have a dress code for students, which would give you a good starting place for checking whether your dress and appearance meet reasonable standards. And do not forget that it is more important to dress in an appropriate way than in a trendy way; students may appreciate a little trendiness, but if there is a code for students' dress, do not break it just to be considered popular or cool.

Bottom line: you represent the school or educational establishment where you work and are essentially part of their public relations campaign, whether they realize it or not. Just consider: if you were the first person a parent or other adult met while visiting the school for the first time, what sort of impression would they have of the school from your dress and appearance? First impressions of the school district could depend on how you present yourself. However, such first impressions are not the only important public relations work you will do. Your ongoing behavior and appearance will continue to inspire confidence in parents.

Confidentiality and Use of Information

Confidentiality is one of the aspects of professionalism most often discussed in training and orientation for paraprofessionals, largely because of the Family Education Rights and Privacy Act (FERPA), IDEA 97, and the Americans with Disabilities Act (ADA). We discussed these laws in Chapter 4, but you can read more specific information on what they say about confidentiality in the Extending Your Learning section at the end of this chapter.

Confidentiality might best be described as the appropriate use of information. Just as in certain situations it would be wrong to disclose information, there are also situations in which it would be wrong to withhold information. You need to know what sort of information you can and cannot share, as well as who you should and should not share information with and whether that changes according to circumstances.

The different sorts of information you may have access to as a paraprofessional may include the following:

- Personal information about a student: name, age, address and telephone, family circumstances, health status.
- Information on a student's academic skills and progress: test results and knowledge gained through working with the student or discussing the student's progress with a teacher or other paraprofessional.
- Information about student goals, such as an IEP for a student in special education or student goals that a teacher has shared with you.
- Information about a student's social skills, particularly for those students following a formal behavior plan or a behavior modification program.
- Information about other adults you work with—your supervising teacher, other paraprofessionals, school administrators—which may include personal or professional details.

Notice that some of the information to which you have access may have been gained from formal written sources (such as test results or reports) and other pieces of information will be from less formal and undocumented sources. Such information may have been gained from personal contact with the student, from conversations with other students, or from other adults who know the student personally or professionally. Alternatively, you may have actively sought the information by asking questions or consulting a written document, or you may have been given the information unasked or accidentally as part of a casual conversation. For purposes of confidentiality, the source of your information is not important. The important question is whether you should share the information, and who you should or should not share it with.

In a rather unfortunate legal case, a paraprofessional informed a Boy Scout leader that one of the students in the classroom—who was going on an excursion with the Scout troop—was on medication and should be watched carefully. Giving out this information, no matter how helpful she intended to be, landed her and her school district in a court of law.

Here is a good rule of thumb, when it comes to confidentiality of information: Do not share student information with anyone, except with your supervisor. Your supervisor can then tell you if you may share that information. In the case of information about other adults, always seek permission before passing on personal or professional details.

Putting It into Practice. Of course, keeping confidentiality is quite simple in theory, but in practice it is one of the most difficult aspects of professional behavior. Most paraprofessionals are members of the local community with many personal contacts among the families of the students they serve. And this is where the greatest difficulties arise. Take a moment to respond to the following situations, which are quite common for paraprofessionals. We have provided a short commentary after each scenario.

■ In the local market, you bump into the mother of one of the children in your classroom. She says, "So how is my boy doing?" What do you say to her?

_____

_____

_____

_____

_____

Commentary: Even though this is the mother of one of your students and parents are entitled to know about their child's progress, you are not the most appropriate source of that information for the parent. Also, the market—a public place where you can easily be overheard—is not the proper setting for sharing information. An appropriate response to this type of question would be to refer the parent to the teacher, stating in a courteous and friendly manner that you have been specifically told not to share information about students because that is not your role and especially not to talk about students in public.

■ One of the other paraprofessionals in your junior high approaches you while you're both on lunch supervision duty and asks about one of the students you both work with. He works with the student as a job coach, and you provide individual support to the student in math. He is a bit concerned about the student's understanding of money and change and wants to know whether there is anything on the student's IEP stressing math skills and what you've been asked to cover with the student. What do you say to him?

_____

_____

_____

_____

_____

Commentary: Even though this conversation concerns a student you both work with and is on a topic relevant to both of your responsibilities, you should not share information freely with another paraprofessional unless you have checked with your supervisor whether it is appropriate. Even if you have been given permission to discuss a particular student's needs or goals, because you both serve those needs and goals, the lunchroom is not an appropriate setting for exchanging information. Despite the difficulty of finding time to get together with another paraprofessional, that is what you should suggest, rather than sharing information in such a public place.

■ At a Saturday soccer game where your daughter is playing, you get into a conversation with your sister-in-law about the soccer skills of the various girls on the team, which leads her to say, "Look at that Danielle—she's a fabulous little player! But it's all very well saying that playing soccer helps her work out her aggression and she learns self-control. I don't think she should be allowed on the team when you hear how she behaves in the classroom. What on earth happened last Friday in the math class? My girl came home with some story about chairs being thrown about and I was ready to go up there and complain, but she wouldn't let me—just shrugged it off and said, 'Oh, it's just Danielle.' But it sounds to me like she's putting the rest of the kids in danger. So I thought I'd check with you and get the real version of the story before I go and confront the principal." What do you say to her?

_____

_____

_____

_____

_____

Commentary: Even if you were present at the incident your sister-in-law described, you are not the appropriate source of information on the "real version" of anything that happens in the classroom, unless you are asked by a teacher or administrator to provide that sort of information. Again, you should politely decline to comment and refer your sister-in-law to the teacher for information. The teacher is also the most appropriate person for your sister-in-law to consult about her concerns, rather than taking them to the principal first.

■ Your supervisor wants to contact the parent of a student who used to attend the school, to ask if he will come and talk to her careers class students about his work as a lawyer. Knowing that you live locally, she asks, "I want to get hold of Ken Grover, to see if he'll come and talk to my ninth-grade class, but his number doesn't seem to be in the directory. He's a neighbor of yours, isn't he? I don't suppose you have their number?" You and your family are close friends of the Grovers, so of course you have their telephone number, but what do you say to your supervising teacher?

_____

_____

_____

_____

_____

Commentary: Confidentiality of information must be observed in both directions: you should not share information about a student with members of the community, nor should you share information about community members at school. Although you can be the source of much useful background information for a teacher who is not local, only share information if it is truly necessary and will benefit the student's education. Personal information such as telephone numbers of friends or neighbors should not be shared. In this case, you could offer to pass a message on to Mr. Grover and ask him to phone the school with a response, rather than providing his telephone number.

Be proactive:

■ Find out more about FERPA. If you have not been given a summary of FERPA requirements, ask your supervising teacher, then

■ Read the information. If you do not understand the implications of the law, ask your supervisor for help in knowing how it applies to you and the information to which you have access.

■ In some cases, you may find that getting hold of this information is difficult. The appendix lists Internet sources such as professional associations that offer additional information. If you believe your school could benefit from the information you obtain, we encourage you to share it with your teacher and administrator.

■ Keep written documentation secure. No documents, reports, or personal information should be left around (e.g., on a desk) where they can be viewed by chance; special education testing and personal information on individual students must be kept in a locked filing cabinet. A teacher and/or administrator has responsibility for these files and will have the keys.

■ Check with your supervisor whether students are allowed to grade each other's papers or tests (i.e., whether local interpretation of the FERPA requirement for confidentiality prevents students from knowing each other's results). Although a 2004 court case ruling stated that students grading each other's papers was not a contravention of FERPA, your school district may still advise against the practice.

Bottom line: you are under a legal obligation, as a paraprofessional who is privy to a great deal of information on students, to keep it confidential. Although it is sometimes difficult to withhold information, particularly when you are approached by a member of the school or local community, you must pay close attention to the information you share and adopt the practice of referring requests for information to your supervisor.

Consider how you would feel if information about your child or your family/home circumstances was freely circulated and came back to you from someone who had no need to know. This also applies to information that a teacher or school administrator may request on a student's family: although you can be a very useful source of community data for the school, no unnecessary information about students and their family backgrounds should be shared with school personnel. As you keep confidentiality, you will acquire a reputation as a person who does not give out information inappropriately, which will help build relationships of trust with your students, your supervisor, and other adults such as parents and school administrators.

Collaboration with Teachers and Parents

Collaboration, something of a buzzword today, is used in a variety of situations, but it can mean many different things. Sometimes we may refer to it as *teamwork.* With your students you may use the term *cooperative learning* for situations in

Collaborative activity: This is what we do	People I collaborate with on the activity

which they collaborate on a project. Whatever the precise term used, *collaboration* means working together with someone else. Before we go on to talk about effective collaboration, take a moment to list some of the collaborative activities in which you currently engage. Using the nearby box, make a brief note of each collaborative activity, and state who you collaborate with on that activity. If you feel you do not have many opportunities to collaborate, think carefully through your day and who you spend time with. Almost the only time when you are not collaborating with someone is the time you spend on your own!

Here are some collaborative activities we thought of. We have grouped them according to the people you may be collaborating with. Did you leave any of these off your list?

- *Students.* Whether you work in an instructional capacity or have more clerical or organizational responsibilities, the chances are you spend a great deal of your time collaborating with students: gaining and *focusing their attention*; engaging in the *teaching/learning* process; *responding to their interests* and concerns as you teach and motivate them; coordinating and *negotiating homework* and assignments; *facilitating work placements.*
- *Your supervising professional.* You may feel your role is simply to carry out the teacher's instructions, but this does not mean collaboration is not required. The simple act of *following the instructions of your supervisor* is collaboration. But in addition, you undoubtedly *discuss ways of carrying out those instructions* in the most effective manner, you *provide feedback* to your supervisor on the results, you may *observe your supervising teacher's methods* for hints on how to be more successful in your work.
- *Parents.* Most paraprofessionals have fairly limited contact with parents, unless their duties specifically relate to organizing and facilitating parental involvement activities on behalf of the school. Nevertheless you may find that at your supervising teacher's request you *phone parents* to arrange meetings with the teacher, or if you are a bilingual paraprofessional you may have *translation duties or participate in teacher-parent conferences* and IEP meetings.
- *Other adults.* These contacts may include other paraprofessionals, other professionals (such as an itinerant speech pathologist), and of course those who have overall authority and responsibility for the school such as administrators. For example, you may be accountable to the special education teacher who is your supervisor, but you travel with the student to various classrooms each day. You are working under the supervision of each of those teachers, although your ultimate supervisor is the special education teacher. This arrangement requires a good deal of collaboration. Working with multiple teachers can be both challenging and rewarding.

Notice the variety of words used when we talk about collaboration: *negotiating, coordinating, responding, facilitating.* For most of us, the working day is made up of interactions with other people—students, supervisors, other paraprofessionals, parents, school building administrators. When we collaborate, we are not just making contacts with other people; those interactions are purposeful and effective. They serve our purpose of helping students learn and develop.

We are not merely bumping into people or exchanging casual remarks but are exchanging appropriate and useful information, learning how to do our work better through observing others and seeking advice, and taking care to notice others' strengths and preferences so we can build on and use them for the benefit of the students.

Collaboration is a two-way process—there have to be two (or more) people involved—you really cannot collaborate without someone else as part of the team. You cannot force another person to collaborate with you, but you can do many things to promote a sense of teamwork and to show you are willing to work together.

Be proactive:

- *Ask advice.* When you ask another person for advice it sends a very definite message: "I am willing to learn from you." There are two parts to that statement: (1) an indication of your desire to learn and improve, and (2) your confidence in the other person's ability to help you learn and improve. People are flattered when you ask their advice, but this is not just a device to win them over. If you really wish to improve in your ability to help students and honestly seek advice from those who are more expert than you are, with the intention of changing your behavior according to the advice they give, the benefits are universal. You will be more able to help students; the students will learn more effectively and easily; and you will be promoting a collaborative learning environment in which adults and students gain in knowledge and skills.

- *Share information.* Although we have cautioned you about keeping confidentiality, it is important that—when appropriate—you willingly share information with those who need it. The person who most often needs information from you is your supervising teacher, who must know what you have done with the students and what the results were. But you do not need to wait until you are asked. You can offer that information. Good teaching cannot happen without information being exchanged. Just imagine standing up in front of a group of students and always talking but never asking for a response from the students—no questions, no assignments, no information from them to show their understanding. As we already discussed in Chapter 8, you would not know whether to reteach any points or whether to move on. You could not be effective. Whether you have an instructional role or perform other sorts of duties, you are essentially the teacher's deputy. You are doing work the teacher cannot do because of time or resource constraints. Any information you have about the students you work with would be useful in helping your supervising teacher plan students' work. Ask your supervising teacher how you should share information—in writing, during scheduled planning time if you have any, and so on. Again, this is a proactive measure for showing your willingness to collaborate. It is also likely to promote an exchange of information in the other direction.

- *Respect other people's preferences.* You will have noticed that not everyone you collaborate with works in the same way. Some of your colleagues are more or less organized than you are; some of them pay more or less attention to punctuality than you do; some of them seem more absentminded than you feel you are, or perhaps they seem to you to be more able to think clearly and remember important facts and events; Some use planners, some don't. In short, we are all very different and complex people, and this shows up very clearly in the way we approach our work, not just our personal lives. One of the words that relates to collaboration is *compromise:* there has to be give-and-take, which is what we are doing when we pay attention to and respect other people's preferences. Compromise can sometimes feel negative if it seems that the other person is always getting his or her own way and you are the one making all the concessions. But if you can learn to respect and work according to other people's preferences, that is a tremendous strength and contribution to effective collaboration. We have discussed the need to work to your students' strengths—drawing diagrams for those who learn better through visuals, writing lists for those who have trouble remembering or organizing, and so on. It makes just as much sense to work in this way with adult colleagues. If one of your colleagues (particularly your supervising teacher) does not remember what you tell him or her unless it is written down, make a point of leaving notes or keeping a log. If your colleagues like things to happen on time, make a real effort not to be late when you are working with them, which will reduce the likelihood of conflict and show you are willing to cooperate.

Bottom line: Whatever your precise role as a paraprofessional, you are likely to engage in a variety of collaborative activities, both instructional and organizational, during your working week. You also probably collaborate with a fairly large number of other people, including your students. You can enhance the effectiveness of those collaborations through your willingness to ask advice, share information whenever appropriate, and work to the strengths of your fellow team members. Although all of your work should be carried out under the supervision of a professional, take the initiative in collaborative activities and approach your supervisor with suggestions and requests relating to your shared responsibilities for students.

This is a good place for a reminder: although you can take initiative when working with your supervisor or other adults, be careful not to assume unassigned responsibilities. In Chapter 2 we discussed the importance of knowing your roles and seeking clarification when expectations are not clear. Take the time to discuss with your supervisor any tasks that need doing and that you would be prepared to take on, but do not assume responsibility for them until you have checked with your supervisor.

Communication and Conflict Resolution

Communication and conflict resolution are really two sides of the same coin. Conflict often arises because of a lack of communication or understanding between two people. Clear and effective communication not only can prevent conflict but also can resolve conflict that has arisen. That is not to say effective communication prevents disagreement. We all have different views, but they should not prevent us from working well with other people. In a certain sense, conflict can be very positive. When two people have very different or conflicting ideas, it can provoke thinking and learning and improve understanding. Clear communication can help our natural differences from becoming difficulties that would impede our collaborative work with and for students.

Teachers and paraprofessionals are frequently assigned to work together in schools and are generally considered part of the same instructional team. The precise nature of that working team, however, varies considerably not only between schools but between teams within the same school. This situation arises largely because of the varying job descriptions and responsibilities of paraprofessionals and teachers, as well as the funding source for the paraprofessional's employment.

View the scenario by going to the companion website Scene B, or read the dialogue below. Consider the following situation.

Case Study

Para Ed: So, what would you like me to do with this reading group?

Teacher: Well, I'd like you to spend time with this particular group. . . . Now, I've listed their names down here. If you would spend 10 minutes a day with each one of these kids . . . then they will have been able to spend time with you twice during the week. Is that all right?

Para Ed: Oh yeah, I've helped out with reading a lot over the years and I really enjoy it.

(The following week . . .)

Teacher: Ed, how's the reading assignment going?

Para Ed: It's going really well, ya know, I mean, um, . . . I've hit all the kids twice, um . . . oh, except for, um, Jim, I think it was, . . . and, um, he was absent Tuesday. So I caught him on Wednesday.

Teacher: So, exactly what is it that you are doing?

Para Ed: Well, um, I'm having them read to me, and, uh, then I ask them questions. Ya know, things like—what do they think is going to happen next. Kids are coming up with some really neat ideas. Um. Mandy was telling me about her grandma, . . . because she was reading a story about a dog that got lost in the snow . . .

Teacher: But how's the vocabulary testing going? Are you paying attention to the vocabulary words in the back of the book?

Para Ed: Well, I haven't actually done the lists, but, um, the kids get all the words. I mean, uh, they're in the stories, and sometimes they stumble first. But by the time they're done with the stories, they're doin' pretty well. Um, . . . you really wanted me to use the lists?

Teacher: I would appreciate that. You see, I have to keep track of the scores on their vocabulary in my grade book. But are they finishing their readings?

Para Ed: Yeah, . . . well, yeah, except for Jim and Patrick. Ya know, I mean, they . . . they just got their books, Monday.

Teacher: Well, are you keeping track of the books that they're going on to read?

Para Ed: Well, um, . . . Mandy's going into the *Emperor's New Clothes.* And then, um, . . . Tim, He's reading a book by Roald Dahl . . . um . . . I can't remember the name of that book. And, of course, now, Jim and Patrick, they haven't gone to the new book yet. . .

Now answer the following questions about this conversation.

Describe briefly what happened in this interaction.

_____

_____

_____

_____

_____

_____

_____

What would you say are the issues in this situation?

_____

_____

_____

_____

_____

_____

_____

How could those issues be resolved? Whose responsibility is it to resolve them?

_____

_____

_____

_____

_____

_____

_____

The case study provides an excellent example of two members of an instructional team who think they understand each other because they are using vocabulary familiar to both of them. However, they each have their own definitions that indicate their differing personal approaches to their work. It would have been appropriate for either the teacher or the paraprofessional to ask for clarification and to check that they had clearly understood what the other person was trying to say, but because neither of them did that, the situation became a little strained. This situation can easily be resolved, however, by following the principles of effective communication and collaboration we have been discussing and elaborate on next.

Communication happens all the time—through words, actions, attitudes, and body language. We pick up and broadcast signals to those around us. What we pick up, however, may not be what the other person is meaning to broadcast, and likewise what we broadcast may not be picked up or understood in the way we meant it to be. What we need in our work as members of an instructional or educational team is effective communication skills, so we can send clear messages and know how to glean the most accurate meaning from the messages sent to us.

Be proactive:

- Ask for clarification. If someone makes a request in vague terms so it is unclear what is expected of you, go back to him or her and discuss it. Say you are not quite clear on what is wanted and would like more detail. Summarize what you think you have been asked to do, and have the person confirm that you have understood correctly. Or use questions like these: How would you like that done? Would you prefer me to . . . or to . . . ? How soon do you need that done? Would you like the information in writing?
- Reflect on the working preferences of the teachers and administrators with whom you work. Each will be somewhat different from the others. Focus on each person one at a time. Explore that person's preferences and ways of working (e.g., I notice that she tries to always arrive on time and expects the same of others). Defining each person's preferences will help you communicate better and avoid unnecessary conflict.
- Cultivate an attitude of learning. If we meet new or different ideas with hostility and distrust, we are likely to promote conflict in a working relationship. But if we keep an open mind and are willing to consider another person's opinion and ideas, rather than automatically assuming that "different" means "wrong," we are much more likely to learn from the situation and reduce the likelihood of conflict.

Most of us encounter conflict in some small way in our work. Complete the blanks in the box on the next page relating to the conflict you may encounter, and make plans for reducing the likelihood of its recurring.

Health and Safety

The school environment or climate can affect all areas of student and staff functioning. Although definitions of school climate vary, upon entering a building both students and adults can usually sense if the environment is friendly. Principals and staff who greet students each day as they enter the building are contributing to a

Person with whom I sometimes experience conflict	Situation in which this conflict is most likely to arise	What I will do to reduce the likelihood of conflict when the situation arises again

positive school environment. Greeting students can provide them with a sense of importance and individual appreciation. This small gesture demonstrates that students are important and educators enjoy their relationships with them. A positive school environment is emphasized when school personnel use positive, proactive measures to build a positive school environment rather than imposing punishment to discipline for infractions. Positive communication between students and staff is vital to building and maintaining a positive school climate.

The best prevention and intervention programs depend on the support of students, teachers, teaching assistants, administrators, school support staff, secretaries, custodians, and parents. All must be involved in building a school climate that is healthy (emotionally and physically) and safe. Here are some suggestions:

- If you are working with students with health issues (e.g., those in special education with physical difficulties) or curriculum areas that have a predominantly practical approach like shop, seek training for such specialized situations.
- Health and safety is vital for both students and for you and the other adults in the classroom. Take a CPR class through your health department, school district, or community.
- In a safe workplace, no dangerous substances or objects are left lying around.
- Train students to know what things they should and should not use/touch. If you are doing art projects, are they allowed to use your craft knife, for example? Do they need to be supervised when using the craft knife or scissors? Teach students the way you would teach any procedural rules (as discussed in Chapter 4).
- Know the fire, tornado, or earthquake drills. You have to know what to do in those situations and be able to assist the students calmly and confidently, which only comes from knowing what to expect and what to do.
- School personnel are required legally to report information on child abuse and/or neglect. In most states this reporting is mandated. If you do not know what to do, ask your teacher to help you find that information and write it here:

If I suspect abuse or neglect, I must

_____

_____

_____

_____

This is the penalty for *not* following this law:

_____

_____

_____

_____

In my school I would report my information to:

_____   _____
Name   Job Title

C-H-A-P-T-E-R—S-U-M-M-A-R-Y

Specifically defining professional behavior is like trying to trap an armful of feathers when the wind is blowing. There are many little pieces and parts to it. Yet you must know there are certain standards to which you are expected to adhere, defined by professional organizations. We have also given you many examples of what to do and what not to do in defining the standards for your employment.

By now you should be able to state the requirements for your paraprofessional position. These should include dress codes, confidentiality and collaboration, limits of your role and responsibilities, and appropriate steps to take to resolve conflict.

Health and safety is everyone's concern. You should also be able to identify things you can do to ensure the heath and safety of students in your school.

E-X-T-E-N-D-I-N-G—Y-O-U-R—L-E-A-R-N-I-N-G

Confidentiality and the ADA

Note: This information on confidentiality is an extract from the Americans with Disabilities Act (ADA) of 1990.

Confidentiality

An employer must keep any medical information on applicants or employees confidential, with the following limited exceptions:

- Supervisors and managers may be told about necessary restrictions on the work or duties of the employee and about necessary accommodations;
- First aid and safety personnel may be told if the disability might require emergency treatment;
- Government officials investigating compliance with the ADA must be given relevant information on request;
- Employers may give information to state workers' compensation offices, state second injury funds, or workers' compensation insurance carriers in accordance with state workers' compensation laws; and
- Employers may use the information for insurance purposes.

Here are some commonly asked questions about the ADA's confidentiality requirements:

1. May medical information be given to decision makers involved in the hiring process?
   Yes. Medical information may be given to—and used by—appropriate decision makers involved in the hiring process so they can make employment decisions

consistent with the ADA. In addition, the employer may use the information to determine reasonable accommodations for the individual. For example, the employer may share the information with a third party, such as a health care professional, to determine whether a reasonable accommodation is possible for a particular individual. The information certainly must be kept confidential.

Of course, the employer may only share the medical information with individuals involved in the hiring process (or in implementing an affirmative action program) who need to know the information. For example, in some cases, a number of people may be involved in evaluating an applicant. Some individuals may simply be responsible for evaluating an applicant's references; these individuals may have no need to know an applicant's medical condition and therefore should not have access to the medical information.

2. Can an individual voluntarily disclose his or her own medical information to persons beyond those to whom an employer can disclose such information?
Yes, as long as it's really voluntary. The employer cannot request, persuade, coerce, or otherwise pressure the individual to get him or her to disclose medical information.

3. Does the employer's confidentiality obligation extend to medical information that an individual voluntarily tells the employer?
Yes. For example, if an applicant voluntarily discloses bipolar disorder and the need for reasonable accommodation, the employer may not disclose the condition or the applicant's need for accommodation to the applicant's references.

4. Can medical information be kept in an employee's regular personnel file?
No. Medical information must be collected and maintained on separate forms and in separate medical files. An employer should not place any medical-related material in an employee's nonmedical personnel file. If an employer wants to put a document in a personnel file, and that document happens to contain some medical information, the employer must simply remove the medical information from the document before putting it in the personnel file.

5. Does the confidentiality obligation end when the person is no longer an applicant or employee?
No. An employer must keep medical information confidential even if someone is no longer an applicant (for example, he or she wasn't hired) or is no longer an employee.

6. Is an employer required to remove from its personnel files medical information obtained before the ADA's effective date?
No. (American with Disabilities Act Public Law 101-336, JULY 26, 1990 104 STAT. 327).

Note: Many of the references here are for action to be taken by an administrator or supervisor. As the paraprofessional, make sure you do not assume that role.

FERPA

The following information regarding Family Rights is published by the U.S. Department of Education.

General Information About FERPA

The Family Educational Rights and Privacy Act (FERPA) (20 U.S.C. § 1232g; 34 CFR Part 99) is a Federal law that protects the privacy of student education records. The law applies to all schools that receive funds under an applicable program of the U.S. Department of Education.

FERPA gives parents certain rights with respect to their children's education records. These rights transfer to the student when he or she reaches the age of 18 or attends a school beyond the high school level. Students to whom the rights have transferred are "eligible students."

- Parents or eligible students have the right to inspect and review the student's education records maintained by the school. Schools are not required to provide copies of records unless, for reasons such as great distance, it is impossible for parents or eligible students to review the records. Schools may charge a fee for copies.
- Parents or eligible students have the right to request that a school correct records which they believe to be inaccurate or misleading. If the school decides not to amend the record, the parent or eligible student then has the right to a formal hearing. After the hearing, if the school still decides not to amend the record, the parent or eligible student has the right to place a statement with the record setting forth his or her view about the contested information.
- Generally, schools must have written permission from the parent or eligible student in order to release any information from a student's education record. However, FERPA allows schools to disclose those records, without consent, to the following parties or under the following conditions (34 CFR § 99.31):

  1. School officials with legitimate educational interest;
  2. Other schools to which a student is transferring;
  3. Specified officials for audit or evaluation purposes;
  4. Appropriate parties in connection with financial aid to a student;
  5. Organizations conducting certain studies for or on behalf of the school;
  6. Accrediting organizations;
  7. To comply with a judicial order or lawfully issued subpoena;
  8. Appropriate officials in cases of health and safety emergencies; and
  9. State and local authorities, within a juvenile justice system, pursuant to specific state law.

Schools may disclose, without consent, "directory" information such as a student's name, address, telephone number, date and place of birth, honors and awards, and dates of attendance. However, schools must tell parents and eligible students about directory information and allow parents and eligible students a reasonable amount of time to request that the school not disclose directory information about them. Schools must notify parents and eligible students annually of their rights under FERPA. The actual means of notification (special letter, inclusion in a PTA bulletin, student handbook, or newspaper article) is left to the discretion of each school.

For additional information or technical assistance, you may call (202) 260-3887 (voice). Individuals who use TDD may call the Federal Information Relay Service at 1-800-877-8339. Or you may contact them at the following address: Family Policy Compliance Office, U.S. Department of Education, 400 Maryland Avenue, SW, Washington, DC 20202-5901.

13 Reflection and Self-Evaluation

New laws are demanding accountability in education and, as we discussed earlier, evaluation is a large and important aspect of any accountability system. In this chapter we briefly discuss the importance of evaluation as a general principle and look at the need for all educators to reflect on and evaluate their own work. This chapter also identifies methods for documenting your own classroom practices, along with listing some of the major resources available to you as an educator to enhance your evaluation and reflection.

By the end of this chapter you should be able to answer the following questions:

- What are the similarities and differences between evaluation of students and evaluation of adults?
- What is meant by the phrase *the reflective practitioner,* and how does it apply to me as a paraprofessional?
- What are some of the ways in which I can reflect on my own work, in order to make a self-evaluation and document improvements?
- What are the benefits of reflection and self-evaluation for my students?

Evaluation of Students and Evaluation of Adults

Evaluation of Students

It seems that educators are constantly evaluating student performance. We test students at the beginning of the school year to see what knowledge and skills they bring to the class. We test them daily and weekly with end-of-chapter tests and end-of-level exams. Then there are the term exams, midterms, and final exams to see what they have gained. With all the testing going on, you should not be too surprised to hear teachers say, "It's a wonder we have time to teach the students!" And yet, as you have already learned, it is critically important when students come to us that we know where they are in their learning, how much progress they are making as we teach them, and what skills they have yet to learn.

As students progress through a hierarchy of skills and knowledge—with careful monitoring and adjustments to their workload as necessary—they are able to know success. This helps boost student esteem and the desire to learn. Research suggests that this building on previous knowledge, with monitoring and adjusting to support student learning, is the only way to be truly effective in teaching.

Defining Terms. You know the teaching cycle from Chapter 8: *check for prerequisite skills*, *teach new content in small steps*, and give plenty of *guided practice*, which leads to successful *independent practice*, then *review* knowledge and skills on a regular basis. So you also know you must assess and monitor students continually. But before we proceed, let's clarify some of the commonly used terms:

- *Assessment* is generally considered any activity you undertake to identify where students are currently functioning. It may be as simple as looking at their frowning faces or yawning and stretching behaviors and drawing the conclusion they are bored. It may be as complex as administering a national exam.

- *Evaluation* is often used interchangeably with *assessment*, and to simplify we consider them synonyms here. Both indicate not only a measurement of performance but also a judgment about the quality of the performance. After all, writing all the answers on a math test is one thing, but writing the *correct* answers is another! You would evaluate or assess not only that students knew they had to fill in the blanks, but also that they could fill those blanks with appropriate information.

- *Testing,* in contrast, usually focuses on a specific topic, such as math, language arts, social studies, or history. Almost everyone knows the spelling test at the end of the spelling unit or the physical education test in which success is measured by the number of sit-ups and pull-ups performed. Testing is really a tool for evaluation purposes: it provides information or data on which to base our assessment.

- *Monitoring* is another word sometimes used in place of *evaluation*, although the term generally has a less formal application. For example, when you are working with students you are constantly *monitoring* or watching to see what is happening and if they appear to understand or if they look confused.

Common terms and their definitions

Assessment. Activity to identify at what level students are functioning.
Evaluation. Measurement of performance and judgment about the quality of the performance. Evaluation and assessment are often used interchangeably.
Tests and examinations. Assessment tools that may have a written, oral, or practical format.
Monitoring. Less formal than assessment and evaluation. May be as simple as watching students to see if they appear to understand.

Evaluation of Adults

There has been—and to some extent continues to be—a negative connotation to the evaluation of adults. It can be intimidating for adults to feel they are being judged, and it is often difficult for the evaluators, who may feel they should not criticize other adults' work. Teachers typically do not enjoy evaluating the paraprofessionals who work with them. There is a real art to assisting another adult in the learning process, and very few teachers have received training in how to conduct effective staff evaluations.

Evaluation is usually viewed as the last step in the educational process and often found in the last chapters of books on school improvement. Indeed, we have included it in the last chapter of this book. But this is not because it is an afterthought. We believe evaluation can be a positive and meaningful activity for adults and should be an integral part of what you do as a paraprofessional. Like student evaluation, it can be used to identify where you are now, what you need to learn, and what you need to do to succeed: it is part of the cycle of teaching and learning for both students and educators.

For you as a paraprofessional, the most formal version of evaluation is probably the annual personnel evaluation conducted by your administrator or supervisor. This evaluation is usually standardized so the same form is used for all personnel with job descriptions similar to yours. Ideally, the person conducting the evaluation observes your work according to the checklist or form being used, writes additional comments or notes, and meets with you afterward to discuss the items. In most schools, the form is then signed by each of you and a duplicate copy is filed in a central location such as the district personnel office. This is the ideal and uses the same principles as the effective instructional cycle we described in Chapter 8, with feedback always provided to students. How well you are doing should not be a secret that is kept from you!

On a less formal level, an evaluation may be as simple as you monitoring your own teaching, for example keeping notes of the questions you ask to see if the students can answer correctly. If students appear not to understand, you may decide to adjust or adapt your questions. As we already discussed in Chapter 9, "Monitoring Instructional Effectiveness," this simple form of evaluation may appear only to evaluate students' learning, but it is also an evaluation of the effectiveness of what you do and say as an educator to facilitate student learning. It is an informal process that good teachers use constantly as they teach and that we have encouraged you to use as you become more aware of effective teaching techniques.

Apart from the level of formality between the two types of evaluation we have listed here, the other distinct difference between the two is that the second one is a *self*-evaluation. You look at your own practices and reflect on them, thinking about (or evaluating) whether or not you are accomplishing what you wish to accomplish—in the way you wish to do so—and identifying the steps you need to take as a result of your reflections. This type of evaluation is often overlooked in staff development plans, but it can be very meaningful if applied earnestly and frequently. It has real value and many advantages. Self-evaluation is generally less threatening than having another person watch your work and pass a judgment, and it can occur much more frequently than the formal once-a-year evaluation by an administrator.

Summative and Formative Evaluation	
Summative Evaluation:	Occurs infrequently—usually annually or semi-annually. Lacks detail and specificity. Purpose is to provide a summary of performance.
Formative Evaluation:	Occurs frequently—monthly, weekly, or even daily. Provides detailed information. Purpose is for making improvements.

Figure 13.1

Summative and Formative Evaluation

Formative versus Summative Evaluation. We hope these distinctions ring a bell for you and take you back to Chapter 9, where we discussed formative and summative evaluation. Just as a reminder:

- Formative evaluation is ongoing, with the purpose of making personal improvements. It operates at the level of daily details and changes in knowledge and skills. When you engage in self-evaluation, this is a formative evaluation activity because you make an assessment of your performance in order to make changes and improvements.
- Summative evaluation, in contrast, is an end product and generally used by the administration for job retention or remediation. Summative evaluation typically occurs once or twice each year for teachers and administrators, and it is beginning to be more widely applied to paraprofessionals across the country.

Summative evaluations are not always met with cheers. Many people view them much like IRS tax returns—unfortunate but necessary. In fact, we know of a school district that actually chose to conduct paraprofessional end-of-year evaluations on April 15! You can imagine the paraprofessionals there viewed their annual evaluation less than enthusiastically.

Ideally, a summative evaluation includes the results of several formative evaluations, if an administrator discussed your annual evaluation in the light of the goals and progress you had already made during the course of the year. This system would recognize it as part of a continuous process of improvement, describing the learning process over time, rather than merely an end product. But by definition, summative and formative evaluations have different functions, and both are a necessary part of the educational system (see Figure 13.1).

The Reflective Practitioner

A phrase often used to describe a thoughtful and deliberate approach to teaching is *the reflective practitioner*. The practice of having teachers reflect on their work is now used in many teacher education programs. Reflective practice is generally recognized as a very useful tool to assist teachers in developing a deeper understanding of personal and professional philosophies, the complexities of classroom dynamics, and the close relationship that exists between teaching and learning.

These concepts are becoming essential in an education system where teams of teachers and paraprofessionals are held accountable for the services they deliver to students and government agencies are requiring annual testing and academic progress of all students to a "proficient" level (e.g., in Title I of No Child Left Behind). As part of a reflective activities program, teachers—or student teachers—may be required to keep daily journals, build portfolios, or engage in group discussions with colleagues to talk about their work with students. These are some of the same activities we will be encouraging you to engage in as part of the self-evaluation process. Reflection is the tool that enables you to conduct a self-evaluation: you have to reflect on or think about your work before you can assess how well you are doing.

Reflection: New to Paraprofessionals

Although reflection has been considered a vital aspect of a teacher's professional development for some years, the practice has rarely been required of paraprofessionals. Yet it is equally important that you reflect on your work as a member of the instructional team. Through reflection, you can identify your skills and knowledge in specific areas relating to instruction, curriculum, or interacting with students and your teacher. Having identified your current skill level—areas where you are comfortable and where you are not—you are able to identify the areas in which you would like to make improvements.

Reflection has many definitions and formats. Models of reflection have been proposed by a number of authors who categorize reflection as follows:

- *Retrospective* (relating to past actions)
- *Contemporaneous* (relating to what is happening now)
- *Anticipatory* (relating to future actions)

We believe all mature adult learners can engage in meaningful reflection and self-evaluation. This assessment sequence parallels the teaching sequence with which you are already familiar (see nearby box).

The teacher . . .	You . . .
Assesses a student's knowledge and skills relating to a specific area of the curriculum.	Can reflect on and assess your own levels of skill and knowledge relating to one of your areas of responsibility.
Through information and modeling, provides instruction to the student according to the needs identified.	Can seek information and training to increase your knowledge and skills in the areas you have identified as needing improvement.
Gives the student multiple opportunities to practice the new skills, with careful monitoring so additional teaching can be provided if necessary.	Can practice what you have learned or seen other educators do, monitoring what you do and making adjustments or seeking further guidance if difficulties arise.

Much of the assessment and monitoring of student progress you carry out is informal: you follow your instinct about what is working well and what is not, based on your classroom experiences. Likewise, when you monitor your own work, the assessments you make are often informal, which usually works well enough. However, in this data-driven era, you need to be able to present facts to your administrator or your teachers—or even to yourself—to show you are making a difference with student learning. Thus in the next section of the chapter we discuss several things you can do to take a more systematic approach to your reflection and self-evaluation activities. First, we briefly consider motivation for learning. We made reference to student motivation earlier and noted that motivation really can determine whether students engage in the learning process or not.

What Is the Motivation to Improve? As an adult learner you have some distinctly different needs from those of your student learners. Over the years, we have observed paraprofessionals attending training sessions, conferences, and workshops and noted that many of them were not paid to attend, nor did it increase their pay or status in a career ladder system. We were curious why they would participate in training without the traditional recognition of added salary or status. We asked more than two hundred paraprofessionals in three different states, "What is your motivation to attend training?" Take a minute or two and think about why you are attending classes and training sessions, before we share the results of our research with you.

I attend classes, workshops, or training because

1. _____
   _____

2. _____
   _____

3. _____
   _____

The answers we received from the paraprofessionals who participated in our survey grouped into five major themes, but by far the most common response (just under half, or 46 percent) was that paraprofessionals wanted to increase their job-related skills and knowledge (see Figure 13.2). Some of their responses were general (e.g., "I just want to be better at my job") and others more specific (e.g., "I have a student who really needs help with his math"). Then almost one-fourth (23 percent) said they were attending training because it could be counted toward formal qualifications, and another 15 percent said they just had a personal interest in the topic (e.g., "The topics will be helpful for me as a parent"). The remaining 16 percent of responses related to the training being convenient, or paid for by the school district, or to encouragement they had received from a teacher or administrator.

Reasons Paraprofessionals Attended Training	
Reasons given for attending training	**Percent of responses in this category**
Wanting to acquire job-related skills/knowledge	46%
General	*27%*
Specific	*19%*
Wanting to acquire formal qualifications	23%
Personal interest	15%
Factors relating to the training	7%
Third party influence	9%

Figure 13.2

Reasons Paraprofessionals Attended Training

From this research we concluded that paraprofessionals attend training mostly because they just want to learn how to do their jobs better. They want to gain the skills you need to be successful with students and with their own children. This research was carried out before the No Child Left Behind Act came into force, so if we asked the same question now, many more paraprofessionals would probably say they want to acquire more formal qualifications. However, we feel this strengthens the point we are making: when paraprofessionals were not required to have formal qualifications, they nevertheless attended training because they wanted to be more effective in their work. We believe this is still true: paraprofessionals may *need* more formal qualifications, but they *want* to be more effective. This is far greater motivation than the possibility of a pay increase or other formal recognition. These skills and knowledge need to be useful so you can apply them in the classroom the next day.

Making Improvements

If you, as a paraprofessional, want to improve your skills, what would be the best way to go about it? Think first: how do you proceed when you want to improve your performance in other aspects of your life (such as learning a new language, sport, or practical skill)? Write some of the steps you take when you have decided you want to improve or learn something new.

If I want to learn something new, I _____

_____

_____

_____

_____

You may have listed such strategies as getting a book on the subject (from the library or bookstore), asking about classes that may be available, or talking to someone who already has the skill you want to acquire. Any of these could be first steps in the learning process because they put you in possession of the information you need to develop the skill or knowledge.

Once you have decided how you are going to acquire the skill—through self-study with a book or other materials, by attending a class, or by talking to an expert—what do you do to track your progress? How do you decide whether you are making progress and acquiring the new skill or knowledge? List some of the things you do to check your own progress as you go through the learning process:

_____

_____

_____

_____

_____

_____

_____

Lastly, what do you do if you feel you are not progressing as well as you would like? Write your thoughts here and then compare them with our ideas.

_____

_____

_____

_____

_____

_____

_____

Here are some of the questions we thought you might ask yourself if you think you are not progressing as you would like:

- *Was I too ambitious?* Did I expect too much of myself? Did I expect too much too soon?
- *Did I select the best method for learning the new skill?* Should I have taken a class, rather than just getting a book from the library, for example?
- *Did I actually do what I had planned to learn the new skill?* Did I spend as much time practicing the new skill as I had planned? Did I attend all the classes I signed up for? Did I take the advice of the expert I consulted?

Essentially, with all of these questions, what you are asking is this: were my plans adequate to carry out the learning program, and did I follow them? This type of reflection on what worked and what did not is the first step in making improvements.

Then, when you come up with an answer to the question, the next step is to adjust your learning plan or goals. Sometimes this only takes a subtle adjustment—like a basketball player shooting foul shots. If the ball falls to the left of the basket, the shooter adjusts the angle and shoots again: adjusting again, if the ball misses the target. This happens so quickly, it may be overlooked as reflection, evaluation, or adjustment and be merely credited to chance. However, note that reflection is common to all the phases.

Ultimately the responsibility for learning belongs to you—the learner. As an adult learner and educator, you must take responsibility for your own progress. You can take deliberate steps to increase your ability to deal with the challenges of the classroom. You can increase the rate and extent of your learning by making opportunities to monitor and enhance your own skills.

Documenting Reflection and Performance Improvement

In the practical environment of daily schedules and challenges, it may be difficult to find opportunities to engage in in-depth discussions of instructional techniques with colleagues. However, you can be proactive in assessing your effectiveness and in gathering information that will be helpful on those occasions when you meet to discuss student progress with your supervisor. Here are some practical suggestions:

■ Keep a daily journal of your successes and areas in which you feel you could improve your skills. This can just be a collection of notes, rather than a series of long essays. A few minutes spent each day in recording what you did and how well it succeeded will eventually build into a substantial piece of documentation and provide ample material for further reflection and self-evaluation. If you keep a schedule or lesson planner, allocate space beside each lesson segment or assignment for jotting down notes and reflections.

■ Some teacher-paraprofessional teams keep a daily log, especially if they work apart for much of the time. The teacher can write requests and advice for the day's activities, and the paraprofessional can make notes on how well the students received the activity and any concerns that may have arisen. The log can be kept in a place where both the teacher and the paraprofessional can easily access it, but out of reach of the students, because it is likely to contain confidential information about individual students' progress.

■ Portfolios can be an excellent method for documenting what you do and the training you have received, as a starting point for reflection and setting goals for improvement. Many school districts are now requiring teachers and paraprofessionals to develop a portfolio as evidence of their growing expertise and to meet the requirements of legislation (such as No Child Left Behind and IDEA). We gave some examples of what you may wish to keep in a professional portfolio in Chapter 4 (Extending Your Learning), although your school district or state may already have guidelines for what it should contain. Whatever you decide to include, date each item and include evidence of the results or progress you made because of that item of training or experience.

Monitoring Through Observation Data

Here we provide a detailed description of an observation and discussion procedure you can use as the basis for reflection and self-evaluation. This is a simple procedure to try during the course of the teaching day. It was developed in conjunction with teachers and paraprofessionals and has been extensively field-tested with those working in both general and special education and with students of all ages. The underlying principles of this procedure are those we already referred to earlier in the chapter and should be used daily by the teacher as he or she provides instruction to students:

- The teacher assesses a student's knowledge and skills in a specific area of the curriculum by observation and discussion and by providing assignments that require those skills.
- Having ascertained the current skill level, the teacher provides instruction to the student through sharing information and modeling skills.
- The teacher gives the student multiple opportunities to practice in meaningful ways and monitors progress so further support or teaching can be provided as needed.

Using these concepts but applying them to you, these are the parallel steps:

- You select an activity or task that is part of your job description and classroom assignment on which you would like to improve your skills. You ask your teacher to observe you as you carry out the activity or task so your current level of competence can be assessed.
- Next the teacher performs the same task, providing a role model of good practice as you observe and record the specific details. Here is an example: the teacher has observed you conducting a small group activity and has noted that not all students were involved. The teacher reminds you of the importance of involving all students and makes a point of modeling ways to engage all students. You write what you see the teacher do to make that happen. You may record the number of times the teacher calls on each student or the ways the teacher helps students to refocus on the activity if they become distracted.
- Soon after the observation, you meet with your teacher to discuss the information you recorded on her teaching session. The two of you discuss the highlighted practices and the associated benefits, and then you, as the paraprofessional, set goals for your work in this specific area, with the teacher's guidance and example as a yardstick. For example, the teacher may have made a point of using a student's name before asking some of her questions, but with other questions, she may have told the class to take time to think about the question before she called on someone to respond. You could set a goal to use the same techniques as you conduct group discussions.
- You take the same assignment—conducting a small group activity—and this time the teacher observes and records the same type of information you recorded for her. Later, as you meet again to discuss the information recorded, you can evaluate your performance on the techniques the teacher modeled

and draw your own conclusions about the extent to which you succeeded in using the techniques yourself. Under the teacher's supervision, you can then set new goals for improvement in the same activity or, if you both feel you have used effective methods, you can focus on a new area or technique.

Here are some things to note in relation to this reflective learning sequence:

1. This activity is not exclusively for the paraprofessional and the teacher, but it does require support and participation from your supervisor. If your supervising teacher cannot assist you in this way, ask permission to carry out the activity with another paraprofessional. Your supervising teacher will be able to recommend someone you can observe who can model effective techniques, so you do not learn poor habits or practices. If your teacher does not feel it is appropriate for you to engage in such an activity with another paraprofessional, you must respect that decision. You can continue to monitor and reflect on your own practice and on what other adults do that seems to work.

2. Taking the previous example of involving all students, if the recording sheet shows that only two of six students were asked to respond during ten minutes of observation, you will be able to draw your own conclusions that you are not calling on all students and need to make more efforts to do so. The teacher does not always need to pronounce judgment on your work for you to know whether you are meeting your goals. Thus, as you work unobserved, you can continue to make note of what you do and see whether it matches up to the example you have seen from your teacher and the standard you have set for improvement.

3. When you are observing and recording, record information on a plain sheet of paper or on a form like the one shown in Figure 13.3. If you date the papers or forms and keep them in a binder, a record of progress develops that will remind you of the principles of effective practice you can use. This procedure focuses only on the pedagogy of teaching. That is, the *activity performed* or *the instruction given* that elicited participation from the students, rather than how the students react. If you do not have time to record both, the teacher's actions are the more important of the two. As you participate frequently in this process, you will find you are able to write faster and record information more accurately. You may even develop a type of shorthand in which you write only one letter instead of the full word (e.g., S for *student* or T for the whole word *teacher*).

4. Write only what you see or hear. Do not write any conclusions or evaluative comments. Write only the observed actions and not comments like "You did a nice job" or "I think you were trying to . . ." These types of evaluative comments would be totally inappropriate if you are a paraprofessional observing a teacher's work, and they are not at all helpful for a self-evaluation. Especially avoid personal comments such as "I really like your suit" because they are not appropriate or useful for the purposes of the observation.

Observation Form

Name: _____ Date: _____ Observer: _____

Activity Observed:

_____

_____

_____

The Educator did this . . .	Students reacted in this way . . .

Beginning Time _____   Ending Time _____

Number of minutes the activity was observed _____

Figure 13.3

Observation Form

Self-Evaluation and Goal Planning

Name: _____ Date: _____ Observer: _____

Activity Observed:

_____

_____

_____

My reflections based on the data from this observation:

This is what I think I am doing well:

_____

_____

_____

_____

This is what I would like to do better:

_____

_____

_____

_____

This is the specific action I will take to improve:

_____

_____

_____

_____

I would like to be observed again on this date: _____

Figure 13.4

Self-Evaluation and Goal Planning Form

This process of observing a good role model and using the data you collect during the observation to reflect on your own practice provides guidance and instruction to you in three ways:

1. By observing, you have access to a role model of effective practices.
2. By recording what you see, you have solid data to review.
3. By engaging in a discussion of what was seen and recorded, you have more opportunity to reflect and conduct a self-evaluation (see Figure 13.4).

Teachers or other adults who know they are being observed are likely to do their best—such is human nature—but when that happens everyone benefits. Paraprofessionals and students benefit from a particularly good example of effective practice; the teacher has an opportunity to use her skills and is reminded of the need to self-evaluate and make improvements. When you are observed, you will undoubtedly try your best, but again, there are only advantages, for both you and the students. As you use the techniques that were successful when you observed the teacher, you will get a more positive response from your students and their chances of success will be enhanced. Then even when you are not being observed, you will be more aware of what you are doing, and you will remember the sense of accomplishment that came from using good techniques. That will be motivation for you to continue to use them even without the presence of an observer.

For the procedure to be most effective, consider carefully the following points:

■ The focus of the observation must be very specific. Change happens in small increments. The information recorded must relate to only one aspect of effective practice, so you can deal with one thing at a time.
■ Observations should occur regularly so the targeted techniques are not forgotten but allow practice opportunities between observations; one observation per a week is usually enough.
■ Observations should continue with the same focus until improvements are evident, but if improvements are immediately obvious, a new focus can be chosen for observation.

This procedure allows the teacher to provide you with on-the-job-training. And it is a simple validated procedure that focuses on job-specific skills.

Setting Your Own Goals for Improvement

Reflection and evaluation should be designed to meet your needs (see Figure 13.5 for a way to pinpoint areas for observation and self-evaluation).

■ First identify your goals and preferences (e.g., I want all students to have an opportunity to learn).
■ Then decide what action you can take to ensure that happens (e.g., I need to give each student some attention or help, leaving no one out).

Making Improvements: Areas for Observation and Self-Evaluation

Area for self-evaluation	Observation data to collect
I want to be fair. Do I call on girls as frequently as I call on boys?	Count the number boys and the number of girls I specifically call on for answers.
I want to get all of the students involved. Do I ask enough questions?	Count the number of questions I ask.
I want the students to learn to think. Do I ask enough high-level questions?	Please write the questions I ask.

Figure 13.5

Making Improvements: Areas for Observation and Self-Evaluation

- Then decide what an observer could look for as he or she watches you work with your group of students (e.g., I want to know which students I call on).
- Then decide how that information can be obtained (e.g., I will ask an observer to mark the seating chart each time I call on a student).
- When you get the information, you can discuss it with the observer to make sure you understand what was recorded.
- Finally, use the information to reflect on the effectiveness of your teaching. If you only called on the same three students throughout the lesson, leaving the other fifteen out, you will surely conclude you need to set a goal for yourself to spread the questions around. That will be your focus for the next observation. You will continue to have data taken on that specific teaching skill until you feel you have mastered it. If you find you called on all of the students at least once and some of them more than once, however, you can feel good about your performance and start the cycle again by identifying a new goal.

Go back and review the goals you have set for yourself. Look at what you have accomplished; celebrate your achievements.

Of course, you are the person most responsible for your professional development. In most cases, it will be up to you to take the initiative to find professional development opportunities and to choose the pedagogical areas in which you feel you need greater expertise. Consider these benefits of on-the-job training and observation:

- Training is specific to your individual classroom responsibilities and job description.
- Skills are built gradually, but the accumulation over the school year can be substantial.
- The teaching profession as a whole improves as you and your teachers become more aware of your own practice and strive to provide models of excellence for others.

■ The procedure can be used no matter what your job description may be and no matter how intense the students' needs are—because observation and reflection are based on the job requirements.

With the appropriate support, you should be able to shape your learning experiences. You could request that your administrator observe you or approach your administrator prior to your annual evaluation with the suggestion that the principles we have discussed in the job-embedded training be used in conjunction with the formal evaluation. Share your goals and what you think you do well and the areas in which you want to improve. Ask your administrator to focus on one of those areas. It is a good opportunity to show what you know, to show you are willing to improve your skills, and to demonstrate you can be systematic and proactive in your own learning.

C-H-A-P-T-E-R—S-U-M-M-A-R-Y

You have already started the reflection and evaluation process by considering the areas in which you have teaching strengths and the areas in which you would like to improve. Setting your own learning goals and working toward achieving them is something well within the grasp of all adult learners. You are already aware of the critical importance of evaluation in the teaching and learning process. In this chapter you learned the importance of reflection as a tool for conducting self-evaluations. You can now identify ways in which you can evaluate your job performance. You have learned ways to monitor your effect on student performance through reflection and evaluation of observation data. You also know various ways to document reflection and performance improvement.

The Extending Your Learning sections that follow provide you with additional material for considering your current levels of skill and knowledge, as well as areas you might wish to focus on for improvement.

E-X-T-E-N-D-I-N-G—Y-O-U-R—L-E-A-R-N-I-N-G

Questions for Self-Evaluation

Take a moment to consider instructional areas in which you have strengths. Remember to acknowledge that you do already have skills and strengths and to take time to remember the things you do well.

I feel these are my current strengths:

1. _____

_____

2. _____

_____

3. _____

_____

4. _____

_____

5. _____

_____

Now identify other areas in which you would like to make improvements. You may list as many as you wish, but because it is impossible to improve in every area at the same time, identify one area where you would like to begin.

These are the areas in which I feel I need to make improvements:

1. _____

_____

2. _____

_____

3. _____

_____

4. _____

_____

5. _____

_____

6. _____

_____

I will give priority to (select one of the areas you have listed):

_____

_____

_____

_____

Now, focusing on this one area, set yourself some goals for what you will do to improve as well as a date by which you would like to accomplish your goals. You may wish to discuss possibilities with other members of your school team, especially your supervising teacher. Often they have good ideas to share with you that will help. These are my goals for this area of improvement:

1. _____

_____

2. _____

_____

I will review these goals on (set a date when you will review your progress toward these goals): _____

CEC Standards

In Section I we introduced you to the standards for paraprofessionals set by the Council for Exceptional Children (CEC), the largest special education organization in the United States. We pointed out that although these standards were written for paraprofessionals working in special education, many of them apply to all paraprofessionals. We have listed a selection of these broadly applicable standards here. In the spaces in the nearby boxes, write how you could demonstrate you have the skills and knowledge for each of the CEC standards listed.

Standard 9: Professional and Ethical Practice

Skills	Ways to Show I Have This Skill
PE9S1: Perform responsibilities as directed in a manner consistent with laws and policies.	
PE9S2: Follow instructions of the professional.	
PE9S13: Demonstrate ethical practices as guided by the CEC Code of Ethics and other standards and policies.	

Standard 10: Collaboration

Skills	Ways to Show I Have This Skill
PE10S5: Function in a manner that demonstrates a positive regard for the distinctions between roles and responsibilities of paraprofessionals and those of professionals.	

E·X·T·E·N·D·I·N·G—Y·O·U·R—L·E·A·R·N·I·N·G

Items for Inclusion in a Paraprofessional Portfolio

- List of formal training attended/completed, including length of training, place and date, who provided it (school, district, state?) and topics covered; plus documentation of attendance/grade (if applicable).
- Training/qualifications not acquired as part of your paraprofessional training but that enhance your effectiveness in working with students: first aid, secretarial, computer/IT, workshops at parent conferences, and so on. Document as fully as possible.
- Experience not acquired as a paraprofessional but that enhances your effectiveness (e.g., PTA, Girl/Boy Scouts, volunteer work in the community, Sunday school, 4-H).
- Letters of recommendation from previous employers (even if not connected to education).
- Results of evaluations (if any) performed by administrators/teachers or from prior employment if they provide insight into your strengths and assets.
- A statement of your personal philosophy of education.

SECTION

V

Appendix

Bibliography

A–C

Allen, M., & Ashbaker, B. Y. (2004). Strengthening schools: Involving paraprofessionals in crisis prevention and intervention. *Intervention in School and Clinic, 39*(3), 139–146.

Allred, D. M., Morgan, J., & Ashbaker, B. Y. (2000). Available but not accessed: Resources to enhance paraeducators' skills and knowledge. *Theories and Practices in Supervision and Curriculum, 11,* 68-73.

Ashbaker, B. Y. (2003, April). Ideas for paraprofessionals, teachers, and administrators as they work to enhance services to students. *E-News, National Paraprofessional Resource Center,* University of Minnesota/Utah State University Online: http://www.nrcpara.org/index.shtml

Ashbaker, B. Y., Allen, M., Johnstun, M., Allen, D., Johnson, M., Paxman, A., & Jones, N. (2003). Strengthening school support staff in basic crisis intervention. *The PARAgraph, 2,* 3–4.

Ashbaker, B. Y., & Morgan, J. (1998a). Teaching students to think: Improving your questioning skills. *Paraphrase, 4*(3), 18–19.

Ashbaker, B. Y., & Morgan, J. (1998b). *The Pro-Active Paraeducator: More than 200 really nifty ideas for the people who help teachers.* American Fork, UT: Swift Learning Resources. (ISBN: 1-56861-052-2). Second edition (2002).

Ashbaker, B. Y., & Morgan, J. (1999a). The 'S' in ASCD: Teachers supervising paraeducators for professional development. (ERIC Document Reproduction Service No. ED 432 561)

Ashbaker, B. Y., & Morgan, J. (1999b, May). *Super-Vision: A model training program for strengthening teacher-paraprofessional teams.* Paper presented at the Seventh Annual CSPD Conference on Leadership and Change, Arlington, VA.

Ashbaker, B. Y., & Morgan, J. (2000). Bilingual paraeducators: What we can learn from Rosa. *NASSP Bulletin, 84*(614), 53–56.

Ashbaker, B. Y., & Morgan, J. (2001). Paraeducators: A powerful human resource. *Streamlined Seminar, 19*(2), 1–4. Quarterly newsletter of the National Association of Elementary School Principals.

Ashbaker, B. Y., & Morgan, J. (2004). Legal issues regarding paraprofessionals. A legal memorandum. Quarterly single-issue newsletter of the National Association of Secondary School Principals.

Bairu, G. (2001), *Public school student, staff, and graduate counts by state: School year 1999.* (NCES 2001-326r). Washington, DC: U.S. Department of Education, Office of Educational Research and Improvement.

Ballantine, J. (1989). *The sociology of education.* Upper Saddle River, NJ: Prentice Hall.

Banks, J. (1997). Multicultural education: Characteristics and goals. In J. Banks and C. Banks (Eds.), *Multicultural education: Issues and perspectives* (3rd ed., pp. 3–32). Boston: Allyn & Bacon.

Berliner, D. (1983).The executive functions of teaching. *Instructor, 93*(2).

Bloom, B. (1981). *All our children learning.* New York: McGraw-Hill.

Brophy, J., & Good, T. L. (1986). Teacher behavior and student achievement. In M. C. Wittrock (Ed.), *Handbook of research on teaching* (3rd ed., pp. 328–375). Upper Saddle River, NJ: Prentice Hall.

Carney, J. M. (2001). Electronic and traditional paper portfolios as tools for teacher knowledge representation. College Park, MD: Educational Resources Information Center. (ERIC Document Reproduction Service No. TM033702)

Catterall, J., & Cota-Robles, E. (1988). *The educationally at-risk: What the numbers mean.* Palo Alto, CA: Stanford University Press.

Conger, R., Conger, K., Elder, G., Larenz, F., Simons, R., & Whitbeck, L. (1992). A family process model of economic hardship and adjustment of early adolescent boys. *Child Development, 63,* 526–541.

Collier, S. T. (1999). Characteristics of reflective thought during the student teaching experience. *Journal of Teacher Education, 50*(3), 173–181.

D–G

DeKalb County (GA) School District. 28 IDELR 626 (Office of Civil Rights, Region IV, November 1997).

Education Commission of the States. (2003). State accountability and consolidated plans for No Child Left Behind. Denver, CO [Online: *www.ecs.org/clearinghouse/42/65/4265.htm*].

Eggan, P. D., & Kauchak, D. (1999). *Educational psychology: Windows on classrooms.* Upper Saddle River, NJ: Prentice Hall.

Ellis, A. K., Cogan, J. J., and Howey, K. R. (1991*). Introduction to the Foundations of Education.* Englewood Cliffs, NJ: Prentice Hall.

Freiberg, H. J., & Stein, T. A. (1999). Measuring, improving and sustaining healthy learning environments. In H. J. Freiberg (Ed.), *School climate: Measuring, improving and sustaining health learning environments.* Philadelphia: Falmer Press.

Garet, M., Porter, A. C., Desimone, L., Birman, B. F., & Yoon, K. S. (2001). What makes professional development effective? Results from a national sample of teachers. *American Educational Research Journal, 38*(4), 115–145.

Giangreco, M. F., & Doyle, M. B. (2002). Students with disabilities and paraprofessional supports: Benefits, balance, and Band-Aids. *Focus on Exceptional Children, 34* (7), 1-12.

Gollnick, D., & Chinn, P. (1994). *Multicultural education in a pluralistic society* (4th ed.). New York: Merrill/Macmillan.

Gonder, P. O., & Hymes, D. (1994). Improving school climate and culture. *American Association of School Administrators Critical Issues Series*, Report No. 27. ED 371 485.

Graziano, A. M. (2002). *Developmental disabilities: Introduction to a diverse field.* Boston: Allyn & Bacon.

H–K

Haynes, N. M., Emmons, C. L., & Ben-Avie, M. (1997). School climate as a factor in student adjustment and achievement. *Journal of Educational and Psychological Consultation, 8,* 321–329.

Hofmeister, A. M., Ashbaker, B. Y., & Morgan, J. (1997). *The effective educator: A training program for paraeducators.* Lehi, UT: Swift.

Hofmeister, A. M., & Lubke, M. (1990). *Research into practice: Implementing effective teaching strategies.* Boston: Allyn & Bacon.

Hunter, M. (1984). Knowing teaching and supervising. In P. Hosford (Ed.), *Using what we know about teaching* (pp. 169–192). Alexandria, VA: Association for Supervision and Curriculum Development.

Hyman, I. A., & Perone, D. C. (1998). The other side of school violence: Educator policies and practices that may contribute to student misbehavior. *Journal of School Psychology, 36,* 7–27.

Independent School Dist. No. 11. 36 IDELR 81, Anoka-Hennepin, Minnesota State Educational Agency. (2001, September 18).

Individuals with Disabilities Education Act Amendments of 1997. Pub. L.105-17. 20. U.S.C./1415 (b)-(d) 34 C. R. F. 300.506-300.513.

Kosslynn, S.M. & Rosenberg, R.S. (2001). *Psychology: The brain, the person, the world.* Boston: Allyn & Bacon.

L–N

Lee, V. E., Chen, X., & Smerdon, B. A. (1996). *The influence of school climate on gender differences in the achievement and engagement of young adolescents.* Washington, DC: American University Association of University Women.

Leeton (MO) R X School District. 34 IDELR 100 (Office for Civil Rights), Midwestern Division, Kansas City, MO. (September 28, 2000).

Lehr, C. A., & Christenson, S. L. (2002). Best practices in promoting a positive school climate. In A. Thomas & J. Grimes (Eds.), *Best practices in school psychology* (Vol. 4, pp. 929–947). Washington, DC: National Association of School Psychologists.

Macionis, J. (1994*). Sociology* (4th ed.). Upper Saddle River, NJ: Prentice Hall.

Marzano, R. J. (2003). *What works in schools: Translating research into action.* Alexandria, VA: Association for Supervision and Curriculum Development.

Morgan, J., & Ashbaker, B. Y. (2000). Supporting new teachers: Practical suggestions for experienced staff. *The Rural Educator, 22*(1), 35–37.

Morgan, J., & Ashbaker, B. Y. (2001a). *A teacher's guide to working with paraeducators and other classroom aides.* Alexandria, VA: Association for Supervision and Curriculum Development. (ISBN: 0-87120-505-X).

Morgan, J., & Ashbaker, B. Y. (2001b). 20 ways to work more effectively with your paraeducator. *Intervention in School and Clinic, 36*(4), 230–231.

Morgan, J., & Ashbaker, B. Y. (2003, March). A rural teacher is to executive, as a paraprofessional is to . . . ?: Revisiting the concept of the teacher as a supervisor of paraprofessionals. *Conference Proceedings of the 23rd Annual National Conference of the American Council on Rural Special Education (ACRES).* Salt Lake City, UT. (ERIC document)

Morgan, J., Ashbaker, B. Y., & Allred, D. (2000). Providing training for paraeducators: What motivates them to attend? *The Researcher, 15*(1), 50–55.

Morgan, J., Ashbaker, B. Y., & Forbush, D. (1998). Strengthening the teaching team: Teachers and para-professionals build their team power. *Support for Learning (British Journal of Learning Support), 13*(3), 115–117.

Morgan, J., Ashbaker, B. Y., & Young, J. R. (2001). Teaming, supervision, and evaluation: Teacher-para-educator team perspectives of their teaching. (ERIC Document Reproduction Service No. ED 454 200)

National Center for Education Statistics. (2002–2003). *Institute of Education Sciences.* U.S. Department of Education [Online: www.nces.ed.gov/].

National Information Center for Children and Youth with Disabilities. (1999). *OSEP Regional Trainings on the IDEA '97 Regulations.* Office of Special Education Programs (OSEP), U.S. Department of Education [Online: www.nichcy.org/regons/subpartb., 21–22].

O–R

Payne, D. A. (2003). *Applied educational assessment* (2nd ed.). Belmont, CA: Wadsworth/Thomson.

Pickett, A. L. (1996). *A state of the art report on paraprofessionals in education and related services.* New York: National Resource Center for Paraprofessionals in Education and Related Services.

Pickett, A. L. (1997). Paraprofessionals in school settings: Framing the issues. In A. L. Pickett & K. Gerlach (Eds.), *Supervising paraprofessionals in school settings: A team approach.* Austin, TX: Pro-Ed.

Pickett, A. L., Likins, M., & Wallace, T. (2002). *The Employment and Preparation of Paraeducators: The state of the art* [Online *http://nrcpara.org/resources/stateoftheart/index/php*].

Robelen, E. W. (1999, August 4). Title I aides often acting as teachers. *Education Week*, p. 33.

Rosenshine, B., & Stevens, R. (1986). Teaching functions. In M. C. Wittrock (Ed.), *Handbook of research on teaching* (3rd ed., pp. 376–391). Upper Saddle River, NJ: Prentice Hall.

S–T

Salvia, J., & Ysseldyke, J. E. (1988). *Assessment in special and remedial education* (4th ed.). Boston: Houghton Mifflin.

Salzberg, C. L., & Morgan, J. (1995). Preparing teachers to work with paraprofessionals. *Teacher Education and Special Education, 18*(1), 49–55.

Schon, D. A. (1987). *Educating the reflective practitioner.* San Francisco: Jossey Bass.

Shulman, L. (1998). Teacher portfolios: A theoretical activity. In N. Lyons (Ed.), *With portfolio in hand* (pp. 23–37). New York: Teachers College Press.

Sternberg, R. (1986). *Intelligence applied. Understanding and increasing your intellectual skills.* Orlando, FL: Harcourt Brace.

Title I of the Elementary and Secondary Education Act, the No Child Left Behind Act of 2001, PL 107-110.

U–Z

Udvari-Solner, A. (1996). Examining teacher thinking: Constructing a process to design curricular adaptations. *Remedial and Special Education, 17*(4), 245–254.

U.S. Department of Education. (1997), *Roles for education paraprofessionals in effective schools.* Washington, DC: Author.

U.S. Department of Education. (1999). To Assure the Free Appropriate Public Education of All Children with Disabilities Individuals with Disabilities Education Act, Section 618. *Twenty-first Annual Report to Congress on the Implementation of the Individuals with Disabilities Education Act* [Online: *www.ed.gov/offices/OSERS/OSEP/OSEP99AnlRpt/*].

U.S. Department of Education, National Center for Education Statistics. (2000). *Education statistics: Common core of data survey.* (Table prepared February 2000). Washington, DC [Online: *http://nces.ed.gov/*].

U.S. Department of Education, Office of Elementary and Secondary Education. (2002). *No Child Left Behind: A Desktop Reference,* Washington, DC: Author.

U.S. Department of Labor. *The Occupational Outlook Handbook* (2004–2005). Bureau of Labor Statistics. Washington, DC: Author.

Wellington, B. (1996). Orientations to reflective practice. *Educational Research, 38*(3), 307–316.

Willoughby, T., Wood, E., & Kahn, M. (1994). Isolating variables that impact on or detract from the effectiveness of elaboration strategies. *Journal of Educational Psychology, 86*(2), 279–289.

Glossary: Terms Used in Education

Americans with Disabilities Act (ADA). Federal civil rights legislation, enacted in 1990, that protects individuals with disabilities from discrimination in all areas of life. The ADA applies to state and local government entities, private-sector employment, public services, public transportation, and telecommunications. If a person with a disability—given the proper support—can perform activities required for a job as well as a nondisabled person, an employer must be prepared to make reasonable accommodations to enable the person with a disability to do the job. These protections apply in a school setting to students and employees.

Applied Behavior Analysis (ABA). A formal system for modifying a student's behavior through carefully observing the inappropriate behavior; implementing an intervention (e.g., change in the instructional program or in the classroom environment, introduction of a reward system); and collecting data to document any changes that take place. ABA is most often used in special education settings but may be used with groups or individuals. See Chapter 11.

Due process. Principle requiring that parents be informed of each step in the identification and evaluation of their child for special education, as well as the development of the child's individualized education program. Parents must also have access to a system for registering dissatisfaction with the services being provided for their child. In special education, parent complaints are heard by a due process hearing officer.

Elementary and Secondary Education Act (ESEA). The major general education legislation in the United States. Known since 2001 as the No Child Left Behind Act. See also Title I.

Extrinsic motivators. Often assist students who are unable to see the value of learning "for learning's sake." Extrinsic motivation can take the form of a reward (such as free time, extra bonus points toward a grade) for completing a task. See also Intrinsic motivation.

Family Educational Rights and Privacy Act (FERPA). Federal legislation that governs the way in which student information is handled and requires confidentiality. Under FERPA, schools and school districts have a responsibility to keep all documentation relating to a student confidential and to allow access to the information only to parents and a well-defined list of individuals with a genuine educational or legal need to know.

Free and appropriate public education (FAPE). A requirement of IDEA. Requires states to provide education services that meet the individual needs of each student, at no cost.

Fine motor. Refers to movements and responses controlled by the small muscles of the body, including hand and finger dexterity, writing, drawing, and manipulation of small objects. See also Gross motor.

Gross motor. Refers to movement controlled by the large muscles of the body, including those regulating walking, balance, throwing, catching, and running. See also Fine motor.

Inclusion. Participation of students with disabilities in the general education classroom and in the general curriculum, with appropriate aids and support services. See also Regular Education Initiative (REI).

Individualized Education Program (IEP). A requirement of IDEA is that each student who is eligible for special education services must have an IEP. Goals may be behavioral or academic. Students from the age of sixteen must also have a Transition Plan. For children below school age the equivalent of an IEP is an individualized family service plan (IFSP).

Individuals with Disabilities Education Improvement Act (IDEIA). The major special education legislation in the United States, originally known as the Education of all Handicapped Children Act, and subsequently reauthorized in 1990 and 1997 as the Individuals with Disabilities Education Act. IDEA promotes the six principles of FAPE, LRE, nondiscriminatory evaluation, individualized education programs, due process, and procedural safeguards.

Individuals with Disabilities Education Improvement Act (IDEIA) of 2004. In 1975, Congress enacted the Education for All Handicapped Children Act (Public Law 94–142) to support states and localities in protecting the rights of, meeting the individual needs of, and improving the results for infants, toddlers, children, and youth with disabilities and their families. This federal law was enacted as the Individuals with Disabilities Education Act (IDEA), and was amended in 1977. In December 2004, the IDEA was again amended as the Individuals with Disabilities Education Improvement Act (IDEIA) of 2004 (Public Law 108–446). In general terms, the IDEIA asserts that children with disabilities will receive a "free appropriate public education" (FAPE) in the "least restrictive environment" (LRE). In other words, children will receive a free educational program that is appropriate to their needs and the program will be administered in an environment that is most helpful to the child's education.

Intelligence. A trait or construct associated with cognitive or intellectual capacity, related to the potential or ability to learn. Intelligence is an abstract quality associated with all types of intellectual processes, including abstract thinking, mental reasoning, using sound judgment, and making rational decisions.

Intrinsic motivation. The satisfaction or pleasure gained from accomplishing a task successfully, with no external rewards or recognition. See also Extrinsic motivators.

Least restrictive environment (LRE). A requirement of IDEA. LRE provides for mainstreaming a student into the general education program to the greatest extent possible, so the student has access to the general curriculum. Placement in special programs should only be considered if the student's maximum learning potential cannot be reached in the general education setting.

Limited English Proficient (LEP). A term used to denote students whose first language is not English and whose speaking, reading, or writing skills are low in English. Such students are often placed in ESL (English as a Second Language) programs.

Mastery goal. A goal set for a certain level of achievement or skill. A mastery goal is oriented to individual student learning as much as possible, without comparison to another student's learning.

Mnemonics. Techniques to assist in remembering facts or processes, by making a memory link between new information and knowledge. For example, FACE to remember the names of the musical notes in the spaces of the treble staff.

Multicultural awareness. A process designed to give all students an equal chance for an education through raising awareness of the issues faced by exceptional students, ethnic, cultural and racial groups, and so on.

Negative reinforcement. An unpleasant condition that follows a desired response or behavior. In negative reinforcement a particular behavior is strengthened by the consequence of the stopping or avoiding of a negative condition. For example, you may drive in heavy traffic and find it is a negative experience. This prompts you to leave home earlier than usual to avoid the heavy traffic. Your behavior of leaving home earlier is strengthened by the consequence of being able to avoid heavy traffic. Negative reinforcement is often confused with punishment. They are very different, however, because negative reinforcement means that a negative consequence prompts a change in behavior. See also Punishment.

Nondiscriminatory evaluation. An evaluation or test that allows students to show their true abilities, no matter what their language or cultural background or gender.

Peer tutoring. The use of students as tutors to each other. May be cross-age or same age. In its most simple form, it is used for drill-and-practice activities, such as testing each other on spelling words or math facts, although it can also be used for brainstorming and problem solving. See Chapter 8.

Portfolio. A file or folder containing a variety of types of information to document a person's experiences and accomplishments. Portfolios may be used as an alternative to formal testing or when the person has few formal qualifications. The difficulty in using portfolios as an assessment tool lies largely in the impossibility of gauging the quality of the experiences and skills documented.

Positive reinforcement. A reward that maintains or increases the rate or frequency of a behavior by presenting the reward following the behavior. For example, the baby sees Daddy and says "Dadda" and the whole family cheers. Baby says "Dadda" again and again. Or a student gets 100 percent on a spelling test and is allowed to go to the school playground early. He begins to work much harder and is allowed to go early to recess much more frequently. The term *reward* is often used as a synonym for positive reinforcement.

Procedural safeguard. A requirement of IDEA. The law guarantees to parents that the rights accorded to them by the law will be "safeguarded."

Punishment. An action with the purpose of weakening or stopping a behavior. When a negative condition is introduced or experienced as a consequence of the behavior, the behavior is reduced or eliminated. For example, spanking a child *may* reduce a child's swearing. Punishment is sometimes confused with negative reinforcement. However, negative reinforcement strengthens a behavior because a negative condition is stopped or avoided as a consequence of the behavior. See Negative reinforcement.

Regular Education Initiative (REI). A proposal advocating that general education should accept primary responsibility for educating students with disabilities. This involves integration of students with disabilities into regular classes and removal of labels on students with disabilities. See also Inclusion.

Reinforcement. See positive and negative reinforcement.

Section 504. Section 504 of the Vocational Rehabilitation Act of 1973 protects individuals with disabilities from discrimination in programs and activities that receive federal financial assistance, and requires that state and local governments make any necessary accommodations for people with disabilities. Students who have a disability, but who are not eligible for services under IDEA, often have a 504 plan that adapts the learning environment to eliminate obstacles to their learning (e.g., making a classroom more wheelchair accessible).

Special Education. This term means specially designed instruction, at no cost to parents, to meet the unique needs of a child with a disability, including instruction conducted in the classroom, in the home, in hospitals and institutions, and in other settings; and instruction in physical education.

Time-out. A control method that involves removal of a disruptive student from the classroom and moving him or her to an isolated part of the classroom, another classroom, or the principal's office.

Title. A section or "title" within a law.

Title I. Title I of the Elementary and Secondary Education Act (or No Child Left Behind) was designed to provide additional instructional support for disadvantaged students. This most commonly takes the form of tutoring in basic numeracy and literacy skills. Title I programs can exist within a school or can be schoolwide.

Useful Websites

- National Resource Center for Paraprofessionals (NRCP).
  Addresses policy questions and describes training models that will enable administrators and staff developers to improve the recruitment, deployment, supervision, and career development of paraprofessionals. Also contains resources, conference dates, and a chat room for paraprofessionals:
  http://www.nrcpara.org/.
- National Education Association (NEA).
  Features a section on results-oriented job descriptions that explains the need for and provides guidance on how to write job descriptions for paraprofessionals. Look for the pages for paraprofessionals under the section called Education Support Professionals (ESP): **http://www.nea.org/esphome/**.
- The American Federation of Teachers (AFT).
  Includes paraprofessionals in the section on Paraprofessionals and School-Related Personnel (PSRP). The website features news and policy information specifically targeted to paraprofessionals, including the status of paraprofessional standards and certification for each state: **http://www.aft.org/psrp/**.
- The Council for Exceptional Children (CEC).
  Lists standards for paraprofessionals. Check for the Knowledge and Skills for Beginning Special Education Paraeducators: **http://www.cec.sped.org/ps/ parastds.html**.
- The Educator's Reference Desk.
  The search interface to the ERIC Database at **http://www.eduref.org** to access lesson plans and links to paraprofessional information. Use keywords such as *teacher aides, tutors, assistants, technicians*, and so on, to conduct a search of relevant resources on this website.
- The National Clearinghouse for Paraprofessional Pathways into Teaching.
  Multiple resources, training programs, and research articles:
  http://www.usc.edu/dept/education/CMMR/Clearinghouse.html.
- The Para2 Center in Colorado.
  Resources for training paraprofessionals and references to articles and books written about paraprofessional employment, training, and supervision:
  http://www.paracenter.org/resources/references.shtml.
- ASCD offers online training for teachers and administrators. Access the course, *Maximizing Assistance: Supervising Paraeducators in Your Classroom* by B. Y. Ashbaker and J. Morgan: **http://pdonline.ascd.org/pd_online/new/**.
- The Northwest Regional Laboratory.
  At **http://www.nwrac.org/para/guide/resources.html** contains the Oregon Resource Guide to Paraeducator Issues and includes the following:

      Management and supervision of paraeducators
      College programs and career ladders for paraeducators
      Paraeducator roles and responsibilities
      Professional development and training of paraeducators
      Paraeducator roles, standards, and competencies

■ U.S. Department of Education
      Overview of issues and policies relating to paraprofessionals: **www.ed.gov/pubs/ Paraprofessionals/**.

■ Education Commission of the States.
      Special section on No Child Left Behind: **www.ecs.org**.
      You can check to see what your state is doing by going to **www.ecs.org/ clearinghouse/42/65/4265.htm**. The site lists state accountability plans and consolidated plans for meeting regulations of the No Child Left Behind Act.

Acronyms Often Used in Special Education

Acronym	Meaning
ADD	Attention deficit disorder
ADHD	Attention deficit hyperactivity disorder
AT	Assistive technology
BIA	Bureau of Indian Affairs
CSPD	Comprehensive System of Personnel Development
EDGAR	Education Department General Administrative Regulations
EAHCA	Education of All Handicapped Children Act (1975)
EPSDT	Early periodic screening, diagnosis and treatment
ESA	Educational Service Agency
ESEA	Elementary and Secondary Education Act (1965)
ESY	Extended school year
FAPE	Free appropriate public education
FEOG	Full educational opportunity goal
FERPA	Family Educational Rights and Privacy Act
GEPA	General Education Provisions Act
IDEA	Individuals with Disabilities Education Act
IDEIA	Individuals with Disabilities Education Improvement Act
IEE	Independent educational evaluation
IEP	Individualized education program
IFSP	Individualized family service plan
LEA	Local educational agency
LEP	Limited English proficiency
LRE	Least restrictive environment
NPRM	Notice of proposed rulemaking
OHI	Other health impairment
OMB	Office of Management and Budget
PE	Physical education
SEA	State educational agency

IDEIA '04: Terms from Special Education Law

§602 Act.

Act means the Individuals with Disabilities Education Improvement Act (IDEIA) of 2004 as amended.
(Authority: 20 U.S.C. 1400)

Assistive technology device.

As used in this part, **Assistive technology device** means any item, piece of equipment, or product system, whether acquired commercially off the shelf, modified, or customized, that is used to increase, maintain, or improve the functional capabilities of a child with a disability.
(Authority: 20 U.S.C. 1401(1))

Assistive technology service.

Assistive technology service means any service that directly assists a child with a disability in the selection, acquisition, or use of an assistive technology device. Such term includes:

(a) the evaluation of the needs of such child, including a functional evaluation of the child in the child's customary environment;

(b) purchasing, leasing, or otherwise providing for the acquisition of assistive technology devices by such child;

(c) selecting, designing, fitting, customizing, adapting, applying, maintaining, repairing, or replacing assistive technology devices;

(d) coordinating and using other therapies, interventions, or services with assistive technology devices, such as those associated with existing education and rehabilitation plans and programs;

(e) training or technical assistance for such child or, where appropriate, the family of such child; and

(f) training or technical assistance for professionals (including individuals providing education or rehabilitation services), employers, or other individuals who provide services to, employ, or are otherwise substantially involved in the major life functions of such child.
(Authority: 20 U.S.C. 1401(2))

§602.3 Child with a disability.
(A) **In General—**
(1) The term **child with a disability** means a child with mental retardation, hearing impairment (including deafness), speech or language impairments, visual

impairments (including blindness), serious emotional disturbance (referred to in this title as emotional disturbance), orthopedic impairments, autism, traumatic brain injury, other health impairments, specific learning disabilities, and who, by reason thereof, needs special education and related services.

(2)

(b) **Children aged 3 through 9**. The term **child with a disability** for a child aged 3 through 9 (or any subset of that age range, including 3 through 5) may, at the discretion of the State and the local educational agency, include a child—

(i) Who is experiencing developmental delays, as defined by the State and as measured by appropriate diagnostic instruments and procedures, in 1 or more of the following areas: physical development, cognitive development, communication development, social or emotional development, or adaptive development; and

(ii) Who, by reason thereof, needs special education and related services.

(c) **Definitions of disability terms**.

§602.9 Free appropriate public education.

In General a **free appropriate public education** means special education and related services that

(a) have been provided at public expense, under public supervision and direction, and without charge;

(b) meet the standards of the state educational agency;

(c) include an appropriate preschool, elementary school, or secondary school education in the State involved; and

(d) are provided in conformity with an individualized education program required under section 614(d).

(Authority: 20 U.S.C. 1401(8))

§602.4 Individualized education program.

The term **individualized education program** or **IEP** means a written statement for each child with a disability that is developed, reviewed, and revised in accordance with this section and that includes—

(I) a statement of the child's present levels of academic achievement and functional performance, including—

(aa) how the child's disability affects the child's involvement and progress in the general education curriculum;

(bb) for preschool children, as appropriate, how the disability affects the child's participation in appropriate activities; and

(cc) for children with disabilities who take alternate assessments aligned to alternate achievement standards, a description of benchmarks or short-term objectives;

(II) a statement of measurable annual goals, including academic and functional goals, designed to—

(aa) meet the child's needs that result from the child's disability to enable the child to be involved in and make progress in the general education curriculum; and

(bb) meet the child's other educational needs that result from the child's disability;

(III) a description of how the child's progress toward meeting the annual goals

described in subclause (II) will be measured and when periodic reports on the progress the child is making toward meeting the annual goals (such as through the use of quarterly or other periodic reports, concurrent with the issuance of report cards) will be provided.

(Authority: 20 U.S.C. 1401(11))

Local educational agency.

The term **local educational agency** means a public board of education or other public authority legally constituted within a State for either administrative control or direction of, or to perform a service function for, public elementary or secondary schools in a city, county, township, school district, or other political subdivision of a State, or for a combination of school districts or counties as are recognized in a State as an administrative agency for its public elementary or secondary schools.

Special education.

The term **special education** means specially designed instruction, at no cost to the parents, to meet the unique needs of a child with a disability, including—

(A) instruction conducted in the classroom, in the home, in hospitals and institutions, and in other settings; and

(B) instruction in physical education.

Related Services.

The term **related services** means transportation, and such developmental, corrective, and other supportive services (including speech-language pathology and audiology services, interpreting services, psychological services, physical and occupational therapy, recreation, including therapeutic recreation, social work services, school nurse services designed to enable a child with a disability to receive a free appropriate public education as described in the individualized education program of the child, counseling services, including rehabilitation counseling, orientation and mobility services, and medical services, except that such medical services shall be for diagnostic and evaluation purposes only) as may be required to assist a child with a disability to benefit from special education, and includes early identification and assessment in disabling conditions in children.

—**Exception**. The term related services does not include a medical device that is surgically implanted, or the replacement of such device.

Transition Services.

The term **transition services** means a coordinated set of activities for a child with a disability that

(A) is designed to be within a results-oriented process, that is focused on improving the academic and functional achievement of the child with a disability to facilitate the child's movement from school to post-school activities, including post-secondary education, vocational education, integrated employment (including supported employment), continuing and adult education, adult services, independent living, or community participation;

(B) is based on the individual child's needs, taking into account the child's strengths, preferences, and interests; and

(C) includes instruction, related services, community experience, the development of employment and other post-school adult living objectives, and when appropriate, acquisition of daily living skills and functional vocational education.

Definitions of disability terms used in this definition are from IDEA '97.

(i) **Autism** means a developmental disability significantly affecting verbal and nonverbal communication and social interaction, generally evident before age 3, that adversely affects a child's educational performance. Other characteristics often associated with autism are engagement in repetitive activities and stereo-typed movements, resistance to environmental change or change in daily routines, and unusual responses to sensory experiences. The term does not apply if a child's educational performance is adversely affected primarily because the child has an emotional disturbance, as defined in paragraph (b)(4) of this section.

(ii) A child who manifests the characteristics of "autism" after age 3 could be diagnosed as having "autism" if the criteria in paragraph (c)(1)(i) of this section are satisfied.

(2) **Deaf-blindness** means concomitant hearing and visual impairments, the combination of which causes such severe communication and other developmental and educational needs that they cannot be accommodated in special education programs solely for children with deafness or children with blindness.

(3) **Deafness** means a hearing impairment that is so severe that the child is impaired in processing linguistic information through hearing, with or without amplification, that adversely affects a child's educational performance.

(4) **Emotional disturbance** is defined as follows:

(i) The term means a condition exhibiting one or more of the following characteristics over a long period of time and to a marked degree that adversely affects a child's educational performance:

(A) An inability to learn that cannot be explained by intellectual, sensory, or health factors.

(B) An inability to build or maintain satisfactory interpersonal relationships with peers and teachers.

(C) Inappropriate types of behavior or feelings under normal circumstances.

(D) A general pervasive mood of unhappiness or depression.

(E) A tendency to develop physical symptoms or fears associated with personal or school problems.

(ii) The term includes schizophrenia. The term does not apply to children who are socially maladjusted, unless it is determined that they have an emotional disturbance.

(5) **Hearing impairment** means an impairment in hearing, whether permanent or fluctuating, that adversely affects a child's educational performance but that is not included under the definition of deafness in this section.

(6) **Mental retardation** means significantly subaverage general intellectual functioning, existing concurrently with deficits in adaptive behavior and manifested during the developmental period, that adversely affects a child's educational performance.

(7) **Multiple disabilities** means concomitant impairments (such as mental retardation-blindness, mental retardation-orthopedic impairment, etc.), the combination of which causes such severe educational needs that they cannot be accommodated in special education programs solely for one of the impairments. The term does not include deaf-blindness.

(8) **Orthopedic impairment** means a severe orthopedic impairment that adversely affects a child's educational performance. The term includes impairments caused by congenital anomaly (e.g., clubfoot, absence of some member, etc.), impairments caused by disease (e.g., poliomyelitis, bone tuberculosis, etc.), and impairments from other causes (e.g., cerebral palsy, amputations, and fractures or burns that cause contractures).

(9) **Other health impairment** means having limited strength, vitality or alertness, including a heightened alertness to environmental stimuli, that results in limited alertness with respect to the educational environment, that—

(i) Is due to chronic or acute health problems such as asthma, attention deficit disorder or attention deficit hyperactivity disorder, diabetes, epilepsy, a heart condition, hemophilia, lead poisoning, leukemia, nephritis, rheumatic fever, and sickle cell anemia; and

(ii) Adversely affects a child's educational performance.

(11) **Speech or language impairment** means a communication disorder, such as stuttering, impaired articulation, a language impairment, or a voice impairment, that adversely affects a child's educational performance.

(12) **Traumatic brain injury** means an acquired injury to the brain caused by an external physical force, resulting in total or partial functional disability or psychosocial impairment, or both, that adversely affects a child's educational performance. The term applies to open or closed head injuries resulting in impairments in one or more areas, such as cognition; language; memory; attention; reasoning; abstract thinking; judgment; problem-solving; sensory, perceptual, and motor abilities; psychosocial behavior; physical functions; information processing; and speech. The term does not apply to brain injuries that are congenital or degenerative, or to brain injuries induced by birth trauma.

(13) **Visual impairment including blindness** means an impairment in vision that, even with correction, adversely affects a child's educational performance. The term includes both partial sight and blindness.

(Authority: 20 U.S.C. 1401(3)(A) and (B); 1401(26))

Definitions of specific learning disability used in this definition are from IDEIA '04.

(30) **Specific learning disability**:

The term means a disorder in 1 or more of the basic psychological processes involved in understanding or in using language, spoken or written, which disorder may manifest itself in an imperfect ability to listen, think, speak, read, write, spell, or to do mathematical calculations. Such term includes such conditions as perceptual disabilities, brain injury, minimal brain dysfunction, dyslexia, and developmental aphasia.

Disorders not included. Such term includes such conditions as are primarily the result of visual, hearing, or motor disabilities, of mental retardation, of emotional disturbance, or of environmental, cultural, or economic disadvantage.

Index